P9-BIV-656

Miracles in the Last Days

Chapters 1 through 4 by

Hierodeacon Pangratios (Christley)

&

Accounts of Miracles

of the Mother of God and of the Saints

Edited by the Staff of New Sarov Press

New Sarov Press
1999

Cover photo:
Weeping Icon of the Most Holy Theotokos
of New Sarov

Back cover:
Fresco depicting the Apocalypse
Mount Athos, Greece

NEW SAROV PRESS
Blanco, Texas 78606-1049
USA

ISBN: 1-880364-06-9

ACKNOWLEDGEMENTS

So many people have participated in the creation of this book that it is impossible to give them all their due credit. First of all, we must acknowledge the Mother of God herself, whose intercession is the source of the many miracles contained in the very large section of accounts of miracles. Next, the Monks who participated in selecting the approximately 300 accounts chosen here from over 20,000 letters and reports.

Of course, the many faithful people who went to the trouble to commit to writing the accounts of the various miracles and blessings of the Mother of God, St. Seraphim of Sarov, St. John the Wonderworker, St. Benedict of Nursia, and the many other Saints whose intercessions are described herein, deserve credit.

Finally, the actual preparation, textual work, editing and compilation of the account of miracles published herein, and the book itself, could not have occurred without the work of Catherine Penn. Her countless hours of work for over three years will win her not only our acknowledgement here, but hopefully jewels in her heavenly crown.

Lastly, other volunteers, again too numerous to name, assisted in some of the typing of the earlier accounts in the miracles section, and also without their loving efforts, needless to say, this present work would not exist.

The Last Judgment

When Thou shalt come, O Righteous Judge, to execute just judgement, seated on Thy throne of glory, a river of fire will draw all men amazed before Thy judgement-seat; the powers of heaven will stand beside Thee, and in fear mankind will be judged according to the deeds that each has done. Then spare us, O Christ, in Thy compassion, with faith we entreat Thee, and count us worthy of Thy blessings with those that are saved.

—*Vespers, Sunday of the Last Judgement*

TABLE OF CONTENTS

The Ladder of Divine Ascent

Traditional depiction of the spiritual struggle involved in living the Christian life; based upon the famous work, The Ladder, *by St. John Climacus. As we struggle by God's grace, to ascend the ladder to heaven, overcoming vices and building up virtues, the demons try to pull us off. But Christ Himself helps us into heaven, if we remain steadfast.*

EDITORS' PREFACE

Handling the many letters that constitute the heart of this book has been a source of inspiration to all those privileged so to do. The letters range from computer-generated printouts to barely-legible scrawl. They are written on everything from the letterhead of European monasteries to simple yellow notepad pages. Many are on picture note cards. Many enclose photographs of the participants, of vehicles involved in wrecks, and photocopies of medical documents.

The vast majority of the letters and testimonials are hand written. The intensely personal character of these individuals' handwriting, each with its unique flow, conveyed to the editors of this material how personal and individual these accounts are. There is an ethereal quality in hand-written correspondence that is lost to the printed page. It is like an exquisite poem that can be translated into other languages, but never with its full beauty and power. That part of the essence is lost. "Praise God"—written in a multitude of wordings and as many scripts as there are letters—is a constant theme. This is perhaps the especial gift given the editors—that they touch letter after unique letter bearing this gratitude. The editors desire to share this gift with all the readers, even if only by recounting the joy and constant amazement and gratitude to God that doing this work brought with it.

These writings came from people of all educational levels, and a rich diversity of ethnic and religious backgrounds. Some changes were deemed necessary for intelligibility. Some terms for naming the Mother of God were brought into conformity with the titles of the Mother of God that the editors felt would be more familiar to the readership. Some words had to be guessed at. Medical terms that were unfamiliar were left in the writers' original form. Misspellings were common and were corrected to the best of the editors' ability. Grammar and syntax were changed where they varied widely from standard English. All these changes were made for the purpose of intelligibility.

Many letters were not included because their content was too personal. Some were included with initials in the place of names in order to protect confidentiality. Requests for prayers for family members by name, mention of donations and other material not directly related to the healing or grace received from God were mostly omitted. The choices about what to leave out and what to include were sometimes difficult. This part of the editorial process was perhaps the hardest, and the editors acknowledge their own limitations and capacity for error in judgment. They present this material to the readers with deepest humility.

The substance of the healings and graces received comes to the reader as it appears in the letters themselves. The tender mercy of God, touching these men, women and children, the authors of the hundreds of letters, through the intercession of the Most Holy Mother of God and the Saints, is the gift they, the letter writers, pass on to the reader. That God in His mercy cares about our sufferings, our being blind, dumb, lame, weak of faith, fearful, cancerous, infirm in every way—that He desires to help us through His All-Pure Mother and the Saints—that is their message and their gift of love to those of us who surely do and will experience these sufferings in our own lives and the lives of those we love.

Those involved in the production of this book, along with the Monastics who daily receive Pilgrims and hear their accounts, already participate in these blessings. With deepest humility, we now wish to pass them on to all who read this book. We pray for each person who reads it, and we beg each reader's prayers for us, sinners, to Him Whose mercy and love are everywhere present, Who never fails to come to welcome those who come to Him in need and a repentant spirit.

St. John the Wonderworker

Russian Orthodox Archbishop of Shanghai and San Francisco, Saint John (Maximovitch) was a Wonderworker of the latter days, providing an example of holiness and triumphant Christian struggle in the midst of injustice and the trials and temptations of the modern world.

CHAPTER 1
THE LAST DAYS

This is a book about miracles in the Last Days. Many of these miracles are connected to an Icon of the Mother of God that is weeping tears of myrrh at a remote Monastery in Texas.

When we speak of the Last Days, we are speaking about the consummation of all things, when heaven and earth as we know them shall pass away, and Christ shall come in glory to judge the living and the dead. This is a time of joy for the righteous—but who among us is righteous? The prophesies about the Last Days are given to us in Scripture as a warning, so that we will be prepared. Throughout the Old and the New Testaments, we are told what is going to happen at the end of time. Take up the Gospel of St. Mark and read the l3th Chapter. Also, read St. Matthew Chapters 24 and 25. These contain our Lord's clear teaching about the Last Days.

The Last Days have actually already begun. They began with the Incarnation of Christ, and continue to this day. The Apostle John says, *Little children, it is the last time: and ye have heard that Antichrist shall come, even now are there many antichrists; whereby we know that it is the last time.* (I John 2:18.) The spirit of antichrist has been in the world and fought against the truth, but there is a specific Antichrist who will come at a specific time, and he will be destroyed with the Second Coming of Christ.

We are now beginning the Third Millennium since the Incarnation of Christ. Sometimes, people become mindless and forget that our Lord is coming; or people say that they don't believe it. The Holy Apostle Peter says,

> *...there shall come in the last days scoffers, walking after their own lusts, and saying, Where is the promise of His coming? for since the fathers fell asleep, all things continue as they were from the beginning of the creation.... But, beloved, be not ignorant of this one thing, that one day with the Lord is as a thousand years, and a thousand years as one day. The Lord is not slack concerning His promise, as some men count slackness, but is long-suffering towards us, not willing that any should perish, but that all should come to repentance.* (II Peter 3:3-4, 8.)

Because He is merciful, the Lord has not yet come, giving us a chance yet to repent. But He will not delay forever. The Lord will come, like a thief in the night—that is, unexpectedly. This warning is given seven times in the New Testament. (St. Matthew 24:43, St. Luke 12:39, I Thessalonians 5:2, II Peter 3:10, Revelation 3:3, 16:15.)

Even if, in the providence of God, we do not see the Second Coming of Christ in our own lifetime, we will all be judged. We shall each of us individually undergo the judgement, and we have no control over when that will be:

> *Watch ye therefore: for ye know not when the Master of the house cometh, at even, or at midnight, or at the cockcrowing, or in the morn-*

ing: lest coming suddenly He find you sleeping. And what I say unto you I say unto all: Watch! (St. Mark 13:35-37.)

Even though we do not know the exact day or hour of His coming, there are signs which have been given us (St. Matthew 24:32-33), and these signs seem to be coming to pass. We see the love of many growing cold. (St. Matthew 24:12.) We see the breakdown of human society and morality. We see wars and rumors of wars, and we cannot simply go on with our lives as though nothing is happening. We must change our lives now, before it is too late. This is why miracles are happening in the Last Days—to get our attention and to bring us back to God.

THE WEEPING ICON OF NEW SAROV

On May 7, 1985, an Icon of the Mother of God was discovered weeping Myrrh by one of the Monks in a small Chapel at Christ of the Hills Monastery, New Sarov. New Sarov is an Orthodox Christian religious complex outside of Blanco, Texas, in the beautiful Texas Hill Country, not far from Austin and San Antonio. On the property of New Sarov are a number of religious institutions, including Christ of the Hills Monastery (Orthodox Monks), the Convent of Blessed Pasha and Pelagia (Orthodox Nuns), New Sarov Press, New Sarov Pastoral School and the Shrine of the Mother of God. The property is named New Sarov in honor of St. Seraphim of Sarov, who is one of Russia's most highly venerated monastic Saints and one of the Patron Saints of New Sarov.

Saint Seraphim lived in the Sarov Monastery in Russia during the 18th Century, and a number of times in his life was vouchsafed wondrous visions of the Mother of God, who often appeared to him accompanied by other Saints. The first miracle of the Mother of God in his life occurred when Saint Seraphim was only nine years old. The young Saint Seraphim (his name in the world was Prochor) was very ill and his widowed mother had lost all hope for his recovery. At that time, there was a procession through the streets of his city with the miraculous Kursk Root Icon of the Mother of God. Just as the procession passed the house where the sick child lay, there was a sudden downpour and the clergy who were bearing the wonderworking Icon sought refuge in their house. When the mother brought the young Prochor to venerate the Icon, he was instantly healed of his infirmity.

The heavenly patronage of the Mother of God continued to guide Saint Seraphim, the Mother of God appearing to him as many as twelve times during his life. Finally, when the time came for his repose, St. Seraphim died kneeling in prayer before another Icon of the Mother of God known as "Umilenie" or "Tenderfeeling." This Icon portrays the Mother of God at the time of the Annunciation. She has her hands meekly crossed in front of her heart, with her eyes cast down in prayerful contemplation, awaiting in humble submission the will of God as she says, *Let it be done unto me according to Thy word.* (St. Luke 1:38.)

In 1983, Archbishop Theodore, a Schema-monk from Valaam Monastery, one of Russia's greatest and most ancient Monasteries, gave to the monastic community at Christ of the Hills Monastery Relics of St. Seraphim of Sarov. These Relics are valued by the Monks as among the greatest treasures of the Monastery. The Monks very much believe that it is because of the presence of Saint Seraphim that the Icon of the Mother of God began to weep at New Sarov.

In the same year, 1983, the Weeping Icon was painted by a Greek Orthodox Monk in California. The Icon was originally hung in the Altar (Sanctuary) of the Monastery Church of St. John the Baptist at Christ of the Hills Monastery. Soon, however, the Monks outgrew this tiny Chapel, and in December of 1984 the Monks began construction on the Church of St. Seraphim of Sarov, which today is their main Church. By the first quarter of 1985, construction of the Church had proceeded to the point where the Monks had already begun to have Services there. But the Vladimir Icon of the Mother of God remained where it was hanging in the Chapel of St. John the Baptist.

On May 7 of 1985, the Icon was discovered miraculously weeping myrrh. A stream of sweet-scented myrrh flowed from each eye of the Virgin Mary.

When the Icon of the Mother of God began to weep at New Sarov, the Monks' first step was to discern if the manifestation was authentic and to immediately notify their ecclesiastical superiors of the event. All attested to the miracle's authenticity.

Next, they began a time of self-examination to discern what it was that God was trying to tell them.

Accompanied by prayer and fasting, each Monk undertook a thorough examination of conscience, culminating in a lifetime Confession by each to his Spiritual Father. The Monks do not believe that the Mother of God is weeping because she is happy. Rather, they see her tears as a sign of distress over how far we have all gone from Christ. Certainly, the current world situation, and the sad absence of the kind of life Christ calls Christians to lead in His Holy Gospels, are enough to cause our Holy Mother to weep.

They see her call as a call to repentance, prayer, fasting and change of life—from a worldly way of living and thinking to a Divine one. Christ is continually calling souls to Himself. Our God is thirsty for our love and our worship.

Great miracles have come as a result of anointing with the tears of this Icon: cures of cancer, leukemia, blindness, mental illness, and the most precious gift on earth—the gift of peace of mind—given so many, many souls.

The Icon continues to weep even to this day. Often she seems to weep when a soul comes into her presence who particularly needs her healing love, although many have received blessings and miracles without ever seeing the tears. Many have been converted to Christ through her intercession.

Hundreds of thousands of Pilgrims flock to Christ of the Hills Monastery, nestled on a mountain top six miles southwest of Blanco, Texas, and overlooking the

Blanco River Valley. There the Monks and Nuns lead a traditional Eastern Orthodox monastic life, never eating meat, often fasting, struggling to repent of their sins, praying over seven hours a day. Many believe that the prayers of Monks help keep the world intact. These Monastics do a full round of Orthodox Services every day, and the public is welcome to attend the Services. Pilgrims are all received as Christ and taken to the Churches of the Monastery and to the Chapel of the Myrrh-Weeping Icon. All are anointed with the tears of the Mother of God and are invited to stay for the next Service. The hospitality of the Monks, who lead a very simple, God-centered life, is given to all visitors.

The Monks follow the ancient Russian Typicon (tradition of worship). The Divine Services are done entirely in English. The Monks, through their hospitality and humble customs, desire to offer the love of Christ as a refreshing blessing in a time of worldly chaos and uncertain future, burdened as it is with economic, social, and political instability all around.

Pilgrims come for a variety of reasons. Some come out of curiosity. Others come looking for miracles in their own lives. Still others come merely to pray before the Icon of the Mother of God. Groups from all over North America and throughout the world have come to share in the wonders of the miraculous sign. At times the crowds are overwhelming and yet the Monks and Nuns believe that to receive all of those who come is to receive Christ.

In the words of the founder of Christ of the Hills Monastery, "We know we are not worthy to have the spiritual treasure which has been entrusted to our care. However, we are profoundly aware of our deep responsibility to share it with all who come in faith. The Mother of God calls all to her Son. The Mother of God calls all to repentance, fasting, prayer, and an other-worldly way of living. Like Saint John the Baptist, her cry is 'Make straight the way of the Lord, Christ is coming again.'"

Patronal Icon
of Christ of the Hills Monastery

CHAPTER 2
ICONS IN THE ORTHODOX TRADITION

The Weeping Icon of Our Lady of New Sarov was painted in 1983, but it represents an unbroken tradition of Christian iconography dating back at least 2000 years. In fact, the Orthodox Icon has its origins in the Old Testament. Many opponents of Icons like to point to the Second Commandment *Thou shalt not make unto thee any graven image* (Exodus 20:2), believing that these words forbid the use of iconography. However, in the same Law, God also commanded Moses to construct images for use in the worship of the Israelites; most notably, the Cherubim which were above the Mercy Seat in the Holy of Holies. (Exodus 25:18.) Does the Scripture contradict itself? Not at all. On the contrary, Scripture is balanced. By looking at the whole of Scripture, not just proof texts (that is, little snippets pulled out of context in order to support one's own opinion), we can see the profound lesson God is giving to us. By "graven images" the Second Commandment is referring to pagan idols. God leads us from the demonically inspired images of this world to the true, heavenly images. Most everyone uses imagery when they pray. The Saints teach us that the highest form of prayer is without imagery—but this is only attained by those who are very advanced, and they could not have attained that advanced state of prayer unless they had first begun from true, God-inspired images.

Throughout the Old Testament, God gave the Israelites Divine or other-worldly images to focus on, in order to keep them on the right path. He also showed wonderworking power through holy objects. The Ark of the Covenant itself manifested tremendous divine power—yet there was never any confusion, and the people did not worship the Ark instead of God; rather, God manifested His power through the Ark.

We also read how, when the Children of Israel were in the wilderness and they murmured against God, He sent serpents to strike them. The people turned to Moses for help and God commanded Moses to fashion the figure of a serpent out of brass and set it up on a staff, so that any who had been bitten by the serpents would look at it and be healed. (Numbers 21:5-9.) This again was no idolatry, but rather obedience to the command of God. The Holy Fathers have always understood this Brazen Serpent as a prophesy or foreshadowing of the Crucifixion of Christ; so that all who have been bitten by the serpent—that is, who are ailing from the temptations and deceptions of the devil—can look to Christ and be healed. God also used the image of a serpent to heal the effects of the serpent's bite in the same way that Christ used death as a means by which to destroy death.

The Holy Prophets in the Old Testament also saw theophanies (that is, manifestations of God). The Prophet Isaiah (Isaiah 6:1-8) says, *I saw the Lord sitting upon a throne, high and lifted up* (v. 1). He was able to say, with great spiritual dread, *...mine eyes have seen the King, the Lord of hosts.* (v. 5.) Moses spoke to God face to face and God revealed Himself to him. (Exodus 33:11, Numbers 12:8.) God appeared to the Prophet Elias (Elijah) at Mount Horeb. (III Kings [I Kings] 19:11-13.) But even so, they did not see the actual Divine Face, for God says, *there shall no man see Me and live.* (Exodus 33:20.) Rather, they were permitted to see a sort of Icon, an image depicting Him Who cannot be depicted.

In the Old Testament there were images, and there were even visions that the Prophets were permitted to see, but there was no Icon directly depicting God. In the Book of Leviticus we read the explanation of why: *...the Lord spake unto you out of the midst of the fire: ye heard the voice of the words, but saw no form; only a voice.* (Deuteronomy 4:12.) On Mount Sinai, when God manifested Himself to Moses, God spoke but did not appear in a form. This is because God is spirit (St. John 4:24), and the Divinity cannot be depicted by a physical form. The Apostle John confirms this in his First Epistle when he says, *No man hath seen God at any time.* (I John 4:12.) So then, why do we have Icons depicting our Lord Jesus Christ? Because the Icons that depict our Lord do not attempt to depict His Divinity, but rather they depict the Incarnation. The same Apostle John says, *the Word* (the Son of God) *became flesh and dwelt among us.* (St. John 1:14.) When our Lord Jesus Christ became Incarnate, He took on the fullness of our humanity: body, soul and spirit. Because the Immaterial God became material for our salvation, we can now use a material means to depict that mystery. In the Old Testament the Incarnation had not yet happened (even though it is prophesied there), so no form was possible; but in the New Testament we have been given a form: the form of our Lord Jesus Christ, *for in Him dwelleth all the fullness of the Godhead bodily.* (Colossians 2:9.) So now, in the New Testament, the Icon of Christ is not only not forbidden, but many of the Fathers consider it *necessary* as a confession of our belief in the Incarnation.

We also depict the Saints in Icons, because the Saints reflect the glory of God. In a sense, by honoring the Saints, we are honoring God, Who shines forth through them, like light shining through a clear glass. Sin darkens us and makes us opaque. The Christian life is a life of struggle to cleanse ourselves of impurities—by cooperating with the grace of God—so that we may become transparent and the light of Christ can shine through us into the world. The Saints are people who have done this. We venerate the Saints through their Icons because the Saints have become Icons of Christ. God glorifies His Saints through miracles, both through their Relics and through their Icons, so that our faith may be increased and we may follow their example. We honor them and learn about their lives and struggles in order to follow in their footsteps and to go where they have gone—to stand before the face of God. The Saints are our heroes, our role models.

Some people have said that our thoughts create reality. In a spiritual sense, this is very true. If we think of the terrible crimes that we have witnessed in our time—drive-by shootings, deadly rampages in our public schools, mass murders, drug addiction, and all forms of demonic behavior—these tragic people did not just suddenly wake up one morning and decide out of the blue that they were going to do these terrible things; it was the result of years of wrongful thinking on their part—wrongful imagery. We have seen over the last few years younger and younger people committing terrible atrocities. The recent wave of school shootings is really only a symptom of the way our society is going. Make no mistake: these young people are not the lunatic fringe, they are our own children, pointing out the direction our society is headed. Take a look at the images the world is presenting to our youth—images of graphic violence and lack of respect for human life. Images that make ugliness and disharmony seem normal. Images that desensitize our youth to the hideous and the harmful. Children play computer games that expose them to murderous destruction, developing sniper skills with which they shoot people for fun. In our society, abortion is considered normal, and it is taught that it is a woman's right to murder her own child. Is it any wonder that these things are happening? We need to return to God. We need to provide our youth with healthy and healing images. We need to allow them to stand before the Living God and gaze upon His countenance.

THE STYLE OF THE ICON

All Icons are reproductions of older Icons, what are called "types." Each type of Icon ultimately refers to its "prototype;" that is, to Christ or the Saint depicted on it. So the veneration given to an Icon is not given to the wood and paint, but rather to the one depicted on it. An Iconographer does not simply rely on his imagination to decide how to paint his subject, instead he refers to a more ancient type. The type of the Icon of Our Lady of New Sarov, located at Blanco, Texas, is called Our Lady of Vladimir. According to Tradition, the first Icon of this style was painted by the Holy Apostle and Evangelist Luke. St. Luke is credited with painting three Icons depicting the Mother of God with her Divine Infant. These Icons became the basis for all subsequent Icons of the Mother of God. To paint these Icons, St. Luke took boards from the table that had been in the childhood home of our Lord in Nazareth, and painted the Icons on them. After St. Luke had finished the Icons, he presented them to the Mother of God for her approval. On seeing the Icons, she said, "May the grace of Him Who was born of me and His great mercy be with these Icons." St. Luke is also credited with painting the first Icons of Sts. Peter and Paul, and thus with initiating the sacred work of Iconography.

The use of portraiture was very common in the first century Greco-Roman world, and was not necessarily reserved only for the upper classes. In fact, in Alexandria, where St. Luke lived and preached for a period of time, portraiture was very common, even among the lower classes. Numerous amazingly realistic depictions dating back to the first century and earlier have been discovered by archaeologists. The catacombs themselves are full of iconographic images. What this tells us is that the traditional depictions of Christ and the Mother of God are very likely what they actually looked like during their earthly lives; they are not simply idealized portraits, but probably have their basis in historical reality. The earliest surviving portrait of our Lord Jesus Christ is found in the catacomb of Domitilla (Second Century). In this portrait, all of the features required to be present in an Orthodox Icon of Christ are found. This catacomb was a local burial place in Rome that was abandoned and forgotten until accidentally rediscovered near the end of the sixteenth century, and yet it preserves the exact same artistic tradition that is known universally in the Orthodox Icon of Christ to this day. The catacombs also provide archeological evidence of the existence of Icons among the early Christians.

After St. Luke painted the Icon of the Mother of God, known today as Our Lady of Vladimir, it remained in Jerusalem until the year 450, when it was transferred to Constantinople, which by that time had become the capital of the Roman Empire. At the beginning of the twelfth century, the holy Icon was taken to the city of Kiev (also known as Vyshgorod), in modern-day Ukraine. In Kiev the Icon was placed in a Monastery of Nuns, where it was glorified by great miracles.

In the year 1160, Prince St. Andrew Iurievich (called, *Bogolubsky*, that is, "beloved of God"—Feastday, July 4), as he was traveling one day, saw a wondrous vision of the Mother of God. St. Andrew was moving from Vyshgorod to the Suzdal region, and he had taken with him the wonderworking Icon. Near the city of Vladimir the horses that were hauling the miraculous Icon suddenly stopped and would move no further. St. Andrew asked the Priest accompanying him to celebrate a Molieben (service of intercession) before the wonderworking Icon. Afterwards, the Prince retired to his tent and continued his fervent prayer. Near morning, the Prince experienced a marvelous vision: The Most Holy Theotokos appeared to him, holding a scroll in her right hand. She commanded the Prince to leave her wonderworking Icon there in

Vladimir (northeast of Moscow) and to build a Church and a Monastery on the site where he received the vision. She then raised her hands to heaven and, receiving a blessing from Christ the Saviour, disappeared from sight. Ever since that time, this style of Icon has been known as Our Lady of Vladimir. This miraculous appearance of the Mother of God is celebrated on June 18. On at least three different occasions, the Russian people were saved from invasion by the intercession of the Mother of God through her miraculous Vladimir Icon (commemorated by the Church on May 21, June 23, and August 26).

The Vladimir Mother of God Icon was copied many times, and has become one of the most revered Icons among the Russian people. The Vladimir Icon of the Mother of God of New Sarov was painted in 1983 in a Greek Orthodox Monastery in California. The Icon was painted by hand in traditional manner on a solid board that had been covered with gesso. Although egg tempera is the most traditional method employed by iconographers, other media are allowed also. The Weeping Icon was painted using acrylics, in a simple and yet deeply-touching style.

The Icon was originally hung in the Sanctuary of the Monastery Church of St. John the Baptist at Christ of the Hills Monastery outside of rural Blanco, Texas. This was the first Chapel erected on the Monastery grounds.

If we look at the Weeping Icon, we will see that Christ and His holy mother are embracing, and we will see that Mary is looking at the viewer—actually, through the viewer into heaven—and pointing to Christ. The Mother of God is directing us to Christ. This is one of the most important roles of the Mother of God for us: she leads us into a closer relationship with our Lord. Like she did at the Wedding in Cana of Galilee, the Mother of God says to us who would be servants of the Lord, *Whatsoever He saith unto you, do it.* (St. John 2:5.)

St. Seraphim of Sarov

One of Russia's most beloved Saints, St. Seraphim is an amazing miracle-working Saint, like one of the ancient fathers, living almost in our own time. A number of the miracles recounted in this book are attributed to his intercessions.

CHAPTER 3
MYRRH

Myrrh, as it is found in nature, is a fragrant gum resin exuded from any of several thorny shrubs which grow along the Red Sea (on the Arabian Peninsula and eastern Africa). To gather myrrh, slits are cut in the bark of the shrub and the thick resin oozes out and hardens into crystalline globules. These globules are, interestingly enough, referred to as "tears." The tears of myrrh may be placed on hot coals to be burned as incense, but because myrrh is so expensive—two to ten times the price of frankincense—the tears are often crushed and combined with oil to be used as a perfume. It should be noted that the admixture of myrrh with oil is not a combination that occurs in nature. Rather, it requires the agency of man—or, divine intervention. This is part of the miraculous aspect of weeping Icons: it is scientifically impossible for myrrh, mixed with oil, to flow naturally from wood.

Oil itself is also significant. In the Greek language, the word for oil (*élaion),* is similar to the word for mercy (*éleos*, compassion). So an Icon that is exuding fragrant oil is symbolic of the outpouring of the mercy of God upon all mankind.

The use of myrrh is found in ancient writings going back at least 2,700 years. We find myrrh mentioned not only in the middle east, but in China, ancient Egypt, and throughout the Greco-Roman and Asian civilizations. Trade in Myrrh and spices was a major economic factor in the ancient world. (Genesis 37:25.) Myrrh at that time was considered to be as valuable as gold.

From ancient times, myrrh was used not only in religious ritual and as a perfume, but also had medicinal uses. Even today, throughout the middle east one can find myrrh sold in the *suk* (open air market) as a medicine. It is used for the treatment of wounds, sore throat, and mouth and gum disorders. It is also reputed to build up strength, assist the digestive system and treat apathy. Modern science has supported the antiseptic, antibacterial and anti-inflammatory properties of myrrh. It also facilitates the production of white blood cells and therefore is useful in building up the immune system.

In the Sacred Scriptures, myrrh is mentioned in both the Old and the New Testaments. On Mount Sinai, when our Lord gave the holy Prophet Moses specific instructions on how to construct the Tabernacle and how to conduct the Divine Services, He also commanded Moses to make anointing oil. (Exodus 30:23-25.) The principal ingredient in this holy anointing oil was myrrh. The anointing oil was made for consecration. Initially it was used to consecrate the holy things in the Tabernacle and the priests. Later, when the Holy Prophets anointed Kings, the holy anointing oil was used for this also. So myrrh carries with it the concept of consecration. When something is consecrated it is set aside for the exclusive use of God.

Anointing was performed only on those kings who were descendants of David. An interesting Rabbinic tradition states that when kings were anointed in ancient Israel, the oil was poured on their head in the form of a circlet (like a crown), and priests were anointed in the form of the Cross. The word “Messiah” means “Anointed One” (the Greek word for Messiah is *Christos*, from which we get our word “Christ”). Christ is both King of kings and Great High Priest.

In writing to the whole Church, the holy Apostle Peter teaches that we are members of the Royal Priesthood. (I Peter 2:9.) Although there is a particular Priesthood (Bishops, Priests and Deacons), to whom alone certain things are reserved; there is also a general Priesthood composed of all the Faithful. This means that each member of the Church has an obligation, a vocation to fulfill.

In the Mystery of Chrismation (known in the West as Confirmation) we are anointed with Chrism. This Chrism is compounded after the fashion of the anointing oil of Moses, using olive oil, myrrh and other spices, and its use dates back to the time of the Apostles themselves. We read in the Acts of the Apostles how after converts were Baptized, the Apostles would lay their hands upon them and they would receive the Holy Spirit. (Acts 8:17, 19:6.) However, soon the Church began to grow so rapidly—not only in numbers, but also in distance—that it was not possible for the Apostles to lay hands on each and every new convert who was Baptized. So the Apostles met together and prayed, and they laid their hands upon a vessel of Chrism, and the Holy Spirit was bestowed upon the Chrism. The Chrism was then distributed to the Presbyters (Priests) whom the Apostles had Ordained, so that they could Chrismate those whom they Baptized. In this way the gift of the Holy Spirit was made available to all the Faithful. This anointing with Chrism is our consecration into the Royal Priesthood. When an Icon weeps myrrh, we are being reminded to live up to the obligations of our royal and priestly calling.

When our Lord Jesus Christ was born in Bethlehem, Magi (wise men) came from the east, bearing gifts. (St. Matthew 2:1-16.) These wise men very likely came from Persia, where the Holy Prophet Daniel had been taken at the time of the Babylonian Captivity. Daniel's prophesies appear to have been remembered not only by the Jews in Persia, but by the pagan astrologers also. The Magi were members of the Persian priestly caste, and were considered to be diviners who believed that by studying the movements of the stars they could predict the future course of events. They combined the truth of Daniel's prophesy with their own erroneous pagan beliefs. But God had mercy on them and led them from ignorance to the truth. By making use of a star (actually an Angel of God), He led those who formerly worshiped the stars to the Truth Himself—God incarnate, lying in a crib in Bethlehem. Travelling from the East to the West, they journeyed from darkness towards the Light.

When the Magi came to our Lord and worshiped Him as God, they presented their gifts: gold, frankincense and myrrh. These were not only the most costly gifts of the time, but also had symbolic meaning. Gold is symbolic of royal dignity, and the Magi thereby showed that our Lord Jesus Christ is King—not only King of the Jews, but King of kings, and Lord of lords. He is *Pantocrator*, Ruler of All. Frankincense is incense that is offered to God in worship. by offering frankincense to Christ, the Magi witnessed to the divinity of Christ. In ancient times, myrrh was used not only as a perfume and for medicinal purposes, but also as part of the preparation of the dead for burial. Thus, the gift of myrrh signified Christ's humanity: He participated so fully in our humanity, that He even participated in the experience of death together with us. The gift of myrrh prophesied Christ's death on the Cross for our salvation. So myrrh is also symbolic of death: We must die to the old man; we must be buried with Christ in order to rise with Him.

The Scripture tells us that the Magi, *being warned by God in a dream, returned home by another way.* (St. Matthew 2:12.) In mentioning this, the Evangelist is not only recounting an historical fact, but he is also teaching us an important lesson. Having encountered the Incarnate God and His Holy Mother, we cannot return to our old ways. When we see how God has reached out to us, we must be forever different. In returning to our daily lives, we must now live differently—no longer as citizens of this world, but of the world to come. Our lives must be permanently changed.

Most of us are familiar with the fact that when our Lord was crucified, He was offered gall and vinegar to drink. (St. Matthew 27:34.) This is in fulfillment of the prophesy in Psalm 68:22 (69:21 in modern translations): *They gave Me gall for food, and for My thirst they gave Me vinegar to drink.* The Greek word translated "gall" can refer to anything bitter or an anodyne (a narcotic used to lessen pain). St. Mark tells us specifically that it was myrrh that was mixed with wine. (St. Mark 15:23.) Wine (or vinegar) tinctured with myrrh was given to those condemned to crucifixion. Thus, our Lord was offered this to lessen His pain. We should also note that He refused to take this narcotic, preferring to endure the Crucifixion, with all of its pain and anguish, for our salvation. Even so, myrrh is linked to the death of Christ on the Cross, and is itself symbolic of death.

As mentioned already, myrrh was commonly used to anoint the dead before burial. In the Gospel of St. John we read how St. Nicodemos came with a mixture of myrrh and aloes to prepare the Body of our Lord for burial. (St. John 19:39.) Here again we see how myrrh symbolizes death. Each Christian must enter into the death of Christ in order to participate in the Resurrection.

Finally, early in the morning, as the Holy Women came to the Sepulchre of Christ, they were bringing with them "sweet spices." (St. Mark 16:1; St. Luke 23:56, 24:1.) The Greek word used means "aromatics," that is, it is a general term meaning any sweet aromatic mixture. Sacred Tradition refers to these Holy Women as the "Holy Myrrhbearers" because traditionally we are taught that what they were carrying was myrrh to anoint the body of Christ, in accordance with the burial custom of the day. But instead of encountering the dead, they were greeted with the joyous news of the Resurrection. In the words of one of the Orthodox Church's most beautiful Paschal hymns:

> The Myrrh-bearing Women at the break of dawn, drew near to the tomb of the Life-giver. There they found an Angel seated upon the stone. He greeted them with these words: "Why seek ye the Living among the dead?

> Why mourn ye the Incorrupt amid corruption? Go, proclaim the glad tidings to His Disciples."

So here, that which formerly was symbolic of death, has now come to symbolize the Resurrection. Having passed through the bitterness of the Crucifixion, we now partake of the sweetness of the Resurrection. Now we can sing, in another verse of the same hymn:

> Come from that scene, O women, bearers of glad tidings, and say to Zion: Receive from us the glad tidings of joy, of Christ's Resurrection. Exult and be glad, and rejoice, O Jerusalem, seeing Christ the King, Who comes forth from the tomb like a Bridegroom in procession.

Our English word "myrrh" comes from an Arabic word that means, "bitter," because even though its aroma is very sweet it's taste is bitter. The Hebrew word, *môr*, has the same meaning (from *mârar*, meaning, "to make bitter"). This is how it is sometimes with repentance: it is bitter in the mouth. Sometimes, it is hard to admit our sins; to say, "I have sinned," and to ask forgiveness. But when we do, then the aroma it produces—the grace of the Holy Spirit—is very sweet. So myrrh is also symbolic of repentance.

Throughout the Church's history, God has manifested miracles not only through the prayers of the living, but also through Relics of the Saints (IV Kings [II Kings] 13:21), and the Holy Icons. Among the miracles which have been recorded in the Tradition of the Church are miraculous manifestations such as myrrh streaming from Relics and from Icons. Probably one of the most famous Saints from whose Relics myrrh flows is St. Nicholas of Myra (Feastday, December 6). Also, St. Nicodemos the Myrrh-streaming (Feastday, May 7), who made a number of amazing prophesies specifically about the Twentieth Century and the approach of the Antichrist.

There are also many famous myrrh-streaming Icons. Although there have been myrrh-streaming and weeping Icons of Christ and of various Saints, most are Icons of the Mother of God. Often myrrh will flow from the face, from the hands and feet, or from some other feature on the Icon. In all of these cases, the symbolisms associated with myrrh which we spoke of above are applicable.

There have been hundreds of myrrh-streaming Icons of the Theotokos throughout the centuries. Some of the most famous in Russia are the Icon of the Theotokos "Of the Sign" (1170 A.D.; Feastday, November 27), the "Pimen" Icon of the Theotokos (1381 A.D.; Feastday, June 6), the "Chirsk-Pskov" Icon of the Theotokos (1420 A.D.; Feastday, July 16), and the "Mirozh" Icon of the Theotokos. (1567 A.D.; Feastday, September 24.) In North America, more recent famous Weeping Icons are the Iveron Mother of God of Montreal, and the Weeping Icon of the Mother of God in Chicago, as well as Our Lady of New Sarov and many, many others.

When the myrrh flows specifically from the eyes, the Icon is referred to as a "weeping Icon," and bears, in addition to the symbolism of myrrh also the specific call to sorrow over one's sins.

It has been reported many times that the tears of the Myrrh-Weeping Icon of New Sarov are self-replicating, meaning that a cotton ball with the tears on it that has dried out will suddenly and miraculously become moist again with fresh tears of the Mother of God. This marvelous wonder has been reported with other Weeping Icons also, including the Iveron Weeping Icon of Montreal, Quebec, and others throughout the world.

Another phenomenon that should be mentioned is that on occasion the tears have been known to go rancid. This surprising occurrence seems to happen when women have been anointed who have been wearing heavy makeup. It would appear that the Mother of God is calling women to modesty and humility in an age when these virtues are considered to be unimportant. Other occasions when this has been noticed seem to be when the tears are treated with irreverence or light-mindedness. One remembers the manna in the wilderness—when mere men were permitted to eat the bread of Angels, and yet complained about it—how if people abused the great blessing that God had given to them, the manna would become putrid. (Exodus 16:13-20.)

Although this kind of miracle has been occurring for many centuries and is nothing new in the Church's history, there have never been so many Icons weeping at the same time as there are right now. The call of the Mother of God is very urgent. Everywhere she is reaching out for men, women, and children to heed her tender plea. It is because of the lateness of the hour. Her plea is for repentance. In a way, she is saying, "It is later than you think."

Archbishop Theodore

A Spiritual Father in the tradition of Valaam, one of Holy Russia's largest and most ancient Monasteries, Elder Theodore lived the Evangelical life, and instructed his disciples in the little way of humility and obedience, teaching them to live the angelic life while still on earth.

CHAPTER 4
THE CALL OF THE MOTHER OF GOD

To encounter the Myrrh-Weeping Icon of the Mother of God of New Sarov is a wondrous experience. To be a witness of her many Miracles is an experience that touches the soul. Yet, no matter how extraordinary this experience may be, the Monks at Christ of the Hills Monastery do not see the weeping of the Mother of God as a happy event. They see her tears as a sign of deep sorrow. She is weeping over our sins. Her tears are the tears of a mother whose heart has been broken by her children.

You see, she weeps over how far we all are from Christ. Our sins break her heart. Like Saint John the Baptist, her call is *Repent and make straight the way of the Lord.* (St. Matthew 3:2-3.) Indeed, we believe that the signs of the times indicate that we are the Christians of the latter days. How long it will take for these days to unfold no one knows. Christ said that no one would know the hour or the moment of His great and glorious Second Coming. However, each of us is on a personal race with his own death. We will be held accountable for our life before God, based on the condition of our soul at the time of our death.

As mentioned above, Icons have been weeping in the Orthodox Church for many centuries; this is nothing new. But there have never been so many Icons weeping at the same time as there are right now. There are reports of hundreds of Icons weeping throughout the world—not only in America and in the Old Countries, but on every inhabited continent—

everywhere, the Mother of God is gently calling us to turn back again to Christ. To realize that we are not the center of the universe: that God is the center of the universe, and if we are to lead fully human lives—lives lived the way God intended us to live—we must lead them in conformity with His will. We were made for a purpose, and have been bought at a high price—the price of the Blood of her son, Jesus Christ.

The Church has always interpreted the tears of the Mother of God as being tears of sadness. We believe that she is weeping because of our sins, because of our selfishness and because of how far we have fallen away from the Gospel of Christ. She is weeping because we are not weeping. We should be weeping for our sins. But we are not. And so she is weeping for us. Often when we see someone we love weeping, it causes us to want to weep also.

We believe that the Mother of God is calling all who listen to her silent plea to lead a Christ-centered life. We read in the Gospels how a Christian is supposed to conduct his life: he must be in the world but not of the world. (St. John 15:18-19; 17:14, 16.) We hear Christ tell us that to enter the Kingdom of Heaven we must become innocent like little children. (St. Matthew 18:3.) We hear Him tell us that if struck on one cheek we are to turn the other. If robbed of our coat we are to run after the robber to give him our shirt also. (St. Matthew 5:39-40.) Christ tells us to bless those who persecute us, to love our enemies, and to refrain from judgement. (St. Luke 6:28, St. Matthew 7:1.)

• THE CALL OF THE MOTHER OF GOD •

It does not take a genius to read the Acts of the Apostles and the Holy Gospels in order to discover that most people who call themselves Christians today are not leading a Christian life in the way in which the Apostles and the early followers of Christ understood a Christian life. They took the Scriptures and Apostolic Teaching seriously. They strove to live the Gospel life literally, the way Christ called them to. We would do well to follow their example.

It is in this context then that we find the Mother of God weeping, not only here but around the world. We believe that the call of the Mother of God has five specific points. We have outlined them here, so that you will better understand what we believe she is asking and her Son requiring of each of us.

REPENTANCE

First of all, the Monks believe the Mother of God is calling all of us to repentance. Since she is weeping tears of sadness over our sins, our response should be to repent of those sins. Looking upon our own sins, we will be less inclined to judge others. Needing great mercy from God, perhaps we will show mercy to others. Many of the great Saints examined their consciences numerous times a day. We must begin to develop spiritual vision, so as to be able to see ourselves as God sees us.

Repentance is the foundation of the Christian life. When our Lord Jesus Christ was Baptized by John in the Jordan, He went out into the wilderness to fast and pray for forty days. When He came out of the wilderness, He began His preaching ministry. The first words the Gospel records of our Lord's preaching ministry were *Repent, for the Kingdom of Heaven is at hand.* (St. Matthew 4:17.) One can be Baptized and go to Church every Sunday, one can do all of the externals—but until one begins to repent of his sins, he is not yet leading the Christian life. As soon as we stop repenting, we stop living the Christian life. There is a famous Russian Priest who once said, "Our Faith makes no sense to those who are not repenting."

In the Greek language, the word for repentance is *metánoia*, meaning, a change of heart. To repent means to change, to no longer follow our own path, but to return to the path that God desires us to walk on. To do this, we need to first of all realize that we are on the wrong path.

The perfect instruction on repentance is given to us by our Lord Himself, in the Parable of the Prodigal Son. (St. Luke 15:11-32.) We are like the Prodigal—we have left our Father's house and squandered our inheritance (the good gifts that God has given us) on earthly things. We have departed into a foreign country (the world, separated from God). We have sought to fill our bellys with swine's food (the things of this world). Now, we have to also be like the Prodigal and realize where our own self-will has gotten us. We must rise up from the mire and struggle to return to our Father's house. When our Heavenly Father sees our desire to return and our struggle, He Himself will run out to meet us, and give us all that we need to be restored again.

To help us in this process of repentance God has given us the Sacrament of Confession—or, as the Orthodox call it, the Mystery of Confession. We refer to the Sacraments as "Mysteries," not in the sense that they are strange, but rather in the sense that they are mystical. Confession has become very unpopular today. People don't want to admit that they are sinners. But Confession is extremely important in the working out of our salvation. Some spiritual writers have referred to Confession as "the forgotten medicine"—because it is a therapy for the soul. But as with any therapy, if we only go every now and then, the therapy won't do us much good. For the therapy to be effective, we must go regularly and we must go frequently, and be completely honest about our sins.

When we go to Confession, we must remember that it is not the Priest we are confessing to—it is Christ. He is the one Who hears our confession, He it is that forgives our sin. The Priest is there as a witness—for the Scripture says, *Confess your sins one to another.* (James 5:16.) In other words, it is not enough to simply confess silently in your heart. You must go before another—one whom God has chosen for that purpose—and bravely expose your wounds, that the Physician of Souls (Christ) may heal you. The Priest is also there to counsel you and guide you. Often the Holy Spirit will guide the Priest in what he should say to you. Most importantly, the Priest is there as the vessel, through whom God forgives your sins and bestows His grace upon you. Our Lord said to the Apostles, *Whose soever sins ye remit, they are remitted unto them; and whose soever sins ye retain, they are retained.* (St. John 20:23.) The grace of the Holy

Spirit that you receive at Confession is the grace you need to overcome the sins you have confessed. But you do have to cooperate with that grace, if there is going to be any change in your life.

It is recommended that you go to Confession at least once a week. However, you must understand that you cannot make a good weekly Confession of sin, unless you first make a good daily examination of conscience.

A very good practice is to spend some time in silence and prayer every evening, and then sit down with a piece of paper and begin to go through the whole day in your mind and memory. Begin from the moment you woke up in the morning. Remember your first thought of the day. Remember: What was the first thing you did this morning? Who was the first person you spoke to? Were the subjects of your conversations during the day godly or no? How did you react to the various things that came your way? Remember not only what you did, but also those things you failed to do.

That first thought, by the way, is very important. One of the Fathers said that he could tell the direction the whole day will take by his first thought. For this reason, we should strive to seize that first thought and dedicate it to God. So that the first fruits of the day belong to Him. As soon as we gain consciousness in the morning we should stand up, make the Sign of the Cross on ourselves and say a prayer. There are morning and evening prayers said daily by all Orthodox Christians, and regular, daily prayer is very important.

However, if you do not have a prayerbook, you can say a simple prayer, something like, "In the name of the Father, and of the Son, and of the Holy Spirit. Amen. O Lord, I dedicate this day to Thee. Bless me, save, and grant me eternal life."

Then, at the end of the day, as you examine your conscience, notice the ways in which you fell short (the Greek word for sin means, "to fall short" or "to miss the mark," and thus to "not share in the prize"). Remember that we sin not only in our deeds, but also in our words, and even in our thoughts—even a thought can separate us from God. So we have to be very conscious and guard our heart, observing both what goes into our heart and what comes out.

When you remember your sins, write them down. Some people even carry a notepad with them throughout the day, and when they notice that they have sinned, or remember a previous sin that they have not yet confessed, they write it down then and there. This is an excellent practice. Writing down our sins accomplishes two things: first of all, it makes us more conscious of that sin, so that when the same temptation comes along again, we can recognize it and not fall into the same sin again; the second thing it does is to provide us with a written record that we can take with us when we go to the Priest for Confession. If you do this, often you will notice that as you are reading through the list of your sins you will suddenly remember other sins that you might not otherwise have remembered or confessed. Then, after you have confessed your sins, you can burn the paper you wrote them on.

It is also important to go to Confession before receiving Holy Communion. We will find in the Holy Scripture that Saint Paul in his First Letter to the Corinthians says, *Let each man examine himself, and so let him eat of that bread and drink of that cup. For he that eateth and drinketh unworthily, eateth and drinketh damnation to himself, not discerning the Lord's Body.* (I Corinthians 11:28-29.) These are very strong words. But the Apostle is not making an over-statement; rather, he is warning us about how serious a matter it is to receive the Body and Blood of Christ without first confessing our sins. If we receive unworthily, not only will we not receive any benefit from Holy Communion, but it can actually be harmful to us. St. Paul goes on in the next verse to say, *That is why many of you are sick and some have even died.* (I Corinthians 11:30.)

FASTING

Next, we are called to fast. This is another thing that has become very unpopular today. People don't like to fast—at least they don't like to fast for God. There are plenty of worldly reasons why people fast: perhaps in order to lose weight so that they can be more attractive, or for physical health. But this is not the kind of fasting we are talking about: we are talking about fasting as a spiritual discipline.

The reason a Christian fasts is to overcome the passions. A passion is any sin that we have fallen into so many times, it has begun to have control over us. It can be over-eating, smoking, gossiping, lying, watching too much television, etc., etc., etc. Man was created with a free will, and anytime we submit our free will to anything other than God, it is a perversion, it is unnatural, and it must be overcome before we can begin to make progress in the spiritual life. If we look into the Scriptures we will find that our Lord Jesus Christ Himself fasted frequently—not because He had to; He is God, He is not subject to the passions. But He fasted in order to give us an example that we should follow.

If we look at the early Church, we will discover that the early Christians fasted two days out of the week: Wednesday and Friday. Most everyone knows that we fast on Friday because that is the day on which our Lord was Crucified. But why Wednesday? We fast on Wednesday because it was on that day of the week that Judas went to the chief priests and elders of the Jewish people and made the bargain to betray Christ for thirty pieces of silver. So Christians traditionally fast on Wednesday as well as Friday to remind us that we too betray Christ when we don't do what it is that He would have us do.

There is a very ancient Christian document called the *Didache*, which probably dates back to the end of the first century A.D. The name *Didache* means "Teaching," and it is called this because it contains the teaching of the Apostolic Church. Its full name is *The Teaching of the Lord to the Gentiles Through the Twelve Apostles*, and was probably written to instruct those converting from paganism to Christianity. Scholars had known about this document for centuries, but it had been lost until 1875 when it was rediscovered in the library of a Monastery in Constantinople. In the *Didache* is found the earliest admonition for Christians to fast on Wednesdays and Fridays, showing that this was the practice of the Apostolic Church.

There are different degrees of fasting. Some are able to abstain from food all day, or at least until sundown. Others eat only bread and water. If you are unable to fast this rigorously, then on Wednesday and Friday eat no meat, fish, or fowl; drink no alcoholic beverages; partake of no dairy products (i.e., no milk, no eggs, no cheese, no butter); do not use oil in the preparation of your food and refrain from using too many spices. Eat simple fasting-type food: vegetables, boiled grains, potatoes, bread, nuts and fruits. Fasting food should not be unappetizing, but it should be kept very simple. Part of the idea of fasting is to avoid those foods which stir up the passions. But whatever degree of fasting you take on should only be done only with the advise and blessing of your Spiritual Father. A prideful fast is a fast of demons.

When we fast, we are living the life of Paradise. Remember that Adam and Eve were told to abstain from a certain kind of food—the fruit of the Tree of the Knowledge of Good and Evil. So long as they were obedient and abstained, they continued to experience the joys of Eden, but once they abandoned their fast, they were cast out. Through fasting we have the opportunity to be obedient to God and to live in Paradise while still on earth. So fasting should never be a hardship for us, but should be embraced joyfully.

The Holy Fathers teach that mankind is not only physical by nature, he is also spiritual. But these are not two separate divisions within man, they are intimately united. What happens in his soul can affect his body, and what happens in his body can affect his soul. The soul of a man begins to exist at the same moment his body does—the moment of conception. Throughout his earthly life, the soul and the body of a man are united, and using both together he either works out his salvation or not. Even the separation of the soul from the body at death is temporary (and it is unnatural too—originally, man was not meant to die). At the Last Judgment, the soul will be re-united with the body, and both will stand together to be judged and to enter either heaven or hell eternally united. So fasting is not only a physical exercise, it is spiritual as well.

The fast of Wednesday and Friday is more than pious custom. St. Andrew the Fool-for-Christ lived in Constantinople during the Byzantine era. St. Andrew represents a particular kind of Saint in the Orthodox Church, called the Fool-for-Christ. Taking the words of St. Paul, *We are fools for Christ's sake* (I Corinthians 4:10), they intentionally embrace a life of foolishness so that their praise will come not from men but from God alone. Foolishness for Christ is considered to be the most difficult form of asceticism in the Church. To His holy fools, God often imparts special graces, such as healing and clairvoyance (God-given insight into the souls of others). One day, St. Andrew saw a funeral procession passing by. He beheld two Angels walking in the procession, one to the right of the bier and one to the left. When St. Andrew asked who these

Angels were, he was told that they were the Angels of Wednesday and Friday. Since the departed person had faithfully observed the fasts of Wednesday and Friday, these Angels accompanied him on his departure into everlasting life.

We would also like to mention St. John of Kronstadt, a Parish Priest in pre-revolutionary Russia. Although he was blessed by God to die before it began, St. John of Kronstadt prophesied the coming of the Bolshevik Revolution. He said that for this reason alone—that the fasts of Wednesday and Friday were not being observed—God's chastisement would fall upon the Russian people.

We can see from these two examples from the lives of the Saints how important fasting is. We believe that our Lady is calling all to return to this ancient tradition of the Apostolic Church.

CEASELESS PRAYER

Next, we are called to ceaseless prayer. Saint Paul says, *Pray without ceasing.* (I Thessalonians 5:17.) Again, the Apostle is not exaggerating, he is simply saying what is expected of each Christian. Many of the Saints have been able to do exactly this—by God's grace they have been able to pray without ceasing. One of the tried and true methods of praying without ceasing is through what is called the Jesus Prayer: "Lord Jesus Christ, Son of God, have mercy on me, a sinner." It is a very simple prayer, easy to memorize. The object of the prayer is to get in the habit of praying constantly, no matter what one is doing. While one is working, reading, driving the car—at all times. The Jesus Prayer is based, of course, on the name of Jesus: *that name which is above every other name.* That name *at which every knee should bow, in heaven, on earth and beneath the earth.* (Philippians 2:9-10.)

In the 18th Chapter of the Gospel of St. Luke we will find three stories that teach us about the Jesus Prayer. First, we read about the Importunate Widow who constantly called upon the judge to help her. (St. Luke 18:1-8.) This was a worldly judge, an unjust judge; and yet, because of the widow's persistence he finally did as she asked. How much more will the Just Judge help us when we call incessantly upon His name?

The Jesus Prayer is also based on the Prayer of the Publican. Remember the Parable of the Publican and the Pharisee. (St. Luke 18:10-14.) The Pharisee fulfilled all of the external commandments of the Law, but inside he was filled with pride. He was convinced of his own righteousness. So when he came to the Temple to pray, he prayed pridefully and said, *God, I thank Thee that I am not like other men: extortioners, unjust, adulterers, or even as this publican. I fast twice a week and give tithes of all that I possess.* The Publican, on the other hand, was aware of his own sins. And that awareness made him humble. He stood in the back and was so ashamed of his sin he would not even lift his eyes up to heaven. All he would do is beat his breast and say, *God, be merciful to me a sinner.* Our Lord tells us that it was this man—this sinner—who left justified, not that so-called "righteous" man. Also, we should remember the words of our Lord, *joy shall be in heaven over one sinner that repenteth, more than over ninety and nine just persons, which need no repentance.* (St. Luke 15:7.)

Finally, we read of the blind man on the way to Jericho. (St. Luke 18:35-43.) The blind man asked who it was that was passing by, and when he was told that it was Jesus he cried out, *Jesus, Thou Son of David, have mercy on me.* The people in the crowd told him to be quiet, but he cried all the louder, *Son of David, have mercy on me.* Jesus commanded him to be brought to Him and He healed him of his blindness. Are not we all blind and in need of Jesus' healing of our spiritual vision? Persistence is necessary and through continuously calling upon the name of Jesus, even when the world tries to discourage us, we can be saved.

As with any spiritual practice, it is necessary to have help from someone else, because we don't see ourselves clearly—we all look at ourselves with rose-colored glasses. We need someone who is more objective to guide us along the way and prevent us from falling into delusion, because the devil is always there, trying to prevent us from growing closer to God. So the Jesus Prayer should not be undertaken by anyone who does not have a Spiritual Father (or Mother) who is advanced in the practice of the Jesus Prayer. We also very highly recommend a book called, *The Way of A Pilgrim.* This beautiful book was written in Russia by an anonymous author, and is one of the great classics of Russian Spirituality. *The Way of A*

Pilgrim is about a man who hears the call of St. Paul to *Pray without ceasing* and begins to practice the Jesus Prayer. The book is written in the form of a story, during the course of which we are instructed in the practice of the Jesus Prayer.

Each of us should try to seek out as holy a Spiritual Father as possible. We should never take lightly the care of our souls. And having found a good Spiritual Father, tell him everything and confess at least once a week. In many Monasteries it is common for the Monks to go to their Spiritual Father every day and confess their sins.

Elder Anthony was one of the great Elders of Optina Hermitage. Optina was one of Russia's most important Monasteries, which was responsible for a marvellous spiritual renaissance in Russia just before the terrible persecutions that Communism brought upon the land. He wrote the following, echoing the words of St. John Climacus, who is one of the most important teachers of the spiritual life:

> Just as those who went out from Egypt had Moses as their guide, and those fleeing from Sodom had an Angel as their instructor, so you, in the words of St. John Climacus, must have a Moses interceding for you before God and serving as your instructor. Whoever trusts his own understanding and thinks that he has no need of an instructor will soon stray from the straight path. Therefore, you must entreat the Lord God with tears to grant you an unerring instructor or instructress; for an experienced and skilled physician needed according to the putridity of the disease.

The Elder Anthony is teaching us that the purpose of a Spiritual Father is not to be a guru. On the contrary, like Moses he will be a fallible human being Remember that even Moses, because of his sin, was not permitted to enter the Promised Land. (Numbers 27:12-14; Deuteronomy 34:4.) When Elder Anthony speaks of an "unerring instructor," he is meaning that the Spiritual Father or Mother must adhere to the true Faith; that is, must not follow heretical teachings, which lead one away from God rather than towards Him. Not that the instructor will be infallible from a human point of view; but rather, even in their humanness, the grace of God can still operate through them.

God works through fallible human beings. It was this way from the beginning. After creation, among the first words that God speaks about mankind, He says the following, *It is not good that the man should be alone; let us make him a helper like unto himself.* (Genesis 2:18.) This refers not only to the married state, in which a man and a woman struggle side by side to work out their salvation together; but even more profoundly, it teaches us something about human nature: we are intended to help one another spiritually. Even those who live as solitaries in the wilderness must begin by learning from another. Throughout the Scriptures we are taught that we must have a guide, otherwise we will go astray. The mystery of Eldership is the continuation of the prophetic ministry in the Church. It is the most direct means by which the Holy Spirit inspires and directs the lives of individual Christians.

You will also notice, in the passage by Elder Anthony quoted above, he mentions not only "instructors" but also "instructresses." In the Old Testament there were not only Prophets, there were also Prophetesses. The Holy Spirit is not limited to men, but women also partake—in fact, the Saints recognize the fact that often women are more spiritually attuned than men. After all, the greatest Saint in the Church is a woman: the Most Holy Mother of God herself, who is described in the hymns of the Church as "more honorable than the Cherubim and beyond compare more glorious than the Seraphim." In other words, a spiritual instructor does not necessarily have to be a Priest, or even a monastic. St. Andrew the Fool for Christ was a layman. Of course, we can only go to a Priest for the Sacrament of Confession, but we can have anyone as an Elder or spiritual guide. We cannot limit the Holy Spirit any more than we can limit the wind. Wherever you hear the rustling of the leaves, there the wind is. (St. John 3:8.)

We believe that the purpose of the creation of man is to worship God. When we are not engaged in prayer, we are not fulfilling the purpose of our creation. We are made to pray with every breath, with every heartbeat—no matter what we are doing, whether asleep or awake. We heartily recommend the practice of the Jesus Prayer as a means of attaining to this end.

Other useful books on the Jesus Prayer are Princess Illenia's *Introduction to the Jesus Prayer* and Archbishop Theodore's little booklet: *Prayer of the Heart.* There is also *The Jesus Prayer*, written by a

Monk of the Eastern Church, with an introduction by Bishop Kallistos (Ware). Another excellent book is entitled *On the Prayer of Jesus*, originally written in Russian by Bishop Ignatius (Brianchaninov). This marvelous book was translated into English by the late Archimandrite Lazarus (Moore).

LOVE OF GOD AND NEIGHBOR

The fourth call of the Mother of God is the Great Commandment: to love God before everything, and to love our neighbor as ourself. We read in the Book of Genesis that God saw that creation was good and made man to dwell in Paradise with Him. The great sin of Adam, by eating of the fruit of the Tree of Knowledge of Good and Evil, was the desire to achieve a parity with God. Adam felt that by eating of this fruit he would be equal to God, and thus have no further need of Him. Instead, he fell from his exalted place into sin, with its sorrow, sickness and death.

Now we must struggle to recover our innocence. Still, to this day, this is our greatest problem. We make false gods out of ourselves and our material world. We must die to the self and create an empty place in our hearts so that God can come. We must discover the Kingdom of Heaven within. We must truly worship and love God and not the false god of self (and self-will) that reigns in our hearts.

We must live out the Gospel of Jesus Christ. But we are called to live it out fully; not in the watered-down manner of popular religion today. We must love

God more than anything or anyone else. More than father, mother, spouse, brother, sister, or child. We must love God more than our comfortable way of life, more than our friends, more than all material things—more than our very life. We must be like the Martyrs, willing to peacefully and joyfully lay down our lives for the love of Christ, because this is exactly what He did for us. He came and took our life upon Himself and laid down His life that we may live in Him. Some of us may be called to actually suffer blood martyrdom for the Gospel. But whether or not God is calling us to that, we must *all* die to ourselves, to that part of us that is selfish and in love with worldly things. This is beautifully summed up in the words of Abba Athanasius, one of the Desert Fathers, who says:

> Be tortured by your conscience, die to sin, be as a dead man on earth, and you will be a martyr by desire. They (the Martyrs) fought aforetime with kings and princes (that is, endured persecution from kings and princes); you have a king of sin—the devil—and the princes, the demons. Formerly they were idols, heathen temples and those who sacrificed to idols. And these remain as thoughts in the soul. He who is a slave to lust bows down before the idol of Aphrodite. He who is in anger and fury bows down to the idol of Ares. He who is avaricious and blind to the trouble of his neighbor bows down to the idol of Hermes. But if you restrain yourself from all this, and keep yourself from the passions, you have conquered the idols, turned from evil and false belief and become a martyr for the Faith.

So we must every one of us struggle valiantly against the temptations of the world, the flesh and the devil, and be martyrs in this sense: that we can cry with the Holy Apostle Paul, *...they that are Christ's* *have crucified the flesh with the affections and lusts,* (Galatians 5:24) and *...God forbid that I should glory, save in the Cross of our Lord Jesus Christ, by Whom the world is crucified unto me and I unto the world.* (Galatians 6:14.)

A word of warning, however: even if we are called to blood martyrdom, we must be careful, because if we go to death wrathfully or judging others, it will do us no good. We read in the rite of Baptism the words from Scripture, *As many as have been Baptized into Christ have put on Christ.* (Galatians 3:27.) We must literally put on Christ. The "new man" within us must be Christ Jesus the Lord, entirely. Everything we do, we must do with love.

The second part of Christ's great injunction is to love our neighbor. He gives us the Parable of the Good Samaritan (St. Luke 10:33-37) to tell us that our neighbor is everyone on earth. And He tells us that loving our neighbor means we must place our neighbor before ourselves. We must delight in visiting the sick and imprisoned, burying the dead, comforting the afflicted and sorrowing, upholding the broken and downtrodden. We must love our enemies, turn the other cheek, go the extra mile, lend without expecting repayment. We must bless those who persecute us.

Love thy neighbor as thyself. (St. Matthew 19:19, etc.) These are easy words to say, but living them is more difficult. First of all, we must ask: Who is our neighbor? Our Lord teaches us that everyone is our neighbor—and this applies most especially to those people whom we find it most difficult to love: that horrible, nasty person who has nothing good to say about anyone; the alcoholic lying on the street corner; the drug addict; the murderer; the rapist. We must love our enemies, and and bless any person who wrongs us. These people have also been made in the image of God. If one struggles to see Christ in these seemingly unlovable people, Christ will reveal Himself in ways never thought possible before. For our Lord says, *Insofar as ye have done it unto the least of these my brethren, ye have done it unto Me.* (St. Matthew 25:40.)

REFRAIN FROM JUDGEMENT

The final call is to non-judgement; this is the sign of a truly repentant soul. If one is aware of his own sinfulness he won't stand in judgement of another person. This is the promise we have been given in the Gospel. Our Lord says, *Judge not lest ye be judged. The measure with which you judge others is the measure with which you will be judged.* (St. Matthew 7:1-2.) This is very comforting for those sinners who are merciful, but it is very fearful to those of us who tend to be judgmental. What our Lord is teaching us is that we set the standard by which God will judge us.

On that Final Day, when our Lord comes in glory, all of the departed who have ever lived from the foundation of the world will be resurrected, and they will stand before the Judgement Seat of Christ. Every human being who stands there will be a sinner—even the Saints are sinners, for none is without sin, save God alone. But some of those sinners will receive mercy and be sent to the right, to heaven; while some will be sent to the left, to hell. What makes this difference? This one thing primarily: whether or not we have judged others.

If we are merciful and forgiving of others in spite of their sins, then on the Last Day God will be merciful to us, in spite of our great sins. And that is the whole reason we are here on this earth. The whole span of our life has been given us to bring us to that one moment when we stand before the Judgement Seat of Christ and He will say unto us either, *Enter thou into the joy of thy Lord* (St. Matthew 25:21), or He will say, *I tell you, I do not know you. Depart from me, ye workers of iniquity.* (St. Matthew 7:23.) It is an either-or situation. There is no middle ground. This is a very serious matter and it is something that should sober us.

How often do we speak ill of another? How often do we judge? How often do we look down on others? We must absolutely refrain from all judgement. Pray for those who may seem to act or live in a way that you find wrong. Remember, you don't know what makes people do what they do, so never judge them in your own mind, and certainly never speak evil of someone before others, lest you be guilty not only of committing sin yourself, but of inspiring sin in others. In this way, by exercising great mercy towards all other human beings we will receive great mercy from Christ Himself.

So this is the Call of the Mother of God: repentance, fasting, prayer, love of God and neighbor, and non-judgement. Her tears are tears of compassion, because the Mother of God knows the pain that we endure in this life. And like a loving mother, she is reaching out to us, calling us back to her Son, imploring us to heed her call. This is probably the most important message you will ever hear in your life. If today you hear the call of the Lord, harden not your heart.

We are not promised that it will be easy. The way to God cannot but be rocky, narrow and hard. We are promised persecution in this world (St. Luke, 21:12-19); but in the world to come, life everlasting (St. Matthew 10:32-38, 19:27-30). So, in all the trials and tribulations we endure in this life, we should never loose sight of the fact that God will never give us more than we can endure. We should never be faint-hearted, because Christ has already overcome the world (St. John 16:33). When we suffer abuse or misunderstanding, we receive blessings from God. Our Lord teaches in the Beatitudes, *Blessed are they which are persecuted for righteousness' sake: for theirs is the Kingdom of Heaven. Blessed are ye, when men shall revile you, and persecute you, and shall say all manner of evil against you falsely, for My sake. Rejoice, and be exceeding: glad: for great is your reward in heaven. For so persecuted they the prophets which were before you.* For this reason God gives us tokens of His love, signs of His affection—the miracles and wonders that He has performed for our salvation ever since the beginning—to strengthen and hearten us in the battle, and to remind us of our goal: the salvation of our souls and union with God.

Whenever God performs a miracle, whether it be a healing or a manifestation like a Weeping Icon, we must always remember that the miracle itself is not the point. We must not get carried away with the "flash." God is not interested in making us say, "wow;" rather, God is trying to get us to wake up out of our stupor. To see reality. To realize that there is more than just this earthly life. To realize that we are not the center of the universe; God is the center of the universe.

When Christ was asked about His own miracles, He said that they happened in order that those who do not believe may believe. (St. Matthew 9:6; St. John 9:1-3, 11:40-45.) Remember, suffering is a good thing for a Christian, since much suffering causes people to turn to God. So all miracles are more for the purpose of calling us to faith and repentance, than for the healing of this or that person.

This means that we cannot be just bystanders. We can't just hear about a miracle and then go on with our lives as though nothing had happened. We have a responsibility—there is a response that is expected of us. As you read through the accounts of miracles that follow, remember that as you hear of these things, you are being called by God to completely change your life, to live no longer for yourself, but for God. Remember the words of St. Herman of Alaska:

"From this day, from this hour, from this moment, let us strive to love God above all."

ACCOUNTS OF MIRACLES

CURE OF LEUKEMIA

The following report was received on June 6th, 1986, from Marilyn Marzella. Marilyn had received Myrrh from the Myrrh-Weeping Icon of the Theotokos on her visit to Christ of the Hills Monastery on the third or fourth week of May, 1986. Early in June she heard that a close friend of hers, Dr. William Christmas, was dying of leukemia and was given only a few weeks to live. She rushed to see him in Dallas, Texas, and anointed him with the tears and the disease went into complete remission, totally disappearing and showing no signs of leukemia. Both Doctor Christmas and Marilyn Marzella believe that the healing occurred as a result of anointing with the blessed Myrrh of the Weeping Icon. Physicians in the Dallas/Ft. Worth area have confirmed Dr. Christmas' complete and total recovery, much to their surprise. They say there is no scientific explanation for what occurred to Dr. Christmas.

Dr. Christmas is himself an M.D. and normally prone to skepticism of miraculous occurrences.

The following update from Dr. Christmas himself was transcribed from a telephone conservation taped June 19, 1990 with Marilyn Marzella:

"I was originally diagnosed with Chronic Myleogenous Leukemia in 1974. I subsequently underwent some very heavy chemotherapy that wiped out my bone marrow and put me in remission. I had another attack fairly recently in about 1985 or 1986.

I'm not sure which year. I'm sure (the tears from the Icon) placed me into complete remission. I was in Blast Crisis at the time and basically two weeks after I was anointed, the Blast Crisis was over, and my cell lines have basically restored to normal! I am as normal as anyone else! Blast Crisis is always considered terminal and there is no medical doubt about that. I don't have one single trace of Chronic Myleogenous Leukemia."

"In my research, which has been fairly extensive, I have not heard of anyone else that has done this. Medically, I can only put it down to a miracle. I'm an M.D. and a Ph.D."

REGAINED STRENGTH

The following is taken from a letter from Ruth. E. Crum of Leesburg, New Jersey, dated June 11, 1984:

"I don't know what to say or exactly how to say it! So please bear with me. I'll say it this way: I've had broken legs, one a long time ago, and the other four years ago, with a badly broken ankle; I had never regained my strength. Then I had deterioration of the spine and arthritis of the lower part of the spine—needless to say, I lost all of my speed in walking, and I tired out easily.

"I began feeling so much better, and still better each day. I wondered what happened. Now I know, and may God bless you all! I feel as if 50 years was lifted off my back, felt as if I could run if I wanted to, and I did today! I wasn't even out of breath! I'm amazed, I've been doing so much and I'm not even tired!...I am 67 years old; I never thought I'd ever feel this way again!...God Bless You all, and thank you so much!... I'll never forget you...I have two friends, both of them ladies who would like your prayers...I'm so grateful!..."

CURE OF SKIN CANCER

Mr. Herbert Hoover of Natalia, Texas, wrote in a letter dated June 27, 1987 after being anointed with Myrrh from the Weeping Icon: "...the tears have been doing good to my skin cancers, they are curing up...I went to the doctor the other day and he said 'I believe your skin cancers are leaving you.' Thank God..."

MIRACLES IN MILWAUKEE

Father Gregory, Superior of Holy Theophany Skete in Milwaukee, Wisconsin, sent the following account in a letter dated August 19, 1986:

"In this letter, I wish to document several blessings from God. The first concerns the situation of a seminarian, John, and his wife, Linda, who had been childless since 1982. Last February 9, 1986, they both attended Vespers at the Chapel of St. Herman of Alaska, after which I anointed Linda with Myron (Myrrh) from the Icon of the Theotokos which is enshrined in your paraecclesia (Chapel). That evening Linda conceived a child due to the intercession of the Holy Mother of God of Blanco.

"Also after the month of July a parishioner, Mrs. Bertha Kenders lost her daughter's dog. Shortly after praying to St. John (Maximovitch) the Wonderworker of San Francisco, the dog was found. It was at her home that we served the first Molieben (intercessory prayer service) to St. John on July 4, 1986.

"I have had many requests for copies of the Weeping Theotokos Icon, as well as cotton balls of tears, along with prints of St. Herman of Alaska. If you would be so kind as to send me a supply, I would be most appreciative. Also, if ever the Icon could journey to Milwaukee, many would like to venerate it. Let me know what you think."

Postscript: Father Gregory called the Monastery on November 7, 1987 to report that Linda Riccio, after a difficult labor, gave birth to a baby boy, named Paul, in response to a service of supplication, which was served before a copy of the Weeping Icon, of the Mother of God of New Sarov.

CANCER

Beatrice Maurice of Buffalo Narrows, Saskatchewan, gave a cotton ball on which Myrrh from the Weeping Icon had been collected (together with) a picture of the Weeping Icon to a friend of hers by the name of Pauline Nezcroche, who was confined to bed and unable to walk, dying of cancer. Mrs. Maurice writes that "Pauline is now walking around and gets around (the way she did) before she was in bed."

In the same envelope was a letter from a relative of Pauline Nezcroche, Angeline Nezcroche, which said in part, "...I am writing to you to ask for your blessings through prayer that you would help me. I have heard of your healing Icon, that is why I am writing this letter. I have an eye cataract and I am losing my sight. I cannot read my prayerbook in my Dene language, I am always sick in my bones. I also want prayers for all my children so that they would all lead Christian lives. ...I have raised two children: one son and a daughter. From them I have seven grandchildren and two great grandchildren. In my family we pray for a vocation to come from my son's family...we need your prayers."

EMOTIONAL HEALING

L S. from Wisconsin, wrote concerning her son, Mike who had been having emotional problems and had been fired from two jobs.

She writes: "Mike came and visited us this Saturday and returned home yesterday. Saturday night I anointed Mike and I pray Mike will be healed mentally, that he will neither lie or steal. I anointed his hands—there will never ever be any stealing. I also anointed the other senses."

L. S. reports that they already know of the power of the Mother of God: As of 5:00 p.m., after Mike arrived home, he telephoned them to say that he had gone for an interview and had accepted a new job.

BUFFALO NARROWS

There is, in and around the small community of Buffalo Narrows, Saskatchewan an abundance of miracles due to the Myrrh-Weeping Icon at Christ of the Hills Monastery. On September 10, 1986, Mr. Fred Morin wrote to the Monastery and described some of the wondrous events which have taken place in this faith-filled community:

"When I talked with you on the phone the other day, you asked me to give you some information on those people that received the Holy Tears, Holy Water, Blessed Oil, and pictures of the Myrrh-Weeping Icon. Well, for God nothing is impossible, and praise Him.

"I guess the greatest miracle that occurred here is the gentleman by the name of Moise Janvier of La Loche, Saskatchewan, Canada, who developed cancer of the throat. He was unable to speak, eat, etc. Well, since he received the Holy Tears the greatest thing happened. When he went to Saskatoon for X rays, doctors could not find any more cancer. He told himself 'Thank God.'

"Then there is the lady, Mrs. Albertine McKay, who had a bad kidney problem. She would swell up quite a lot. She had to use a wheel chair to keep from swelling up so much. She received the holy tears also. She took your advice on the phone and now she never stays home. Always visiting all over. 'Thank God,' again.

"And my Great Auntie, Flora Aubichon: doctors told her that she would live only a few months (this was in

February of 1986). Then she also went for an X ray in Saskatoon, Saskatchewan. doctors were surprised to find that the tumor did not grow. So otherwise she is doing just great. 'Thank God,' once again.

"Mrs. Celina Dore and Mrs. Main are just doing great. And I'm enclosing a picture of Mrs. Pederson, the lady you talked to that had a bad, bad stroke. She was happy to talk to you on the phone. She's doing just great, her spirit is lifted up, always cheerful. 'Thank God.'"

RELIEF FROM INFECTION AND ULCER

Miss Maude Layne of New York City wrote on August 29, 1986, "Thank you for your prayers. I had an infection in the carotid gland in my neck and a peptic ulcer. I prayed to St. Seraphim of Sarov and he helped me immensely."

CURE OF LIVER CANCER

Exilia Morin called the Monastery on November 22, 1986, to report that her brother was cured of liver cancer and her daughter of scarlet fever by anointing with the Myrrh. doctors confirmed this and have no medical explanation for the miraculous cure. They live in Meadow Lake, Saskatchewan.

HOLY OIL HEALS TUMOR

Annie Shaw of Kailua, Hawaii, wrote on October 26, 1984: "God be with all of you and God's blessing. Thanks so much for the Holy Oil (from Blessed John's sepulcher). The lump that I had on my face disappeared since I prayed and used a little oil on my cheek." *Previously, in another letter she described the lump as a tumor.*

HEALING BY THE MOTHER OF GOD

The following report was written in a letter dated October 13, 1986, by R. N. Victuelles of Des Plaines, Illinois:

"The following incident relates how my wife and I made use of the cotton ball of the Mother of God.

"On October 8, 1986, we arrived at our residence from Virginia Beach, Virginia, where we visited my daughter and family. Immediately, we went to the hospital and had my wife anoint our daughter-in-law, who was confined. Since she was scheduled to undergo an operation the following day, all we had to hope for was her successful operation and eventual recovery. Through the help of God she had a successful operation, uneventful recovery, and is now released from the hospital.

"What my daughter-in-law recounted was her strength and bravery as she faced the operating table, and attributed it to the miraculous power of God through the cotton ball containing the tear of the Mother of God."

On October 10, his wife developed a severe breathing difficulty from a long-standing cold which she has been suffering from. Her chest was painful and tight and they were expecting to call the paramedics for an emergency. She only wanted her husband to anoint her with the tears of the Mother of God. He continues:

"Without hesitation I anointed her, and when I finished anointing her chest, the phlegm became loosened and she spat it out, thereby relieving her difficulty of breathing and tightness. As of this time, she is now well and is back to normal health. We praise the Lord Jesus Christ for these incidents."

A PILGRIMAGE TO THE MONASTERY

The following is excerpted from a letter written by Mary Wright, of Atlanta, Georgia, soon after she and her husband and three sons visited Christ of the Hills Monastery over the July 4th weekend, 1987:

"The Mother of God is with us. There has been such a blessing since seeing the Weeping Icon. We all have been touched. There are others here that want to see the Icon. We do hope and pray that you come here to Atlanta soon. Joshua told me to tell you that he still wants to be a Server when you come.

Every aspect of my life has been touched since our visit there. It is as if the presence of Heaven visited us (I know it did indeed!). We both had a hard time coming back here and picking up our life here in Atlanta. After a few days had passed I knew I had to let the blessings enter into my life in Atlanta. I couldn't just sit around and feel wonderful all my life. I had to go to the grocery store, etc. Life goes on but hopefully we will live each aspect of our life a little differently than before. I guess what I'm trying to say is that the things of this world don't seem to be as important as they were. Thank God."

CURE OF PULLED MUSCLE

Ann Fergerson of Houston, Texas, sent the following letter, dated April 17, 1987, to her niece, Mary K. Blevins, who in turn sent it to the Monastery.

"Two weeks ago I was working in the yard pulling weeds. I have a bad habit of putting all my weight on my leg. Anyway, I pulled a muscle in my leg. It hurt so bad it was all I could do to stand it. I limped on my leg here for two days. If I hadn't had arthritis pills I don't think that I could have taken the pain. I could hardly lift my foot. After working here all day I could barely get into the car. I prayed about it and took that piece of cotton ball with the tears of the Mother of God and touched it to my leg. I could feel it tingle that night and the next day I was 80% better."

PROTECTION FROM SIN

David B., in a letter dated May 12, 1987, the day after he had received the tears of the holy Icon, wrote the following:

"Last night, after receiving the cotton ball containing the tears, I anointed myself with the tears of the All

Holy Virgin and the Holy Oil. "I'll keep you informed on my progress using these items. The last time I used the cotton ball with the tears of the Holy Virgin, I was kept for the longest time from falling into my greatest sin....I'm hoping for the same or better in accordance with God's will."

CURE OF RIB FRACTURE

Mrs. Evangeline Joseph of Bay St. Louis, Mississippi, wrote the following on April 10, 1985:

"I am praying to St. Seraphim. He cured me of a rib fracture on February 18, 1985."

RECOVER FROM TUBERCULOSIS

Thomas Billette of Dillion, Saskatchewan, sent the following to the Monastery on April 24, 1987:

"This letter is regarding my cousin Tracy Billette. We are using the tears of the Blessed Virgin Mary (which) we got from Moses Janvier. We have been using it for about a week now.

"Tracy had been in the hospital for over a month now, he has been ill since the Fall of 1986. The doctors finally found out that he has TB (tuberculosis) in the brain, so Tracy is mentally ill now. He does not know us, he can't talk, and could hardly move. Tracy is six years old and is a native Chippaweyan Indian."

In the next letter they wrote:

"We are thankful for using the tears. Tracy is recovering. I think he is coming to his senses the last few days. All we want is prayer from you, and we are also praying for you as well."

RECOVERY AFTER HEART ATTACK

Veronica Poe wrote to the Monastery on March 28, 1987, to request more blessed oil for anointing. She said that she had received some before and had anointed her husband with the oil after he had a severe heart attack from which the doctors said he could not recover. He has recovered and is alive today. Mrs. Poe says she absolutely believes that this is due to his having been anointed with the blessed oil.

THE JESUS PRAYER

Sarah Caturia of Meriden, Connecticut, wrote regarding her experience of the Jesus Prayer and also to report the healing of a tumor on her sister's face:

"Thank you for helping me in the Jesus Prayer...I have been saying the Jesus Prayer every day. Please forgive my lack of knowledge in it. When I heard it within me, I realized it was a gift to me from our Lord Jesus Christ which I did not deserve.

"Please find enclosed my prayer petitions to the Weeping Icon of the Mother of God, she healed my sister's face.."

A GRANT OF LIFE

Midge Hirst of Etobicoke, Ontario, wrote the following on April 22, 1986:

"Thank you for the Relic of St. Seraphim; he is helping my sister Jeana. She wasn't expected to live. Twice last October they called us to her bedside and here it is April and she is still here. She is bed-ridden and her kidneys and bowels are in bad shape, but even the doctors can't understand how she's living—she talks to us too, which she was not able to do before.

"May I ask you to please send me one of the cotton balls with the Holy Virgin's Tears? I have a very ill little granddaughter who is in need of a miracle. She is 12 years old (June 9, 1986). She has lost a lot of weight and is a mere 65 lbs., her large muscles aren't developing and she is walking so twisted. It breaks my heart to see her like this. She looks so frail as well. I love her so dearly, she is such a sweet child. Please pray to our Lady for her to regain her health, and if you can send me a cotton ball with the Mother of God's tears I will bless my granddaughter Alana and me so I can be stronger too for her.

"May this Blessed Weeping Icon bring countless blessings to you and the Monks. It must be a sight to behold. I appreciate the card picture of the Weeping Mother of God that you sent me. Thank you very much. In a way, I imagine it must be very sad to see our Lady weeping. There certainly is so much evil in the world."

CURE OF CANCER

Fred Morin of Buffalo Narrows, Saskatchewan, wrote the following letter on February 21, 1986, which described the progress of his aunt, Flora Aubichon, who had been totally crippled and paralyzed by cancer.

"Thank you so much for sending me the beautiful print of the Weeping Icon. It is wonderful. It is something that I treasure. My Auntie is sure moving around. She's always visiting every day. She doesn't look depressed in any way (like she used to). Her spirit is just lifted up. For a woman that has cancer, it sure doesn't show.

"I mentioned I had swollen glands myself. I prayed and rubbed the Myrrh from the holy Icon and my swelling went down."

RELIEF OF PAIN

Stanley Bullock, Jr., of Pasadena, Maryland, wrote the following letter on May 11, 1986:

"On April 12, 1986 my wife Mary anointed me with the cotton ball of Myrrh to help the pain in my arm. I in turn anointed her to help the pain in her foot.

"Our pain has decreased. We are still praying. Since it's been four weeks, I'm writing you to report per your request.

"An unexpected miracle did happen for myself, wife and son. The Great Comforter, the Holy Spirit has begun to quench the thirst in our souls that have been dry from the physical pain. Our home is being filled with love more each day.

"May healing be completed and continue for my family through the mercy of our Lord Jesus Christ and His All Pure Mother."

FATHER BENEDICT'S MIRACULOUS RECOVERY

The following was recounted by Father Benedict:

"On October 22 (1986) I spent the night in great agony. It felt as though my insides dropped down to my groin; I was scarcely able to sleep. The next morning I went to the doctor and we decided that I should try taking an injection for pain in the hopes that it was merely diverticulitis and would pass.

"After four hours of this it became apparent that I was getting worse. By now my fever was 105 degrees.

"Finally, an ambulance came and took me to the hospital in San Antonio. Upon my arrival, there was a big commotion in the emergency room because our doctor from Blanco had referred me to a particular hospital and a particular surgeon. The hospital was part of a for-profit chain. Unfortunately, the Monastery has no medical-hospital insurance; a situation which made the admissions people very reluctant to even allow emergency tests that the doctors ordered. I spent the time praying. After several hours, and the arrival of my father with cash, the emergency tests were done.

"The surgeon came in to see me and told me that my colon had ruptured. He explained that if it had been seventeen or eighteen hours since this occurred and that I was very, very badly infected with peritonitis.

"Up until now I had thought only of relief from the pain, but now I realized that I was probably going to die. Immediately, all of my sins came before me. I had a profound sense that I wished I had more time to repent. I began to pray even more fervently. In a few moments I realized that I would have to rely on the mercy of an abundantly merciful God. I asked Father Pangratios, who was there with me, to call the closest Orthodox Priest and to ask him to bring me Holy Communion and hear my confession. I asked the doctor to wait thirty minutes in order that this might be done.

"After making the necessary phone calls, Father Pangratios came back and I gave him a number of instructions regarding the future of the Monastery. I told him to call Abbot Vasili home at once, and gave messages to him for Father Vasili (he had been in Alaska at New Valaam Monastery, which was founded on the site where Saint Herman of Alaska had lived and struggled).

After a short while of this I felt as though affairs were as much in order as they could be, and at that moment the Priest arrived. He heard my confession and gave me Communion and they rolled me into the operating room. There the anesthesiologist noticed my prayer rope and asked me if I was praying for my life. I told him that, no, I was praying for him and the surgeon that God would guide them. He seemed a little taken aback.

"The next thing I remember is lying in surgical intensive care and, looking up, seeing Vladyka John Maximovitch (a recently declared Saint in whose Glorification I participated). He approached me and said, 'It is not yet your time.' Others also saw his presence. At this moment I realized that I was still alive (for at first I thought that I was approaching the Heavenly Realm). Many people had been praying to Vladyka John throughout the surgery for my healing.

"The next day, everyone was prepared to begin the long battle with peritonitis. My fever, however, suddenly disappeared. Vladyka John, no doubt.

"I lay there with tubes running up my nose and down into my stomach pumping bile from my stomach for twelve days. I was not allowed to eat or even take a little water to wet my tongue during this time. Now everyone was concerned because my colostomy had not yet begun to work. Finally, after twelve days, it began to work. The tubes came out, thank God. After three or four more days I was discharged.

"Coming home, I have had plenty of time to pray, as I did lying there in the hospital, fasting those twelve days. Having come close to death—I prepared myself to die. Now it is as though every moment is a gift from God. I know that this gift is not for myself but for the Church. Pray that I may use the gift wisely and that I may be responsive to those things that Christ calls me to do, for the good of the Holy Church.

"My only desire is for the Kingdom of Heaven and the salvation of souls."

RELIEF OF NUMBNESS

Mrs. Bernice L. Seguin of Ontario, Canada, wrote the following on June 5, 1987:

"I am writing you to let you know the Blessed Oil of St. John (maximovitch) and the Myrrh that drips down from the Icon onto a cotton ball that you sent me helped me tremendously.

"My hands (both) were tingling and numb, now, since applying the cotton balls to my hands and making the Sign of the Cross, it has been taken away.

"Hoping to hear from you and receive more Myrrh soaked cotton-balls."

CURE OF VIRUS

Mrs. Irene Staube of Dillon, Saskatchewan, wrote the Monastery on May 20, 1987. She thanks Father Benedict for the Myrrh "from the beautiful Myrrh-Weeping Icon," *and the Blessed John Oil together with his letter. She reports:*

"When your letter arrived, I had my grandmother, aunt, and cousins here visiting us from New York; so I put your letter in a drawer upstairs before we left for the zoo, planning to read it later that day.

"Well, enjoying everyone's company, I'm sorry to say, I forgot your letter. After my family went home I rediscovered it the best way.

"About a week had passed and I could not find one of the prayers to our Lord Jesus Christ that I say at night. I had caught a cold virus, along with some of my family also and was not feeling well. I wanted to find my prayers so I went to the upstairs searching. When I opened the drawer there was your lovely letter, with all of the beautiful blessed gifts. I put some oil on right away, read your letter, and started to feel better right away holding the Myrrh-Weeping Icon card."

RETURN FROM DEATH

Exilla Morin of Buffalo Narrows, Saskatchewan, reported the following miracle of the Mother of God in a letter dated December 2, 1986:

"My brother Julian was ill. I got there just in time. I stood there with my cotton ball tears of the Virgin Mary and (Blessed John) Holy Oil and I anointed him and prayed with tears in my eyes. He died for a second and then he came to life again. I just cried from my heart and said, Thank God. And so I had a miracle from God."

TWICE CURED OF CANCER

On July 3, 1984, Diana Irene Pierre of Minneapolis, Minnesota, wrote the following wonderful miracle:

"God healed me of two terrible cancers and He gave me back the gift of life. I love Him so!"

RECOVERY FROM SURGERY

On March 18, 1987, Mrs. Evangeline Joseph of St. Louis, Missouri, wrote the following to the Monastery:

"I have been so busy taking care of my son-in-law. He had a very serious operation in January. He was given up to die. The doctors gave up all hope for him, but thanks to Saint Seraphim of Sarov and our Lord Jesus Christ he recovered miraculously. He was in the intensive care unit of the hospital for a month..

"I was so happy to hear from you. Also, I was glad to see the prayer to Saint Seraphim of Sarov and also the cotton ball with the tear of the Blessed Mother—when I opened the foil it was wrapped in, a sweet smell of roses or the like was all over the room.

"It was something I had never smelled before.

"My son-in-law asked me what that was smelling so good. I told him I received a letter from you and you send me a cotton ball of her tears to anoint the sick with.

"I anointed my son-in-law, Thaddeus Jackson, with the cotton ball like you told me and said the prayers. I will let you know what miracles happened.

"My son-in-law is home now but has to wear a colostomy also. He had part of his foot cut off. He had seven operations in a week and the doctor can't seem to get over the fact that he is still alive. He was supposed to die—they gave up all hope for him, but I know it was the prayers of Saint Seraphim...and all the Saints and the Holy Oil you sent me—I anointed him each time I went to the Hospital—and of course your prayers. God bless you and keep you."

CURE OF BLINDNESS

Mrs. Angele Collins, whose husband suffered from a terrible eye problem from which he was going blind and in great pain, and who herself was suffering from cramps, wrote the following from Houma, Louisiana, on December 14, 1985:

"I used the cotton ball with the tears of the Mother of God on Darcellie and me. He doesn't complain of his eyes anymore and I don't have cramps anymore. I suffered so much with cramps in my legs and at my waistline. It's good not to suffer.

"My cousin suffers with his leg. He is always hitting it and it gets sore. He has to take care of his old mother of 99. He has to do all the housework and take care of her. She sits in her wheel chair. If you have a ball of cotton with the tears of The Mother of God please send it to him. He asked if he could get one."

APPEARANCE OF ARCHBISHOP JOHN

One night Angela M. Palacio of Mission City, Texas, had a dream in which a Monk appeared to her. Very moved by the appearance, she wrote to the Monastery about her dream, wondering who it might be. The Monks sent her photographs of three holy men whom we thought it might possibly be, including Saint John (Maximovitch) the Wonderworker. This is what she wrote back:

"Thank you for the pictures of the holy Archbishops; they look very spiritual—truly Saints.

"Yes, I will tell you that among the three of them it was Archbishop John who appeared in my dream. He was so vivid in my memory even up to now and even more so now that I saw his picture. It is amazing that I cannot erase from my memory that dream. I only wished I could talk with him face to face. Funny, did I tell you that when he appeared in my dream, I probably was sort of scared and I kind of drove him away from me? As I was starting to drive him away, he cautioned me with a slight move of his hand and a smile in his eyes in my dream, I stood speechless. After that dream, I had been trying to solve the mystery of that man in my dream. I asked friends of mine the symbolism of my dreams. One told me it stands for a father figure, but finally I solved the problem when you sent me those pictures. I am happy and very pleased.

"So he appeared to Father Benedict too. I pray with his help Father Benedict may be able to have a successful second surgery."

CURE OF GOUT

Lida E. Wells of Philadelphia, Pennsylvania, wrote on October 3, 1983, to express her thanks to God. The gout had left her foot and she is able to walk without pain.

THE PERFECT TIMING OF GOD

Dorothy Giosa of Langhorne, Pennsylvania, wrote the following account on January 14, 1984:

"I received your beautiful letters and the pictures. Thank you for sending them. As usual, they arrived at a time when they were needed. Truly, God does work through your ministry in countless ways of which you are not always aware.

"Sometime ago I worked as a companion-housekeeper to a stroke victim. Even after going to other jobs we maintained contact but did not see each other too often. On Wednesday I had some time to catch up on other things and was impressed to call them to arrange a visit. As it turned out I went at 3:30 and had dinner with them also. We had a beautiful visit and talked of many things. Yet, inwardly I sensed this might be the last time I would see her. Even as she hugged me and kissed me 'Goodbye'—the feeling still persisted. Usually, she had said 'See you later.' After she went to bed her husband and I talked a while longer. We had planned that with my work schedule being lighter I could relieve him one day a week so he could do his business and it would be a change for her too.

"Saturday evening while shopping for a vaporizer for my grandson, I fell as I left the store and really messed up my spine and head. The doctor ordered X rays, gave me codeine for pain and muscle relaxants to use until the X ray results came back on Monday. Upon taking the medication before bed—it was a restless, interrupted sleep—at one point I saw her spiritually and she was saying, 'It is time to go now.' I'm glad for the time we spent together.

"This afternoon at 4:00 p.m. her husband called to tell me that she'd had a cardiac arrest and died peacefully in her sleep during the night. He had called because he didn't want me to read it in the paper.

"The point I'm making is that God truly does lead us in the path if we take the time to listen and pray.

"As of now, (I can) see where the accident could be a blessing in disguise. I've been pushing myself, and now am forced to rest—physically as well."

HEALING OF BLOOD DISEASE

Mary McMurry of Fresno, California, suffered from a serious blood disease. She was sent some of the Myrrh from the Weeping Icon. On March 15, 1986, she sent us the following:

"I took a blood test two weeks ago praying that all would be well for my health. The doctor couldn't believe how perfect my blood was. He kept saying to me while reading the report, 'Perfect, perfect.' But I only smiled, knowing that it was a miracle, which of course he wouldn't believe, but in my heart I know it was."

FREEDOM FROM FEAR

Mrs. Madeline Cannizzaro of New Egypt, New Jersey, wrote the following on July 2, 1984:

"Thank you for your prayers. I feel much stronger. I wish some day to be able to take off my brace from my back a few hours a day, or even one hour at a time. I even started to face life with more courage. All my life I've been afraid. My daughter Maria with epilepsy...fell and hurt her breast. It was all black. Thanks to St. Benedict and St. Seraphim of Sarov the lump is getting smaller. I prayed, put the Holy Oil on it and touched it with the Relic of St. Seraphim. I pray it will disappear."

CURE OF NERVES AND CANCER

Mrs. Viola Yosso of Brooklyn, New York, wrote the following on the 17th of March, 1986:

"I want to thank you very much for sending me the tears from the Mother of God. When I felt the cotton ball, I felt so good. I anointed myself and it helped me so much. I had pain in my feet for two weeks—no one could help. I anointed myself and the pain left.

"Please pray for my son. He is a Vietnam Veteran and is so nervous from the war. He anointed himself and for the first time in years I can see a change in him—he now goes to Church—with the help of the Mother of God."

About two months later, on the 8th day of May, Viola wrote the following:

"I have to write and let you know how the tears of the Blessed Mother helped me out. First, I am in remission from cancer; second, my ulcer has been healed. The doctors are amazed at it. Thank you so much for the tears on the cotton ball. I wonder if I can have one more tear on a cotton ball. I would like my daughter, who does not live with me, to have one. She is very depressed. Her lungs are giving her troubles. If I gave her mine, I would not have one, since she does not live here. You see, this cotton ball with the tear means a lot to me. She seldom visits me so I cannot anoint her. May I say, God bless you for praying for me and giving me the tear of the Mother of God."

MENTAL ILLNESS

A woman who writes to the Monastery frequently, and whose anonymity is being maintained, suffers terribly from mental illness and is under the care of a devout Christian psychiatrist. She made the following observation about prayer in a letter dated November 8, 1984:

"I know that the Saints caution against the seeking of mystical experience and sensations for their own merits as a form of idolatry—the experience itself may be sought after rather than God's presence. The

Saints place more spiritual value on an anguished soul in the desert (or dry period) seeking after God, even in the midst of doubt, than on the most spectacular mystical experience Heaven can offer. The latter is from God; the former counts more: we are seeking God with our own free will. I know that contemplative prayer is a valuable and beautiful way of life for those who practice it on a regular basis.

"I have a mental handicap, however: schizophrenia, and am on a medication that affects the chemical balance of the brain. This is probably one of the last frontiers of human knowledge and understanding: the effects of God's presence on a handicapped mind. If the world were not calling me, I would rest in God's presence exclusively."

CURE OF KIDNEY STONE

Lucille Gaydos of Taylor, Texas, wrote to the Monastery on May 3rd, 1984, telling us that she was scheduled for surgery for a kidney stone on May 7th. She related the following:

"When I first went to see the doctor I was hurting badly and I couldn't work. After the X rays, they said that (my left) tube was blocked with a stone in it. He gave me some strong medicine. That Sunday I went to Church as always. I went early and I knelt and prayed to God and to Saint Seraphim to please help me. After I sat down I still hurt, and all at once I heard this voice in my mind, 'You will be all right,' and such a calm feeling came over me. I couldn't believe what I heard. It felt so good. When I went to the doctor again that week the tube was opened and was passing waste. I know that it was St. Seraphim who answered me. I have been praying all the time and believing that he will help me."

REMOVAL OF A TUMOR

Celine Ference of Carteret, New Jersey, writing on May 8, 1986, after anointing with the tears said, in part:

"One of my problems was helped. A uterine fibroid tumor was passed and I couldn't believe it."

THE PERFECT JOB

On New Year's Day, 1984, Helen Noyes wrote the following letter to the Monastery:

"Christ is born!

"I prayed to him (Saint Seraphim) to beg the Blessed Holy Trinity to allow me a job. We are living in dire poverty, even our Priest has given us meals, some of our fellow parishioners have given us money as Christmas gifts, etc. I prayed to St. Seraphim earnestly and the 5th day of petition—through him—I got a good job, in a nice restaurant. Decent pay, friendly co-workers, good benefits, etc. We are paid twice monthly. I was hired December 22nd and began work December 24th.

"Last year, or rather the Fall of 1982, I filed applications in 12 places. No job. In September-December of 1983 I filed applications in 24 places. No job. After saying the prayer to St. Seraphim for 4 days—the Holy Trinity gave me the perfect job on the food service line, serving the public.

"It may not be a grand-scale miracle but it was indeed a miracle to me!

"It seems my lengthy period of intense physical, emotional and financial suffering is nearing a close (it is still hard for me to believe, I was truly at death's door in July). Yes, you surely wrote truth when you said 'So often it is we ourselves who stand in the way of God's glorious blessing.' In our lack of true faith we forget that there is such a thing as Divine Providence. That God allows sufferings of all types for excellent reasons, if not for benefit for ourselves, then to benefit others for the Grace obtained by perfect resignation to His Will.

"A friend at Church told me, 'God must love you very much to choose you to bear such intense sufferings.' I felt somewhat guilty because at times that fact became forgotten and it seemed like punishments for sin, a severe testing of faith or testing of my resignation to His Holy Will."

HELP IN COPING WITH KIDNEY DISEASE

Elizabeth Patterson of Henderson, Nevada wrote the following on December 20, 1984:

"Please include in the prayers at the Pilgrimage to St. Seraphim of Sarov the following: Lisa Leanitt, my granddaughter, who is a juvenile diabetic, that they will soon find a cure for her and others so she can have a long life too; and also my husband, William Patterson, who is a kidney dialysis patient: and myself that God will give me strength to cope with it all and keep me in good health. We have had these problems for years, but since I've been praying to St. Seraphim of Sarov......we have all been coping much, much better."

CURE OF ARTHRITIS AND KIDNEY PROBLEM

On September 18, 1983, Archbishop Theodore reported this miracle which happened to Mamia Olivea Ogtaviaja Novarrette, 47 years of age, of Juarez, Mexico: she had suffered from crippling rheumatism and arthritis and inflammation of the kidneys for years. She was totally disabled. After being anointed and touching a portion of the Relics of St. Seraphim of Sarov, the sickness went away and the lady was able to not only get up, but to take a job and go to work. She is now working and attributes the miracle to St. Seraphim.

HEALING OF A LEG INJURY

Dean P. Henwood of Del City, Oklahoma, wrote the following to the Monastery on October 10, 1983:

"I received your Holy Oil and used it to heal a friend's leg that had three pins in it to hold it together. The next night the cast came off before anyone expected it to."

CURE OF A HEART CONDITION

On July 12, 1987, Mrs. Margaret De Soto wrote the following:

"I am writing to let you know that I have been anointing myself with the blessed tears of the Weeping Icon that you sent me. I had been going through a lot of examinations and testing for my heart and the doctor told me I had a heart condition. He put me on nitroglycerin and sent me to a very good heart specialist. I started anointing myself on June 10th and here the doctor tells me on July 10th that I have a good heart——nothing wrong. He couldn't get over why I had been so sick with all the symptoms I had."

RELIEF FROM SPINAL DISEASE

Mrs. Solange Hayward of Rittman, Ohio, wrote the following on August 29, 1986:

"I do have a lot of pains because of my spinal cord disease. But with your prayers I am able to stand up and walk a little. The Lord is good."

CURE OF HEART DISEASE

Virginia Garcia of San José, California, sent a letter on March 5, 1987, which reported how St. Seraphim of Sarov cured her of heart disease:

"I went for an X ray of my heart to a heart specialist and I had a blood test. The specialist told me that there was nothing to worry about. My blood test was good.

"From the doctor's office my son and I went to church to thank God and our Blessed Mother and to pray to St. Seraphim. Miracles do happen."

GREATER PEACE OF MIND

Raquel Garcia of Harlingen, Texas, wrote to Fr. Benedict on July 7, 1986:

"I am praying the Jesus Prayer like you told me to months ago. I feel better and have noticed a change for the better in health and attitude."

HELP FOLLOWING A DISASTER

On May 27, 1984, Doris Santreau of Shediac, New Brunswick, wrote that her home had completely burned to the ground with all her possessions—she didn't even have a photograph left. Very soon thereafter, by a miracle of God, she writes.

"I was able to borrow the money I needed to build again at a price at which I can afford to repay it. So I think we will be able to move into it in about two weeks. So now I'm worried about furnishing the house, but I guess God provided for us so far. He won't let us down if we pray."

A NEW JOB

Francis Hock of Chicago, Illinois, who has been in correspondence with Father Benedict for spiritual direction, was in desperate need of a job. On March 28, 1985, she wrote regarding the Jesus Prayer:

"The second day of reciting this prayer brought a job for me, of which I really am in need. I am on a fixed income. I am disabled also. The Prayer is extraordinary."

IMPROVEMENT OF HEART DISEASE

Delores Hubbard of Orange, Texas, wrote on June 12, 1984, that through the intercession of St. Benedict of Nursia a friend of hers who had heart trouble had been helped.

LOST MONEY

Benedicta Castro of San Francisco, California, sent the following on May 23, 1984:

"I received the package containing the Holy Oil and read the part in your letter that said, expect a miracle. And, Father, the very next day I was browsing around my one room, looking at this and that. I'm not able to keep a very neat dwelling as half the time I feel tired with this very high blood pressure. By the way, I'm almost 74 years old, so please forgive and overlook my mistakes. I came across a photo of my granddaughter in a small frame. I picked it up from the box and decided to take the photo and put it into another frame a little better than the original. And, Father, as I pulled the picture out from the frame, out fell a hundred dollar bill. The very next day I was leafing through a book and found $35.00. Of course, I was grateful and delighted but not too surprised as I'm a great believer of God's miracles. I've had so many of God's blessings and know deep in my heart that there's no limit to God's love and mercy. One must believe in Him: and that I do, with all my heart, soul, and being. I pray constantly for one and all the world. Especially for those that need His mercy. I attend Church frequently."

RETURN OF FAITH

Virginia Garcia of San José, California, wrote the following in a letter dated April 29, 1985:

"My prayers have been answered. If you remember, I told you my daughter stayed away from Church for one year. She is controlling her drinking. She was drinking real bad. She is now reaching out for God's help.

"A week before Easter she went to Church. She doesn't live with me, she lives with her 15 year old daughter. That Sunday morning I was surprised to see my daughter in Church. On Easter her daughter went together with her.

"There are times when I am so depressed. I go and sit in my chair and say the Jesus Prayer. I feel something good inside me. I open my eyes and thank God for everything."

HELP WITH BREAST CANCER

Sandra Lanni of Sterling Heights, Missouri, wrote the following in a letter to Father Benedict dated September 17, 1985:

"Thank you very much for your kind letter on the Prayer of the Heart. Yes, I'll do my best and pray—I do believe in prayer. God has been very good to me and my family. I would appreciate some cotton balls with Myrrh from the Weeping Icon. I have prayed (before) the Icon and I have had three biopsies on my breasts and she has helped me—and I thank you for thinking of me. Please pray to the Blessed Mother of God for me and my family. We do need help."

CURE OF A BLOOD CLOT

Anna Czyzewski of Pitcairn, Pennsylvania, wrote on July 30, 1987:

"I had an ulcer develop in my leg and went to the doctor and got an injection and got a blood clot in my leg and had to be off my feet for a week. I thank God and the Blessed Mother Of God. I'm walking around today. I was glad to receive the cotton balls from the Weeping Mother of God. I made a Sign of the Cross with the cotton ball and feel better."

IMPROVED LIFE

Josie Aragon of Masquero, New Mexico, wrote the following on May 27, 1984:

"Since you started praying for me, my life has changed in a lot of ways: like for instance: I don't get as lonesome as I used to a while back. I was always so depressed, now when I start getting that way I get outside and do some work around the yard. I can't do too much because I have arthritis in one of my knees and my right hand, but I keep my mind busy on my work so it helps a lot."

CURE OF BRAIN CANCER

On November 9, 1987, James Kamas wrote:

"In the summer of 1987, my uncle Daniel Kamas, 48, was diagnosed as having astrocytoma, an ultimately fatal form of brain cancer. He was scheduled for surgery immediately. I saw him the day after surgery, and with my visit I brought a photograph of the Weeping Theotokos and tears collected on a cotton ball. I told him about the Icon and tears and left them with him, but for some reason I did not find the strength to anoint him.

"For the next six months Daniel underwent radiation and chemotherapy and suffered from the side effects. On February 28, 1987, my fiancée Stacy and I were married at Saint Seraphim's Church. My uncle Daniel was my best man. After the ceremony and reception, I took Daniel to see the Icon. At first sight he was in awe. As I further explained my beliefs, we both gazed upon the Theotokos and before our eyes a tear welled up and ran to the bottom of the Icon. At that moment, I knew that was for him—I anointed him and we cried together.

"In the eight months that followed, Daniel's therapy had changed to Interferon II and the tumor went into remission. However, in late October, 1987, my mother Betty phoned me to let me know that the latest CAT scan of my uncle showed regrowth of the tumor and he was scheduled for a second surgery and again anointed him with tears from the Mother of God.

"To the surprise of the surgeons, at the second surgery there was no sign of cancer, only small amounts of scar tissue. At this time, the doctors believe that no other treatments may be necessary. Glory be to God!"

RETURN FROM CERTAIN DEATH

On November 9, 1987, James Kamas reported the following:

"In the summer of 1987, my wife Anastasia and I were in Fairhaven, New York, where we were participating in the Renaissance Fair. We had made the journey with our five dogs, trusting that God would provide a place to board them during our two month stay. After three days of searching, we were told of an old barn that might be available but that the couple who owned it, Richard and Jean Derby, were quite distraught because their son, Ronnie, was on his death bed. He was in a hospital in Syracuse with pneumonia and was in a coma. The next morning, we received a note at the Fair Office from Mrs. Derby inviting us over to meet her. Our first visit lasted three and a half hours. She is a devout Roman Catholic woman and was enthralled with our description of the Weeping Icon. We gave her a photograph of the Icon and tears to anoint her son with. At the end of the first visit, Mrs. Derby told us that a miracle had already occurred. She explained that for months she had been praying to Christ, asking for assurance that it was proper to pray to the Mother of God for intercession. She told us that her prayer had been answered. She anointed her son the next day. During the next two months we learned of Ronnie's slow recuperation. Our last day in New York, we finally met Ronnie. He was eating a Labor Day picnic dinner at home with his family."

HEALING OF THIRD DEGREE BURN

The Rev. Christopher Williamson wrote from Atlanta, Georgia, on December 26, 1987:

"Thank you for your letter. It was a refreshing breath of the Spirit of Monasticism. I am so thankful for our monastic brothers whose prayers sustain us. It was as though I were at New Sarov again. How easy it is to forget.

"You will be happy to hear that the intercessions of the Mother of God, I believe, one of our children was healed of a serious third degree burn. We allowed the young child to enter the sanctuary and we anointed her with the tears from the Mother of God Icon of New

Sarov. We gave her parents the cotton to use at home, which they did. The child is around two and had spilled scalding water on her arm. The doctors wanted to do plastic surgery, but the arm healed. I believe the Mother of God helped this take place, and she wants her tears to be used especially for homes and children and she wants the faithful in need to receive Her Message. The name of the family is Nelson and Elizabeth Pardomo—the child is Anna. Glory be to God!

"I am intending to make the Pilgrimage for St. George in May, 1988 and I suppose there will be a group of us. We will discuss this in the near future. Regular visits to the Monastery are very important. I am beginning to realize, for maintaining our life of prayer. May God bless you richly and may He preserve the New Sarov Monastery fully, for you are dear to my heart and I look forward to a return visit soon."

TWO MIRACLES OF THE MOTHER OF GOD

Fred Morin wrote from Buffalo Narrows, Saskatchewan, on August 21, 1987:

"These are two cures we had up here from the 'Holy tears' (from the Myrrh-Weeping Icon) of our Lady and Mother of God that we can account for, but there are more in different ways. Here are the two ladies that I want to mention:

The first is named Eliza Jonvier, who apparently had some kind of disease which caused her mouth to begin to twist for no apparent reason. Anyway, Moses

Jonvier gave her the Holy tears and now she is better. Her mouth is back to normal. Thank God for that.

The other lady is named Irene Bellette. Apparently, she has been suffering from headaches for 5 to 6 years and she too was given a Holy tear. Now her headaches have disappeared, which is a wonderful relief for her. Thank God for these miracles.

It's been wonderful since we discovered the Holy tears here in Saskatchewan. A lot of people are receiving wonderful blessings. Thank you for your prayers. The Lord has been so kind to us all, we love Him, and we love you all at the Monastery for praying for us. We pray for you."

CURE OF LUNG CANCER

The following testimonial was received by phone at Christ of the Hills Monastery at 4:30 p.m. on April 20, 1988:

Monique Sylvester of Dillon, Saskatchewan, called and asked for prayers for her husband, Albert, who was suffering from lung cancer. He was experiencing much pain on his left side. She had received a cotton ball with Myrrh from the Weeping Icon from Fred Morin and had anointed her husband with the Myrrh on his left side with the Sign of the Cross and prayed for him. Almost immediately, red spots began to appear all over his side, shoulder and back. He slept very peacefully that night. In the morning when he woke up almost all the red spots were gone and his pain was much better.

Now there is worry that Albert may have cancer in his neck. The doctors have taken tests and we are waiting for the results. Monique asked for prayers and also asked for Holy Water, Holy Oil and another cotton ball with Myrrh from the Icon.

CURE OF BRAIN VIRUS

On April 12, 1988, Father Benedict received a phone call from his aunt, Alma Heyse, to report the following miracle which she attributes to anointing with tears from the Myrrh-Weeping Icon and prayers to the Theotokos.

During the previous Winter, Mrs. Heyse had what appeared to be a stroke. She became paralyzed on one side of her body, her speech was slurred, she was unable to move by herself, and her normal bodily functions were impaired. Someone had to move her from her bed to a wheelchair and she was hospitalized. The initial diagnosis was a stroke. Later, through numerous advanced tests it was determined that she had a brain tumor. There was, however, a conflict of opinions between the original diagnostician and the specialist whom she called in for a second opinion. Yet a third doctor was called in because brain surgery was immediately anticipated. It was finally determined that she should go to the Neurological Center at UCLA. There, brain surgery was performed and no brain tumor was discovered. But there was a liquid-like substance that was spreading rapidly through the brain and was causing intense pressure. They felt this was the cause of the malady. They indicated that the damage to her body was permanent even if the cause of the liquid like substance could be determined and the situation reversed and corrected. They were very, very confused.

Through further testing and consultation with more specialists, now on an international level, they determined that she had a virus in her brain caused by some kind of invasive parasite, unknown to them. Mrs. Heyse's weakened condition prohibited further testing and her prognosis was declared to be terminal. She was told that she was dying and that she should go home and try to enjoy her last days as best she could, unless she would prefer to be in a nursing home. Mrs. Heyse chose to be at home but responded with faith in God, believing that if it was God's will she could be cured of this malady.

She called the Monastery and asked for prayers and for the tears of the Mother of God with which to anoint herself. She has been prayed for regularly since her illness began. She was anointed repeatedly with the tears of the Mother of God and on her most recent examination today it was determined that the invasive virus was receding for no apparent medical reason. Mrs. Heyse called to say that she knew that this was from the direct intervention of the Theotokos and the anointing with her holy tears. The doctors are baffled by the miraculous recovery. The Monks of course glorify God who is praised in all things and His Most Holy Mother.

HEALING OF CHRONIC RASH

On August 28, 1988, Hierodeacon Pangratios reports the following:

"In January of 1988, a man visited Christ of the Hills Monastery suffering from a severe rash on his left leg. The debilitating rash had been bothering him for at least 18 months and all the medication the doctors had recommended had not helped at all. He came with some friends and received anointing with Myrrh from the Weeping Icon of New Sarov.

"On September 10, 1988, he returned to the Monastery and reported that soon after being anointed the rash had completely disappeared. Showing us his leg we could see that all that was left of the rash was a small patch of dry skin. I remembered from his earlier visit that the rash was quite large and runny with lots of discoloration; just the slightest touch would cause him great pain. Now his leg was normal. He attributed his healing to the intercessions of the Theotokos and his being anointed with the Myrrh from her Icon.

"On his visit he brought with him his sister who was in a wheel chair and had been steadily loosing the strength in her right leg. She could stand only with great pain and always had to be supported. It was obvious that she had come with great faith. We served an Akathist before the Weeping Icon. During the Akathist the Icon began to weep and Father Luke, the Hieromonk serving the Akathist, gathered some of the Myrrh on a cotton ball and anointed her with it. After the Akathist she stood up and kissed the Icon with tears flowing down her cheeks."

CURE OF SPINA BIFIDA CHILD

The following statement was given by a Pilgrim to Christ Of The Hills Monastery on June 10, 1989:

"My name is Mary Louise Cantu, and on Memorial Day weekend 1989, we came on Saturday to see the Weeping Icon. We brought my niece and nephew, Espirancita and Francisco Alipia with their little daughter Anna Patricia, who had spina bifida. She was going to have to have an operation because the urine in her bladder keeps backing up into the kidneys and this is what kills most spina bifida children. They have developed one operation in which they can put Teflon in the kidney, but it's not guaranteed. She had been having a lot of bladder infections. The physician at Scott and White Clinic, Temple, Texas, said she did have to have the operation.

"We came here on Saturday of Memorial Day weekend. The following Tuesday she went to the doctor to get the results and to set up the date of the operation. When the doctor examined her again he came back beaming and he said 'I don't know what you've done for this little girl, but whatever you're doing, keep on doing it, because she doesn't need the operation any more.'

"We give all of the glory to our Blessed Lady and her Son for granting us this miracle in our little Anna Patricia."

TWO LIVES MIRACULOUSLY SAVED

Lucy Flores wrote from Lubbock, Texas, on September 21, 1989:

"One of my daughters, Diana Maria, lives in El Paso, Texas. She was going to have a baby last month, so I went to see her to take care of their other little boy. She was having some problems with the pregnancy. A lady from my church gave me a little piece of cotton from the Weeping Icon. She goes to Blanco all of the time. I don't even know her name, but she gave it to me to use on my daughter.

"My daughter was real sick in the hospital and I just kept going to the Chapel to pray for her and the baby, but everything was going wrong. Her heart and the baby's heart kept stopping and my son-in-law was just crying. So I asked the doctor if I could go in to see her. The doctor said, 'Yes, but just for a little bit.' So I went in and then they told me to leave. I said that I wanted to know what was going on, that she was my daughter. He told me everything. He said, 'We have to do surgery right away, because if we don't you are going to lose both of them.' So they did the surgery. The baby was in real bad health. They had to do surgery on the baby's heart. They didn't know if he was going to make it, he was so sick. They told us that Diana was in real bad shape too, so they didn't let us see the baby or her. I just kept praying and praying for them to get better.

"The next day we were able to see Diana. She was doing pretty bad, so I anointed her with the little piece of cotton with the tears from the Icon, and she started recovering. They kept saying about the baby that they didn't know if he was going to make it. So when they let us see him I took the miraculous cotton with me. I anointed and prayed for him. Then they said that he started improving. He was recovering. One of his lungs cleared by itself. I knew that the Lord had answered my prayers with the Mother of God's tears. He is doing real good now and I keep giving thanks to God and to the All Holy Virgin."

CURE OF CANCER

On Christmas Day, January 7, 1990, Dora and Hattie Saldana visited the Monastery. Hattie wrote the following that day:

"Mrs. Dora Saldana was diagnosed with cancer (in the uterus) on July 23, 1989. The prognosis was very poor with a poor chance of recovery. On this January 7, 1990, she is here (at Christ of the Hills Monastery) giving thanks to our Most Holy Lady for a miraculous cure. At this time, she is eating and feeling much better and is gaining her weight back. Mrs. Saldana lives in Austin, Texas. The Mother of God has granted this miracle to her, her family and friends."

"Ms. Hattie Saldana stated that the tumor in Dora Saldana had grown so large that it was visible, causing her to appeared bloated. Hattie had visited her in the hospital, prayed for her and anointed her with the tears of the Mother of God. From that time on Dora began to improve. Dora appeared very healthy and was walking without aid. The only residual effect of the cancer was that her hair had not yet grown back from the chemotherapy treatments."

CURE OF LEG AILMENT

Jo Ann Young of Denver, Colorado, wrote on May 1, 1984:

"Well, a prayer was answered. My feet and legs gave me problems. I got my new boots. They have a slight heel with a heel left inside. My cane is in retirement. Can walk normally. These shoes put the weight in the right place and less on the wrong place. A Miracle. Now if my breathing problems with the moisture would clear up, also hay fever. It will in time, I know.

"Pray for us for improved health, no surgery, tests, change of drugs (prescription) and no accidents or illness. And our breathing problems. Less flu bugs. You have been praying to cure my leg problems. Tonight my friend and I saw it happen. The bones in my foot straightened in perfect alignment. Plus no pain in my knees or hips. (Due to injuries, birth defects, I had serious problems). With God as the head of that team, I am cured of the problem. Praise God."

MIRACLE OF ST. SERAPHIM

Anthony J. Herryman of Steger, Ill , October 17, 1983 wrote requesting a Relic of St. Seraphim, and stating that he had received a miracle from the Saint.

FINANCIAL BLESSING

Lena Castanzo from Kane, Pennsylvania. Wrote on June 11, 1984:

"I wonder if you would be kind enough to send me some St. Seraphim Relics for my family. I asked St. Seraphim for something and made a promise to (give alms) for the poor people. My prayers were answered and I am keeping my promise. Please pray for my brother who is ill."

HEALING THROUGH ST. SERAPHIM'S INTERCESSION

Helen Longo of Torrance, California, on May 2, 1987, wrote:

"I'm sorry to know that Father Benedict suffered so much. By the time this letter arrives, I hope all his illness and troubles are over. I would like another Relic of St. Seraphim. I wasn't feeling good, so I placed the St. Seraphim Relic where I was hurting and I fell asleep. When I awoke I felt much better."

RELIEF FROM DEMONIC ATTACK

The following account of her suffering and relief was written to Fr. Benedict by P. P.:

"What a nice surprise to hear from you. Thank you for the sweet letter—and for being so loving and caring. Your prayers must be very powerful, because since I wrote you the voices and the sensations seem to have lessened on me. They have not stopped entirely, but are less bothersome. I have been under a doctor's care because of it—and have been on tranquilizers for quite some time. Since you are going to be praying for me and since you seem concerned for me, I thought perhaps you might be interested to hear my story.

I just turned 57 and have had the voices within me for 13 years. They call themselves spirits—but I call them demons. They pester me (or have) until I try and scream in frustration. This, of course, upsets my husband. So it has caused unhappiness in our home—and has driven us toward divorce several times.

When I first started hearing the voices it seemed almost miraculous—and like sweet and innocent fun. For three years I talked with them almost every waking minute—and there were many laughs, lots of silliness and what seemed to be really good fun. I talked to them in thought and they replied by words audible to me and not to anyone else. After three years I started to get sensations: they were bubbles which just hung there, unless I sat down and that popped them. Needless, to say, this made me very angry, and I started to say mean things to them—and to tell them to leave me alone. It now no longer seemed fun, but they continued to speak to me in every sound, the sound of walking, water running, eating, breathing, music, cars,—any noise, and if there was no noise they spoke in silence, their voices seeming to come from above. As you can imagine it was most annoying—and annoying was the nicest thing it was. If I prayed, they prayed with me, and if I sang they would sing with me. I had hungrily gobbled them up, fearing it might end, little knowing that I'd soon be praying that it would.

There were both men's and women's voices. One of the men's voices said he was our Lord—and I had many a sweet conversation with that one. Of course, I don't suppose they'd say they were Joe Blow—because then who would be interested in speaking with them. They or whoever, made my statue and my holy pictures speak to me. They were and are clever demons, the one insisted he was Jesus-but some of the regulars said they had pretended to be him.

Anyway, I finally stopped speaking to them and I had to stop praying, because that seemed to intensify their attacks on me. I had a tooth ache and one of the voices said to take my crucifix off the wall and the pain would stop. They can also give and take ailments and do. If I pray or speak to the Lord they give me some pain. If I stop it they take it away. I have kept my sanity, throughout it but, as you can imagine, sometimes I was left with my head spinning. I also had what seemed like many small miracles, but know that they could be, and probably were, done by the demons. If I could remember all that has happened—I should have written it down as it happened—but kept thinking it would end. I could write a book to rival the best of them. Well my Dear, I have rattled on and hope I haven't bored you. Maybe you will know what to make of it.

"Was happy to hear about your dining room, and enlarged garden. That means more work for someone. From the sounds of it you are living well within your vows of poverty. Thank you for listening and for being interested. You have an unusual capacity for love and I am honored that you would take time from your busy schedule to care and share. Much love to you and many thanks."

HEALING OF MULTIPLE SCLEROSIS

Mrs. Charles Garrett of Grand Rapids, Michigan, wrote on October 13, 1989:

"Thank you so very much for your kind letter of October 2. You have been on my mind (and I have wanted) to write to you for quite some time but I just did not take the time to do it.

"First of all, when we visited you on August 16 of this summer, we left with such a highlight to our trip. When we were there I left a picture of our daughter-in-law and her son and you put it next to the Weeping Icon. She has multiple sclerosis and I asked for prayers for her and her son. When we arrived home we found that she had improved. She has been in a wheel chair before we left for Texas and when we got home she was walking by holding onto the walls or someone's arm and has been improving ever since. The doctor that checked her just shook his head and said that he cannot understand her improvement. When we arrived home I anointed her with the tears from the Icon.

"I am asking you again at this time to pray for her and also her husband (our son) and their three children. Their names are Denny and Kathy Garrett and their children are Matthew, Jennifer and Stephen. Also, I ask for your prayers for my husband Charles who is having a very difficult time with his job. He is a teacher and the students of today are so difficult to handle. I ask also for myself that I be able to carry all burdens that God allows me and also to be more kind and charitable to people. I also ask prayers for my mother-in-law and her daughter....

"Is it possible for you to send me another piece of the cotton with the tears of the Icon and also could you put me on the mailing list for your newsletter and two of the holy cards with the picture of the Icon on it. I thank you so very much for all your prayers and may God Bless you all for your devotion to Him. I will most certainly include you in my daily prayers for your health, Father Benedict."

POWER OF MONASTIC PRAYER

On October 31, 1988, Mimie Davis, of Irving, Texas, wrote to request another of the tears from the Weeping Icon. She comments:

"It is always good to know that you're there and that the prayers are continuous. I also remember you daily in my prayers. As Ruth Barnhouse says: 'Anyone who doubts the reason for the existence of Monasteries has never had the occasion to call on the prayers of one!'

"You have no idea how I long to see you. Dr. Ed Sylvest mentioned trying to work out a trip down there-he's teaching the class on Mary again at Perkins School of Theology. I was going to join them but my schedule doesn't permit. I'm back in school, commuting to Denton and Fort Worth. Have only so much time and energy and must budget it. (As if you didn't know about THAT). I do miss you—and I will get there!"

PEACE OF MIND AND HEALING OF SON

Rose Marie Cummings of Port Jefferson, New York, wrote on December 5, 1988 about the healing of her son.

"I received your most precious gift and prayers, and the tears of our Blessed Mother—I can only say, that when I held the tear in my hand, and smelt the fragrance, ecstasy overwhelmed me.

"One of my sons, Matthew, is epileptic. He had taken an overdose of medication. I rushed him to the hospital, our Lord Jesus Christ and His Holy Mother bestowed blessings. He was saved and safe, and a Priest walked by. I've been praying for this opportunity, and the Lord Blessed all of us."

She continues, "I ask you to please mail to me, as many tears as one is allowed to have. I anointed Matthew, but I long to have her gift (of tears) preserved and available. I shall spread the devotion to all whom I encounter in my life. Blessed is she who comes to us, always and ever, and gives us heavenly gifts!"

HEALING THROUGH PRAYER

On December 6, 1988, Nadine Reynols of San Francisco, California, wrote:

"I am now back home from the hospital, having had the flu, inflammation of my stomach, and also had to have three pints of blood. (I was) healed through your prayers. Please pray for me that I stay well for the rest of the year. As of now, I feel just fine.

"I have a place of my own now, thanks to your prayers. You must have stormed heaven with prayers for me and I want to thank you and all the Monks and Nuns.

"I pray that God will let me live in peace with my youngest, who is 18 now and will be graduating from high school in June, 1989."

FOR HIS MOTHER

On December 20, 1988, Elizabeth V. Clee wrote from Beacon, New York:

"When your letter arrived I was feeling definitely down in the dumps. The first thing I thought was, 'Oh no, not another one.' ...I am a widow of the past 26 years. I am 85 years of age and live in the low income housing tract. I put your letter aside, still annoyed, but thought, 'I'll just send $5.00.'

I still can't get over it, but I distinctly heard a voice. I was amazed as I live alone. What did the voice say?

'But Vera, it's for my Mother!! I know how much you love her.'

"As I said, I am alone—Whose voice was it? Whose Mother did I love? No wonder He was so hurt. He knew how much I loved His wonderful Mother.... I lost my mother when I was six."

RELIEF OF STOMACH CRAMPS

Mrs. Eugenia Llanos of Maxwell, Texas, wrote on January 27, 1990:

"Thanks to God for healing with God's Grace and the Mother of God Myrrh-Weeping Icon. My Father was sick for about 3 to 4 hours with pain in the stomach. At the same time, when I was about finished reading your letter, they called me and told me that he was sick. I went over to his house to see him. I used a little bit of anointing oil and at the same time I asked God and the Myrrh-Weeping Icon to heal him. In less than 10 minutes his pain was going away. It was a miracle."

HEALING OF CHRONIC PHLEBITIS

From Scranton, Pennsylvania, Lynne Hease wrote on October 10, 1989:

"We are still finding out how blessed we are from our visit with you all. In fact, they border on miracles.

"In the five days before we arrived at the Monastery, I had been suffering from phlebitis for the fourth time last summer. That is why I tried to walk as little possible while I was there. It took the wise observation of a friend here to point out that I have not been bothered by the health problem since I was with you in August. She also has pointed out that I've lost 28 pounds since August."

Ms. Hease then describes how Fr. Benedict gave her an extra tear, 'for someone you will meet.' This had puzzled her at the time, but later that day she met a man in San Antonio whose illness had cost him several jobs. When she gave him the tear, he wept for joy and professed his unworthiness. She thanks the Monks for the tears and closes with this remark. "Allan and I see the tears as very miraculous in themselves, since the smell of Myrrh does not fade and every time someone is blessed with them, the traces of oil is left on the skin-oil that does not evaporate."

PEACE OF MIND AND FORGIVENESS OF WRONGS

To Fr. Benedict and Fr. Vasili came the following letter from Eleanor A. Wandke of Spring, Texas, on January 5, 1990:

" I appreciated hearing from you and most grateful for the opportunity of visiting the Monastery in October of 1989. It was a most moving experience. I have enclosed my yearly traditional Christmas letter to you because I wanted you to know how my visit to see the New Sarov Icon has affected my life.

"I have been a faithful child to my parents all these years and at age 51, they turned against me and fired me from their business after I had devoted most of my life to them, their needs and their business. It was a difficult time for me to not harbor hate in my heart for them and their actions. But my visit to the Monastery changed all the hate I was holding within me and for that I am truly grateful.

"I have enclosed my intentions although I've never requested anything openly before, maybe now is the time! Whatever prayers you can say for me and my family will be appreciated.

"I am enclosing a small check and hope you have some tears for me. May God richly bless you and everyone at the Monastery for their truly good works."

HEAVENLY AROMA

Ruth Green of Arvada, Colorado, conveyed the following from her niece in Kenneth, Michigan, on January 28, 1990:

"When I opened (your) letter I removed the picture and tear and placed them on the end table. I started to read your letter, then decided to read the literature you sent concerning the picture and tear. I took the Icon picture, looked at it, read the back and laid it down. I picked up the foil wrapped tear, held it in my hand, gently felt of it (still in foil) and then smelled it, no smell. Then placed the tear on the picture and continued to read. Again, I stopped reading and picked up the Icon picture and tear. (I) looked at the picture a few minutes, felt the foil-wrapped tear and again started to place them on the end table, when at that moment, I smelled this beautiful smell. I laid them down and smelled my hands—thinking it was hand lotion—though I hadn't any on my hands. I couldn't understand where the beautiful, indescribable scent came from. "I then smelled the picture and the foil wrapped tear and there was no odor coming from either of them.

"I finished reading your letter, then read the letter you sent from the Monastery signed by Father Benedict. It stated there was a beautiful Myrrh scent to the tear. So I picked up the foil wrapped tear, turned the foil back a little and smelled the cotton. Oh what a beautiful smell. The same smell I had smelled, when I placed them on the table.

"How I wish I could take a trip to that Monastery! Perhaps our All-Holy Mother will grant me this desire someday. I can't thank you enough for sending me the picture, the tear, and the information.

"May the love and protection of the Sorrowful Mother of God clothe and protect you as you journey to everlasting bliss in heaven."

Mrs. Green then writes:

"Please remember me and Kenny and Shannon (our 13 year old) daughter in your prayers. The world is in such a state of perversion and for many the love of God has grown cold.

"We only need to reflect on the sadness of our Lord Jesus Christ and His Holy Mother to know and understand the great danger that is waiting to overcome our young people. I constantly consecrate my young daughter Shannon to the Mother of God.

"As soon as I had read your letter and that of the Monastery, Kenny, Shannon, and I washed our hands, knelt down in front of the Icon. We had Shannon anoint Kenny and I with the tear. It was a very blessed and inspiring moment. I sent for another tear and literature and received it from you and gave it to a lady at church whose husband is very ill with cancer.

"I put on a white sweater one afternoon, felt in the pocket, and there was a tear. I do not know how it got there. It's a mystery where it came from. I gave it to a lady on the first floor, who has been at death's door many times. She has a bronchial problem."

RELIEF OF TENSION

Linda Uhrhan of Chaffee, Missouri, wrote on January 16, 1989:

"I am sorry to hear of your health problems and I will remember you in my prayers. I want to thank you for remembering us in your own prayers. It seemed that within a week from my asking for your prayers, that at least some of the tension and burdens were lifted. All is not solved, but our son, Mike, has shown great improvement. Larry does off and on. Yet, it has only been about a month, but I am pleased.

"Thank you so much for the tear. I loved the smell when I opened the envelope. I want to bless each member of my family with a tear. I first blessed

Michael and asked that he carry the cotton in his bill fold. Surprisingly he did, as if he were a young boy again. It makes me feel better.

"I truly believe the Weeping Icon is God's sign to all of us. The world has taken over so many lives.

"Also I did bless my daughter, Amy, my sister Barbara, and myself with the tear. I don't know if more than one person can use the tear, but I hope that it will help. Michael was the intended member and he is carrying the cotton with him. I pray he finds his place in life and it be a happy one."

LOVE OF CHRIST

Mary E. Kalukiewicz of Alexandria, Virginia., wrote on February 1, 1989, to say she is having problems and must have surgery and feels that the Mother of God has helped her.

She continues:

"Thank you and the Monks for your prayers. I have shared the Icons with a lady here at the Senior Citizen Complex and she has written you and tells me today of another lady who will write you.

"The Mother of God has enriched my life so much and filled me with a great love for her beloved Son's presence in the Mysteries.

"Thank you for the wooden Icons you sent my daughter. I have distributed them all and if possible could have more to give to friends during Lent. I have a ministry of writing to persons and ask you to please pray for them and for me that I will continue to share the Icon with them."

ICON PRINTS WEEPING

On March 8, 1989, Emily Harma of Pleasant Hill, California, wrote to Fr. Vasili of her great interest in holy Mount Athos:

"I hope one day if you have the time you will write and tell me about your trip. I am very much interested. Most of all about Mount Athos in Greece. 'The Garden of the Mother of God' as it is called.... I had word that my son Don was to have an operation and I wanted to go, when two days before I was to leave, my husband had a heart attack. It has kept me busy and this is the first chance I have to catch up on my mail. Both are fine now and home from the hospital.

"I wish to thank you for the two Icon cards you sent me. I have been so busy that until I received your letter I had not looked at them. They do not look like the way I first received them. At least I do not remember them this way. On the small one both Mother and Child are weeping. The large one has faded and her tears are quite pronounced. Surely a Miracle.

"Fr. Benedict was kind enough to send me a note and the large mounted Icon. It is lovely. I know at the time he wrote he was in much pain and I do hope he is now feeling better. I'm sure when he has the surgery over and done with, he will be well on the road to recovery once again. I remember him in my prayers and all at the Monastery. You all have been most kind to write me and I appreciate it. Enclosed find a small donation. Sorry it can not be more at this time."

RELIEF OF FLU

Claudette Henly of Orange, New Jersey, wrote on March 18, 1989:

"I will not be able to make the Pilgrimage, because of short notice, but please send me the Icon of St. Patrick and the prayer. I would like to tell you that during this week I had a very bad case of the flu and put my picture of the Weeping Icon on me and felt much better."

HEALING OF ARTHRITIS

Catherine Hinson of Colorado Springs, Colorado, wrote on March 23, 1989, that a friend came to visit her and brought a print of the Weeping Icon. She says:

"I have had arthritis of the back and knees for about three years. I almost walked doubled over. This morning I got out of bed and for the first time in a year I can walk straight. It is a miracle and I am so happy. .... I am sitting here writing and looking at that beautiful Icon and really believe she did it. My son who lives in San Antonio told me to ask you for some cotton balls. Please keep me on your prayer list."

MIRACULOUS HEALINGS

Sister Dorothy Belongie, S.F.P., of Cincinnati, Ohio, wrote the following report on February 3, 1989:

"With spiritual delight I am writing this letter to express my sincere thanks and appreciation for your most precious gift ñ'a tear of the Mother of God from her Myrrh-Weeping Icon.' Also I thank you for the prayers, your Monks and Nuns, have said for me.

"I acknowledge I owe a profound debt of gratitude to your kindness and generosity in sharing with me these spiritual treasures. I have used the tear on the following Sisters and one lay person and herewith I am stating its results:

"Sister M. Consolata received healing of back pain and peace of heart.

"Sister Dorothy Belongie received healing of heart and peace.

"Sister M. Irmengard received improvement in speech and healing of deafness and peaceful resignation to her illnesses.

"Sister M. Jerome had a stroke and received peace.

"Sister M. Louise received healing of the eyes.

"Sister M. Norbertine received healing of deafness.

"Mrs. Mary Suyot received healing of cancer of the breast.

"We Sisters are most grateful to our Blessed Mother for her loving protection and assistance in the healing project. Surely she is our health of the sick. Also we thank you most sincerely for sharing these spiritual treasures with us. May our Blessed Lord and his Blessed Mother richly bless you and reward you with their loving care."

MIRACLES OF THE THEOTOKOS AND SAINT JOHN THE WONDERWORKER

Fred Morin wrote the following from Buffalo Narrows, Saskatchewan, Canada, on April 4, 1988:

"As I had promised, I would write you this letter. And also enclosed is a donation, to help the church. Please accept my offering, because it does cost you a lot when you send me all those beautiful, wonderful things.

"Things are just working great for us. We never give up. Just pray always to the good God. Diane and the girls are doing just great. So is my grand son Andrew, my daughter Jackie, and my son Robert Morin. And Janice—all doing great!

"Otherwise, everything is fine up here in Northern Saskatchewan, Canada. Thank you all, for always remembering us in your prayers. The rest of your friends are okay also. They send you all their love and thank you for sending me the wonderful book of "Blessed John the Wonderworker." He sure was a great man of God. He had a lot of love for mankind. You know I've never even heard of him or seen his picture, but just by reading and judging from the miracles he performed, he was a truly beautiful man of God.

"The first miracle I'd like to mention performed by Vladyka John, is concerning my Grandson Andrew Morin. My daughter took him to the hospital for his usual check up. Then the doctor discovered he had a lump on his breast, close to the nipple, which of course had us quite worried. The doctor suggested that he be taken to the City to a bigger hospital for an operation. Then I told my daughter and her mom not to worry. Just to leave it up to the Lord, but to take him anyway just to make sure. I would pray that it was not cancer or anything serious like that. So I began to pray to Blessed John asking him please to spare my Grandson and prevent him from getting an operation. Because I will go for the power of prayer first. Before anything else. Sure enough, Blessed John, answered. My Grandson Andrew didn't have to get an operation, even after they took him to the city hospital. Thanks be to God and the prayers of the Blessed John. He is such a man of God. Beautiful, wonderful Wonderworker. We love him so much.

"The second miracle occurred when Diane had been suffering from a swollen and painful leg. She had a hard time walking most of the time. She wanted to go to the local hospital here in Buffalo Narrows to see a doctor because it was getting worse. I suggested, maybe we try prayers first. And so we did. I rubbed the holy tear on her leg and foot. We also asked for the intercession of Blessed John. And again another miracle was performed. Thanks to our Blessed Mother of God and Blessed John. The swelling and pain have vanished and have not returned. So many miracles have happened since we discovered Blessed John the Wonderworker.

"Another miracle happened to me in March of this year, 1988. The power had gone off due to a big snow storm we had up here. You see, we get our supply of power from the City of Saskatoon, Sask. They supply power to all the surrounding communities here. So the whole north country was without power for the whole day and part of the evening. Anyway, I was at work and I just stayed there, hoping the power would come on.

"In the meantime, still waiting for the power to come on, I had turned on one of the burners on the stove for the coffee to boil. But anyway it didn't (due to the power failure). So I decided to leave the office. In the meantime I had forgotten to turn off the burner on the stove. I was already gone about four to five hours. I just happened to be reading the book you sent to me of Blessed John, laying in the bedroom. It just popped into my head about the office! Stove? etc.?? I came running into the kitchen telling Diane, I was sure I had left the stove on at the office. I just happened to be reading a part of how Blessed John helped a burn victim. I told Diane we better go and check the office. Sure enough she was the first to enter. The place was just full of smoke. Coffee pot red hot. The plastic handle on it was ready to burst into flames. Once again blessed John had helped. God is my witness of these miracles performed by Blessed John. He surely was a man of God. In many other ways he's helped also. Yes! we believe that. I wish I could go to San

Francisco to visit Blessed John's Sepulcher. He truly was a wonderful, beautiful man of God. I'm sure glad I've discovered him.

"I believe these miracles were from God through his prayers. I believe in the true Orthodox way, because it has brought me closer to God. I've tried every other way, but always failed.

"My older brother Paul Morin has a lot of family problems too, he tried to even become a born again Christian. But that has failed him too. Please I ask all of you at the Monastery to pray for him.

"We would like to go to Texas as soon as possible. Oh yes! Please send some more pictures of the Weeping Icon, and the tears, and blessed oil. So my good friend, say 'hi' to everyone for us at the Monastery. We love you all and pray for you."

ICON PRINT WEEPING

The Reverend Ronald Long of Irvington, New Jersey, wrote to Father Vasili on February 22, 1988:

"Hi! Just a letter to answer yours, I have received today in the US Mail. Yes, Christ is in our midst. It is with great joy and wonder that I write to you, Father Vasili. Just recently my wooden Icon Print has also began too weep too; as those in Tulsa, Oklahoma, Palas Verdes, California, and Albuquerque, New Mexico. I too know that the Mother of God is calling us more deeply to a life of repentance, fasting, and prayer. Like you, I also realize that she is trying to reach as many souls as possible with her call. I am sending my prayer intentions to you at once with this letter. Please tell Father Benedict that he has my prayers for a successful surgery."

HEALING OF STOMACH

Agnes Richard wrote to Father Vasili from Windsor, Ontario, on December 16, 1988:

"Thank you for the soil from St. Herman of Alaska's grave. I must say the tear we received from the Blessed Mother Icon has healed my stomach problems... I am grateful for all we do have. I always try to remember you all in my prayers. God bless you all in your good works."

COMFORT AND HEALING OF RELATIONSHIPS

B. W. wrote from Pomona, California, on December 20, 1988:

"My grandsons have not yet returned from a sexually abusive father. However, the tiny flames of love are growing into a great fire and the intercession of our Lady has brought comfort, solace, and some healing of relationships to my heart.

"Please pray to the Mother of God for the safe return of these children to their earthly Mother and Grandmother.

"May The Peace of the Newborn Christ Child be with you as you continue your path to Him."

SMALL MIRACLES AND PRAYERS FOR GREATER ONES

Three days later, B. W. wrote:

"Our family prays for your speedy recovery so that you may continue the works of our Lord that you have started and that are still on the drawing board. Our wish is for a Blessed and healthy New Year. After receiving many graces and blessings from the first tear I received, I gave the tear to my daughter who was in great distress. Sending for a new one I keep it close to me always, and have been literally showered with the blessings from our Lady.

"After putting up a lovely tree I blessed it with Holy Water and asked the Mother of God to help keep its branches lively for the season, and it has drunk over a quart of water each day. Praying to our Lady has become the blessing it was once when I prayed to the Mother of God repeatedly in my head to her, and lost the blessings due to despair and judgment in our lives. Praying to her for an answer to a problem horse, I found a trainer willing to do exactly as I need on my very first phone call. How can we ignore such blessings? Many people say to me that God is too busy to bother with my every day things, but I say He wants to be involved in all I do, and the more I involve Him, the more the devil ignores me and this I like very much.

"Prayer on your behalf will be sent your way—and we ask your prayers for my daughter's two boys who must be given back to her care from their sexually abusive father, who paid a judge to get custody. That is the big miracle we await."

CURE OF TERMINAL BACTERIAL MENINGITIS

Father Arlen Jones of Round Rock, Texas, wrote the following account on August 25, 1988:

"With deep feeling and praises to God and the Blessed Mother I feel I must relay to you what I can only describe as a miracle.

"On Thursday, August 18, 1988, we received a telephone call from our daughter from a Fort Worth hospital. In anguish she told her Mother that our granddaughter had just been admitted with bacterial meningitis. This is the worst kind. Of course, she was extremely ill, with a fever of 103 to 105. After the conversation, my wife called the hospital in Austin for some information. They offered little hope of survival with that type of meningitis, and if she should somehow survive, there would probably be several after effects.

"Pretty soon we found that ministers and Christians from various denominations were going by and calling my daughter with prayers. Priests from around the state and other states were calling me. Whole congregations of various faiths were having prayer for little Sara. As, of course, we were also. We could not go to Fort Worth until Friday afternoon, the following day.

"That night, Thursday, we had been invited, along with other Priests, to the home of Father Les Harber. We called and canceled, preferring to remain by the telephone. However, during the evening, Father Harber gave to Father Thomas Logue a cotton ball with myrrh from Christ of the Hills Monastery, and asked that he deliver it to us.

"On Friday evening we arrived at the Fort Worth hospital to find that little Sara's condition was the same (that is, it had not gotten worse), for which we were thankful. We had traveled there with such a dread of what we would find. The doctor said she has stabilized, but he was not at all optimistic. The prognosis was still terminal, as is expected with bacterial meningitis. Her fever was very high. We feel, especially now, that God had stabilized her in answer to so many prayers until we could arrive.

"I gave my daughter the pamphlet about the Weeping Icon from Christ of the Hills Monastery. I had to tell her most of it, because she was in no mental condition to read it. Then I showed her a plastic vial into which we had put the cotton ball and told her what it was. She was so excited, demanding immediate anointing, which we proceeded to do.

"The next morning, Saturday, there was no fever. The doctor came in totally amazed. He said there had been a miracle. Whereas the white blood count had been 1,500 (count of 5 is normal) the count was down and dropping. All tests now show viral meningitis (the least severe type). He said he could not understand it. He would have bet everything he owned, including his condominium on the coast, that his previous diagnosis was correct...bacterial meningitis. But now the tests were showing viral meningitis. She was in no danger whatsoever. There would be no after-effects. And he would release her to go home right then, but it was so unusual that he wanted to monitor her through the day and would release her the next day, Sunday. She was well.

"We knew you would want to know of this. Please pray to the Most Holy Mother of God for us."

HEALING OF FINGER

Soledad D. Eugenio of Napa, California, wrote to Fr. Benedict on January 12, 1989:

"Thank you for the tear from the Weeping Icon and the literature that you sent. I can hardly contain myself for what happened to me and I don't quite know where to begin.

"Father Benedict, let me tell you about the little finger on my right hand—just below the nail, the first joint, to be exact. I have some arthritic condition on my fingers but the joint on my right pinkie is worst of all—it had swelled to an ugly size and not only that, it caused me so much pain, I could not even hand write without wincing from the pain and distorting my penmanship. Anyway, just before Christmas, for some reason, the swelling burst open, creating a little crater, which further aggravated the pain. I had to cover it with a Band-Aid to protect it from being touched—besides, the crater oozed some kind of wetness. It could not be arthritis, I thought, because arthritis does not burst open. This condition has been there for a year or so.

"Saturday morning, I received your letter with the tears and the picture of the Weeping Icon. I read everything you sent and smelled the unusual scent. I do not know what myrrh smells like—frankincense, yes, but not myrrh—but I know this scent is unlike any I have smelled before. That Saturday night, I changed the linen on our bed, and in so doing, hurt my little finger so, I had to tell my husband to finish changing of the bedding. Before I go to bed, I often read some kind of spiritual literature—maybe, the life of a Saint, or some contemplative readings. That night, I read your letter again, and for some reason, decided to touch the cotton to my little finger. I had to barely touch it to the wound because it really hurt. And I prayed what you told me to pray. Then I went to sleep.

"Next morning, I said my morning prayers as usual and did not remember what I did to my little finger and went about my usual chores. I continued until around mid-morning as I did something in the kitchen, and noticed I felt no pain in my right pinkie. And I looked and saw that some sort of scab had formed and there was absolutely no pain, even though I struck it again and again on the kitchen counter top, to prove to myself there really was no pain!

"O, Father Benedict, I don't know how providence sent your letter to me but it must only be from the hand of our Blessed Mother! As I told you, I am Catholic but I am not a fanatic who believes everything and anything. On the contrary, I am inclined to need some proof in order to believe in a miracle. But this! I know God wants something of me.

...(Can you send me) some more tears and pictures of the Weeping Mother, that I can distribute to friends and relatives. My sister has leukemia, discovered last November, and I have sent my tears and the picture of the Weeping Icon to her. I have an older brother who is suffering so much from painful knees he can hardly walk and I would like to send him one too. Of course, I would like one for myself too, that I may be able to touch those near me who may need our Lady's healing grace.

"Again, I thank you, dear Father Benedict. My pinkie is now almost as good as new. The swelling has gone down considerably, the crater is now covered with a tiny scab which is almost disappearing. I wish I could send you a picture of my finger, but am sure you are familiar with many, many other miracles."

RELIEF OF SEVERE PAIN

Bernice L. Seguin of Ontario, Canada, wrote on October 24, 1988, that,

"The Weeping tears of the Icon, you sent me in the past has taken away severe pain and tingling that used to be in my hands and fingers.

"I would appreciate one sent to me to help the pain in my left knee due to arthritis in the knee. I'm sure it will help my knee, the way it did my fingers and hands."

HEMPSTEAD WEEPING ICON

On November 12, 1988, Dorothy Merando of Farmingdale, New York, wrote:

"Thank you for the post card and wallet size print of the Weeping Mother of God. My daughter is going to decoupage the larger one for me, and I shall treasure it.

"When at first I looked at the Icon copy I remembered I had seen one like it before and I want to relate to you that memory.

"Some many years ago a happening occurred right here on Long Island. A sensation! The newspapers and television covered the account.

"Some 10 miles away from here at Hempstead—in the Greek Orthodox Church of St. Paul's Cathedral, there was an Icon of the Virgin Mary, weeping tears!

"People flocked from far and wide to observe the Icon. Some were very fortunate to see the tears, others just stood in awe. I was one of those persons.

"The church was ablaze with candles. The atmosphere was electric. Even with hundreds of people treading in and out—a silence beyond belief reigned.

"The day was beautiful and the weather perfect, and I had collected my mother and daughter, and decided we would go and see 'our Lady.' At the time I was fortunate in having a car, and we went to St. Paul's.

"To describe the crowds, the general feeling, the electricity in the air; I cannot, for I do not have the words.

"We stood in a long line and slowly progressed, until I had the honor to stand before the Icon, transfixed, bow my head, and murmur a short prayer and move on. Her face was damp. I felt very sad, and words cannot describe how I felt. We lighted candles and moved along to the outside again.

"As I have said, this was many years ago, and something that I never could forget. When your letter arrived, I was so surprised, but had immediate recall as to the event. Many things have happened since then.

"It is good sometimes to not have any idea of things to come, because when I think of the problems and sufferings of others, my problem does not seem so large."

CURE OF LUNG CANCER

From Apple Valley, New Mexico, Maryanne Frank wrote to Fr. Benedict:

"Thank you for the Icon of the Mother of God. A dear friend of mine was being tested for cancer. The doctor was sure it was lung cancer. They went ahead with the operation. The week before I had sent him the Holy Water you sent me and the picture of the Weeping Icon. He said the prayers and washed in the water. He has almost no religious interest. When the doctor operated, they found no cancer. It had disappeared. We feel this is a great miracle and we are so grateful. Thank you for introducing us to the Weeping Mother."

ANOTHER CURE OF LUNG CANCER

On March 1, 1989, Jane Blanchard of Gilmore City, Iowa:

"I anointed and gave the tear you sent a long time ago, (probably a year ago) to Mildred Sudek who had lung cancer. As to this date, she has had no sign of cancer return and she has kept the tear.

"Now my brother-in-law has brain cancer. It is not operable. They thought it was in remission, but he lost the use of one leg and a CAT scan revealed two more spots. I would like to give him a tear also. I have great faith in the Weeping Icon."

ICON WEEPING

From New York City Mr. Goldstone wrote on March 3, 1989, "The picture of the Weeping Icon has changed. The tears have gone more to the left, and have gotten white and very wide."

AID IN SURGERY

From West Palm Beach, Florida, Mrs. Anna Di Nicola wrote to Fr. Vasili on February 3, 1989:

"I asked you for a tear from the Weeping Icon and I have received it. I have blessed myself with the tear before I had a heart operation and I thank God and the Blessed Icon that I'm alive today. I have shared a piece of the tear with my family and hope it will help them as it did me. I would appreciate if you would send me another tear. As I would like to share it with my children. I thank you very much."

HEALING INTERNAL MALADY

Mrs. Charles Hammond wrote to Fr. Benedict on February 23, 1989, from Washington, Pennsylvania:

"Thank you so very much for all the kind and considerate attention you have given to my correspondence. I especially appreciated your last letter, wherein you enclosed a tear of the Mother of God from her Myrrh-Weeping Icon.

"As you suggested my use of the tear, I anointed myself with the proper prayer before going to the specialist's office.

I prayed fervently that medication could be given me without hospitalization or operation or scope treatment. And thanks to the All Holy Mother of God, the internist discharged me, saying he was so pleased with the X ray results. I was healed."

ICON WEPT ON CHRISTMAS

Virginia Vild of Cleveland, Ohio, wrote to Father Vasili on March 3, 1989:

"I am enclosing five dollars. I live on a small income from S.S. I am not able to work. I am 64 years and I have chronic anemia. My small Icon Print of the Weeping Icon that is mounted on oak wept on Christmas day 1988, as I prayed before it.

"I will be praying for Father Benedict. May his surgery be successful! Please send me a tear from the Weeping Icon so I may be healed."

AID IN SURGERY—TUMOR NOT MALIGNANT

Agnes Vaicunas wrote from Mechanicsville, New York, on March 3, 1989:

"All praise to Jesus Christ and His Holy Mother. As I wrote previously, I used the Holy tear from the Myrrh-Weeping Icon on my cousin William, who had an intestinal growth. He had surgery February 15, 1989, and thanks be to God and the Holy Virgin, the growth was not malignant. He still needs prayers, as he is subject to asthma and has a heart condition.

"Dear Father, your letters to me are so full of love. I have never experienced anything like it. I'm sure Our Holy Mother will make it possible one day for me to visit the Weeping Icon at your Monastery.

"I ask your prayers and those of all the Monks and Nuns for my Mother. She says it is so hard to die.

There have been times in the past few weeks when I thought she was going, but she rallies and is able to be up and around. It is all in God's hands."

CURE OF RENAL FAILURE

Anne B. Covalesky of Dalton, Pennsylvania, wrote on February 4, 1989:

"Received the tears of the Weeping Icon of our Blessed Lady two weeks ago. I applied them and prayed to our Blessed Lady to cure my sister that very day. She had renal failure—she was in intensive care and very critical. She was undergoing renal dialysis. Today I phoned her. Her voice sounded young and beautiful (she is 74 and the mother of a Priest). She told me she passed her water (excuse the clinical details-but it was important). The nurse told her she was dreaming (it was 11:30 at night). Indeed, she was not. She said she felt it was a miracle through the anointing of the tears of the Blessed Lady's Icon. Her name is Rosalie Slavetskes, Binghamton, New York.

"Please thank our Blessed Lady. I would appreciate a small tear with cotton for myself, as I have hypertension. I thought it was under control, but it has flared up. I'm needed here to take care of two brothers here on our farm. And money is not that plentiful for all kinds of medical care, since there is no insurance. I couldn't afford some medicine, which is expensive enough. Please pray for me."

HEALING OF CHRONIC CONDITION AND CONVERSION

A moving account was sent by Agnes Salens of Pinellas Park, Florida on January 8, 1989:

"I must confess that never before in my 80 years of life, have I ever received personal written notes, (so profound) in the spirit of heart and soul, humility, and love and so I say, may God continue to bless and guide you, very specially every moment of your life!!

"And so I wish to assure you of my prayers for the healing of your physical being and for the strength to carry on your great mission of love and service to heal and guide the hearts of men.

"I will take this time to relate to you the grace of healing, that happened in the life of Margaret Fowery and her two daughters, one of whom is a foster daughter. When the mailing sent by you, was opened and she held in her hand the tear drop of the Blessed Mother.

"It had been such a close 'touch and go' for her life for so long. After four important surgeries, the doctor allowed her to go home: thinking the home atmosphere would help to enkindle her outlook and lift her spirit with her own special nurse to provide care. She had fallen on the second day and was in terrible pain day and night four days in a row. Then your Tear of our Blessed Mother arrived. She held it in her hand and immediately all the pain went away! She and the daughter wept and wept together, declaring it all a miracle. She believes very deeply that she will live and be able and strong again, as she was before this long ordeal all began. Her own blood daughter was converted spiritually. She is back in the church. They pray together, as they read your letters and prayers and drink spiritually from the well, the Monks and the Monastery. They dream of making a trip as soon as they are well enough to do so."

HEALING OF DESPAIR

Giving thanks, Mary Bandy wrote to Fr. Benedict from Fall City, Washington, on June 27, 1988:

"June 18th will mark six years, that I came through a cancer operation, that would give me a chance to live longer, (without it I would have lived less than six months). So I know what you mean when you say the mystery of God is awesome. It truly gives you something to think about. I also believe that He tries us. When I was at my lowest, and told God I was very tired, a friend gave me a book. It said to start giving Thanks to God for our illness, and that there would be a change. So instead of asking God to make me well, I started praising him for this illness. It turned my life at once to him. I started getting better and have never looked back six years later. Some times it takes time, but when we suffer, count it as pay. The Lord has some wonder for you. Suffering borne properly is a great opportunity to grow closer to God.

"My prayers are with you in your time of need, and thank you for praying for me. Keep your faith strong and turn it over to the Lord. We sometimes forget how powerful He really is."

HEALING OF CEREBRAL HEMORRHAGE

From Tucson, Arizona, Rose Mary Rico wrote on September 20, 1985:

"I received the beautiful card of the Weeping Icon of the Ever–Blessed Virgin, Mother of God. I'm very happy to tell you, it could not have come at a better time. You see my very dear son-in-law was dying from a cerebral hemorrhage and I prayed with all my heart and soul for his salvation. I asked God to please grant me a miracle and not take him yet. You see he has a limited time. He has kidney trouble and the time is almost here. So we thought, this was it. But the doctors said that this had nothing to do with that. Anyway, God granted my petition and the miracle I asked for. He is now convalescing and the doctors say he can't work until six months have passed, certainly a far cry from being at death's door before being anointed with the Tear of the Mother of God.

"So I'm begging you, can you please send me another piece of the cotton saturated with Myrrh. I'm also very sick and my diabetes is giving me a lot of problems and pain. So please if you can dispense with a little of your precious Myrrh, I sure will appreciate it. Please pray for us and I will for all of you and the whole world.

DEATHBED CONVERSION—ICON WEEPING

Olga M. Colon wrote from Coamo, Puerto Rico, on November 30, 1989:

"It is with great sorrow that I write you to tell about my brother Jaime's death. He died on September 23, a week after hurricane Hugo. For many years he was away from religion and my mother used to pray to St. Jude for him. After he died I continue to pray for him.

"It was his sickness that made him come back to religion. One day I saw in his room an Icon of the All-Holy Virgin and I thought perhaps a friend of his that is very religious had given it to him. It looked to me similar to our Mother of Perpetual Help.

"As I was going to fix his room, I took everything out and placed the Icon flat on a small table. It was then that your letter came and I knew about the Icon. It was new to me, all this, but I thanked the Mother of God of New Sarov for the help she has given my brother. As my brother lived in my house, I was near him when he died. He died in his sleep about 2:00 a.m. on Saturday 23, of September.

"As I was telling the story of the Icon, I noticed the tears were very clear and that they had run down near the end of the picture. Clearly the Icon print had wept. I kept quiet. Last Saturday, Nuns visited me and when they looked at the picture they saw that the tears ran down all the way to the end of the frame.

"Yesterday a friend of mine came to my house and when she saw the Icon I told her the story. I had to translate it for her as she wants an Icon. It would be a good idea if you have this leaflet in Spanish.

"I want to thank you for your prayers for my brother Jaime. I am sure they helped him a lot.

"I am glad to know about the good things happening in your Monastery, because God is rewarding your sacrifices.

"Please pray for my brother and me, as I will pray for your mission on the Mother of God's behalf."

MULTIPLE HEALINGS

Fred Morin's family in Saskatchewan, Canada wrote again on October 21, 1987:

"I have promised I would write you this letter, to explain of the wonderful help 'our Blessed Mother' has given to the people in this town. Anyway, this is the information that was given to me by Beatrice Billette:

"This lady, Pauline Billette, has been suffering from cancer. The doctors told her that she wouldn't live very long. She was bedridden. Well, with prayer, and the help of our Lady, she goes up to the bushes and goes hunting, etc. It's a real miracle.

"Then there is the other lady, who is her daughter, Beatrice Billitte. She has been suffering from chest pains. And the doctors also told her there was nothing they could do. She was always very sick and unable to do very much. She too was given the holy tear and is now able to do things which she could not do before.

"And then the little girl, Michelle Hayro, from LaLoche where Moise Jonvier is from, who was paralyzed. She too is able to move her hands slowly and is improving quite well. I gave her the Holy tears. Thank the good Lord, she is slowly improving.

"Many wonderful things have happened here, since we were introduced to the Holy tears of The Mother of God. Many, many thanks to her.

"Well my friends, that's pretty well all the information I can give you. I will say good bye for now. We all love you up here. Please remember us in your prayers, as we will do the same for you."

RELIEF FROM DIABETES

Pauline Machuta wrote to Fr. Benedict on May 31, 1989, from Lincoln Park, Michigan, that her "blood sugar was very high, over 500 and near 600. It is now much lower. The Weeping Icon of the Mother of God helped me very much, in other words I am a diabetic, and the doctors could not control it—the Mother of God can."

HEALING OF PARALYSIS

From East Hartford, Connecticut, Monica J. Jesensky wrote to Fr. Benedict on August 22, 1989:

"Thank you for the Myrrh tear from the Weeping Icon. I appreciate your generosity. My Grandmother regained use of her legs a week after anointing with the tear. She had a stroke and a heart attack prior to it. Thank you for remembering me in your prayers. It is nice to know that you all think of one when you pray.

You speak of prayers in all of your letters. I again want to say thank you for your prayers."

INSPIRATIONAL

On August 15, 1989, Dorothy Giosa wrote from Langhorne, Pennsylvania:

"You and my spiritual family have been in my thoughts and prayers. Last time I wrote to tell you about the beautiful work God has been doing for Josh Compton. I promised to send a picture for your use. The changes in this child through the prayer efforts of your community is truly an inspiration to all of us. The Shriner Hospital has taken care of the medical needs and Josh is doing so much better. Know that my love and best wishes are with all of you. Please do continue in your efforts in Josh's behalf."

MULTIPLE MIRACLES

Fr. Vasili received the following report from Doloros Robledo of San Antonio, Texas, on December 10, 1989:

"My sister invited me to go with her to Blanco and visit the Weeping Icon. I went at first out of curiosity. But the closer we got to the little hill, the more spiritual I began to feel. We got lucky that day we went. There was no line, so Father showed us the Icon at once. He told us all about the Icon and then asked if anyone wanted to be anointed...I went forward. He anointed my five senses. I felt so incredibly peaceful after the blessing. We went through the whole tour and headed back home. My prayer was that my children be healed from their asthma. Instead I was healed of my failing eyesight, but I hadn't realized the miracle until a week later.

"We went out of town for the Thanksgiving Holidays and our relatives invited us to a football game. I failed to mention that everything was blurry to me at night, so I recently paid $240, for exams and glasses. Anyway at this game I could see the band, the football players' numbers on their shirts, the score board, etc. It didn't hit me that I didn't need any glasses till we got home on Sunday. I remember how I told my husband that I was taking the car around the block. I couldn't figure out why I was driving and I noticed the signs were not blurry and everything looked clear to me. I was stunned and could not believe my eyes. My husband tested my eye sight one evening on the way to the store and he could not believe it either.

"The other recent miracles are: We have a Doberman pinscher and last week she could not get up and walk. She was struggling to walk. It was almost as if she was crippled from her two front legs. I told my husband and he looked at me and asked me to pray for her. I looked at him and said "I've prayed for people but never an animal." He replies "why not"? God created them too. So I said, O.K., give me the cotton with the Blessed Mother's tear. As I approached our dog, she gave me a look of despair. I blessed her two front legs and they began to shake. I blessed her with the Myrrh on her front legs and her forehead.

Miraculously, she has been healed. She can walk just fine, as a matter of fact, I saw her run the other day. Thank God.

"My eight-year-old son became ill with a headache, fever, and nausea. All he wanted was me by his side. I felt so sorry for him. So I began to rub his head and a voice within my heart told me to anoint and pray for him. I did just that, the next thing I knew, he closed his eyes and slept all night and woke up feeling fine. He did not complain again. Thank God.

"The other day my husband said that during the night I covered him with a blanket and placed my hand over him and prayed. I do not remember doing such a thing. Now I see why I did. The next day he said he was very close to having a bad accident at his job. He says God saved him from getting severely hurt or even killed.

"After my second visit to the Monastery on the hill, I believe the Lord has strengthened my faith and the gift that He gave me many years ago.

"I am praying for a spiritual father or mother to help me when I fall. I truly believe God will send him/her at this time."

RELIEF OF SPIRITUAL DRYNESS

On January 4, 1989, Kathy Freeman wrote from Snohonish, Washington, to thank the Monks for their letters and gifts:

"Last night, I received a small Icon in the mail. I was so moved by the power of prayer behind the Icon that I stared at it all night and then put it on my bed table and dreamed of Icons. I really am amazed at what a holy community you have. It is inspiring that our Mother is weeping in the United States. Please send me the largest mounted print you have for my home.

"I have been at a total low point in my prayer life for about three months and I just felt in one night like I'm over the hump and on the spiritual path again. Thank you that holiness and love of the Mother of our Lord Christ is so near to us in the United States."

STRENGTH FOR PRAYER

From North Hollywood, California, Bob Carter and his family wrote to Fr. Vasili on August 5, 1987:

"For each and every time I have corresponded with all of you at the Monastery...I have found a sense of spiritual strength. It is for certain that your prayers for me are answered without fail.

"And so as I continue to gain in strength and understanding, my faith continues to re-assure me the direction of my life is being guided by the Almighty Father.

"For although my ability to understand His direction for me is limited, I continue to trudge forward in my life, by trusting in God, in my prayers and trying to carry out His will for me as best I can.

"But when I fail and my life begins to show a doubtful pattern, I have no doubts whatsoever that your personal prayers for me have removed the darkness of doubt beyond my conscious ability to perceive it.

"So it is by your prayers I am finding a newer and more positive direction, even when the going gets rough. Perhaps in the year to come the many prayers of my family will be answered. God will bring us all together for a more prosperous life. Rewarded by his Grace for our long and hard efforts through the hardships and trials."

CURE OF CANCER

V.C. of San José, California, wrote on August 27, 1985:

"I have been praying to St. Seraphim. If you remember, I told you I was operated on last year for cancer. I went back to be examined again and had tests. My prayers have been answered. I am cured from cancer. I also had a pap test. Everything came out fine. I believe in my miracles. The doctors were baffled.

"My son that was apart from his family (it was a broken marriage) is re-united with Mom. My younger son told me that his brother is back to his marriage. I pray it works now. They were apart six months.

"My Jesus Prayer is coming fine. My sleep has improved. I can sleep better. The problem I have is with my daughter, I. She drinks very bad. It is making her daughter very unhappy.

"I always say the prayers you told me to. I never forget. Pray for my other son, J. His marriage is having problems too. I'm telling you, if it's not one thing, it's another.

"But I believe in prayers and faith. I was so ill last year. I am feeling fine with your prayers and the intercession of the Mother of God.

"My doctors told me I looked very good. I know it is a miracle. When I went to the hospital for the operation last year, I was very ill. They told me if I would have waited one more week, they could not do anything for me. But I pray as I always have. My doctor was very concerned. So he talked to another doctor into doing the operation fast. I am so thankful. Isn't it wonderful.

"...Please give my best regards to all and please pray for my intentions to St. Seraphim and St. Benedict and our Lord. I believe and have faith in all the Saints."

HEALING OF BREAST CANCER

Fr. Benedict received a letter from Sandra Lanni of Sterling Heights, Michigan, written on September 17, 1985:

"Thank you so much for your kind letter on prayer of the heart. Yes, I'll do my best and pray. I do believe in prayers. God has been very good to me and my family. I would appreciate some more cotton balls. I have prayed (before) the Icon and I have had a biopsy on my breasts and she has helped me. I was healed of cancer. I thank you for thinking of me. Please pray to the Blessed Mother of God for me and my family. We do need help."

MULTIPLE HEALINGS

Romulo Victuelles of Des Plains, Illinois, wrote on November 12, 1989:

"Last time I asked you to pray for my daughter, Dominica, and a friend, Eduardo, that they get well from their ailments. It's now over four weeks. Through the anointing with the ball of cotton containing the Tear of the Mother of God and your prayers, her friend and my daughter are apparently well now.

"Eduardo Abina is now working, and I hope to see him again next time. My daughter, Dominica has resumed her job and I hope that next time that she will be X-rayed, her tumor should have disappeared."

RELIEF FROM SORROW AND HOPELESSNESS

Fr. Benedict received the following letter from E. S. of Decatur, Georgia, on December 19, 1987:

"I've wanted to write you for some time now, but always some distraction would rear its ugly head and cause the thought of writing you, or calling you to leave my mind. Please forgive me. Please continue to keep me and Jo Ann in your prayers. I feel that I have no hope, but for the prayers of others and the mercy of God.

"I want you to know how precious the week you and the Fathers shared is for me. When I have been engulfed by sorrow, or hopelessness, I remember the blessed tears of the All Holy Virgin and bring to mind her sorrows, and open the vial containing her holy tears, and inhale of their sweetness, and my darkness is lifted. And then I remember Christ of the Hills Monastery, the cycle of prayers, the Holy Icons, and the great love and humility of the monastics there and I am filled with peace and blessedness."

HEALING OF SEIZURES

Virginia Prewett of Memphis, Tennessee, wrote the following account on December 21, 1987:

"My Mother has been very ill: she had a severe reaction to some medication, and was hospitalized with mental confusion, slurred speech and other neurological symptoms. The next day she began having seizures (she has never had epilepsy), and even had a grand mal seizure.

"When I went to her, the doctors had transferred her to a large medical center for neurological examinations. It was evening and soon everyone left and I stayed the night. I showed her the photo of the Weeping Icon and asked if she remembered my telling her about it. 'Oh yes!' she said. 'Would you like me to bless you with the tears from the Icon,' I asked. Her face brightened, and she smiled and said 'Oh yes!'

"I anointed her with the cotton moistened with the Icon's Tears. She then went to sleep for more than two hours, although she had not slept for many days prior to this. The rest of the night she was restless and talkative, and her mind began to clear. When the doctors visited her the next morning, they were very surprised. The doctor said to me, 'What happened? When I looked at the chart written last night, then I look and talk with this patient, I see two different people. I can't believe the difference.'

"The next night I blessed her with the tears again. She was discharged from the hospital the following day and has improved steadily since, although she is still a little anxious and afraid. I am sure she will be fine now, however—the goodness of the Mother of God has touched her.

"Would it be possible for me to get another tear from the Icon? I would like to give it to my mother. Thank you for your prayers and work for our Lord Jesus. Please say a prayer for my husband, Jim, for our Blessed Lady to heal his heart."

TWO HEALINGS FROM TEARS OF THEOTOKOS

James Lewkowski of Riverdale, Illinois, wrote on July 28, 1989:

"A few months ago you had sent us a tear from the Weeping Icon, which my wife and I cherish greatly. We keep it on a little table in the bedroom next to the picture that you had also sent.

"I must tell you of two miraculous happenings. First, my brother had recently passed away as result of cancer of the jaw. He had developed a sore in his mouth which would not heal. Finally surgery was performed. But after two years he died. Well, a couple of months ago, I developed a similar sore in my mouth, which would not heal. After trying to heal it myself for a whole month, with no success, I felt that I should go to a doctor. But remembering the Tear of the Weeping Icon, I decided to place the Tear directly on the sore and pray to the Mother of God for healing. Two days later, I noticed there was no longer any pain and the sore seemed to be going away. It's been over a month now and the sore is completely healed.

"Second, my wife injured her back when we took our grandson to an amusement park. I had to carry her from the car. She did have back surgery a few years ago. I was going to take her to the hospital, but she didn't want to go. So we decided to place the Tear on her back where the pain was and pray for healing. The next morning, the pain was gone and she was able to go to her part time job. Praise God.

"I felt that I must write to you and once again say thank you.

"The Tear still retains its fragrance, although the cotton is beginning to get raggedy from our repeated use."

HEALING OF SKIN PROBLEMS

Charles Yost of Lincoln, Nebraska, wrote to Fr. Benedict on November 14, 1986 to report:

"Greetings! I thank you so much for the wonderful tear of the Mother of God. I received your note along with another from Mother Pelagia saying you were in the hospital. We keep you in our prayers.

"The myrrh of the tear has such a wonderful smell—so heavenly. I have used it according to your instructions to anoint my wife Deborah Yost, who has had recurring skin problems. We believe she has improved already. Please remember her in your prayers."

RETURN TO SACRAMENTS

In gratitude, V.S. of Las Vegas, Nevada, wrote on January 9, 1989:

"I have recently undergone important decisions, which have demanded me to walk away from my past life of twenty–five years, for a life with Christ.

"During this difficult time, our Pastor anointed me with Myrrh of the Icon. Though I am still in transition from my former life. I have experienced many blessings. The most beautiful of which was being reinstated in the Church. I am now able to receive the Sacraments and this is the greatest joy I've known in a long while, if ever. It has been a long, hard journey back to the church and it is due to her tears that I have now returned at last.

"Could you send me a tear? It is my hope to make a Pilgrimage there someday soon. So if you have information for me, I'd be ever so thankful."

HEALING OF EYES

Mrs. R. Gardner of New Brunswick, New Jersey, wrote on January 5, 1988:

"I want to tell you of a miracle that happened, because of the tear you sent to me. My eyes were in pain for weeks. I used the tears to anoint my eyes. The pain at once went away and I am getting better. Thank you so much. God bless you and grant you many more years in His service.

"Please pray for me and my family. Please send me some Theophany water."

HEALING OF DOWN'S SYNDROME CHILD

Fr. Benedict received the following report from Gerald M. Long of Cherry Hill, New Jersey:

"Once, months ago, I received a card of the Myrrh Weeping Icon—and a cotton ball. Well, about six months ago, I anointed a twelve–year–old child I know, who has a speech defect, related to Down's syndrome, at bedtime before his prayers every night for three weeks. I did this while I was visiting his house—I did not tell his guardian of this. However, when I later saw his family, he had been cured. I was told the child has been speaking clearly for six months now. I had prayed for the gift of speech and understanding for this child and made the Sign of the Cross with the Tears on his forehead. I was very happy to hear the child speaking clearly.

"All these years the child had these problems, since he was 3 years of age, and only now his speech is completely comprehensible. I do believe in prayers and they were answered. Thank you for all your prayers and pray for all who are in need of prayer. I, too, will pray to Almighty God for you and others.

"I also received your letter with the Palm Cross, which I put with the Weeping Icon. I must tell you I do believe our Blessed Virgin has given healing and peace to this child."

GIFT OF PEACE

From Petrina Mandala of Brunsville, North Carolina, the Monastery received the following letter on April 8, 1988:

"I can't tell you of the joy I received upon opening the letter you sent me, and the cotton with the Holy Virgin's tears of Myrrh. The fragrance was so overwhelming. I bathed in the aroma for two days. I was flooded with perfume and (joy)—and my heart was previously so full of pain and sorrow. I received peace. It was like I was bathed in peace. I truly believe the Mother of God, through her intercession with our Lord

Jesus Christ, will obtain for me my restored health and hearing. I feel better now than I have all year, which was a terrible year that almost cost me my life. Thank you for your prayers and petitions on my behalf.

"I felt the silent message from our Holy Mother—'the tears are a symbol of my love to the faithful.'

"My husband anointed me as you requested. God bless you all. In the Love of Christ and his Most Blessed Mother."

MULTIPLE HEALINGS

From Brisbane, Australia, Helen Margetis wrote on October 18, 1987:

"Mrs. Stathes has asked me to write on her behalf...and convey her heart–felt thanks for the prayers that you and the others offer up for her daughter Natalia.

"I am pleased to report that there has been a definite improvement in her. (a) Her periods of concentration are increasing, (b) she has begun to eat soft foods in small quantities. Mrs. Stathes has enclosed two photos of mother and child. Little Jonathan, the miracle baby is progressing very well, and is being cared for by Natalia's mother-in-law. At this stage, we request special prayers for the guidance about Natalia's future. The hospital can do no more—the rehabilitation hospital for brain damaged people will not accept her because she is not a 'hopeful case.'

"The parents do not know which way to turn. They are considering a hospital in Melbourne that deals with comatose cases, but that would be a big decision to make.

"The doctors keep waiting for her to die, but she is becoming more alert in her mind and regaining her strength in her paralyzed leg.

"Now as far as the others, there are no dramatic changes, but the abundant grace 'to run with patience the race set before them.' As for myself, since I have been anointed, I have successfully come off my medication. Bretos got a good report for his practical teaching, though does not enjoy it. He is waiting for an interview with the ABC.

"Theodora has been promoted to Teller A which is an enormous responsibility."

FAITH AND HEALINGS

C.G. of Austin, Texas, wrote to Fr. Benedict on December 18, 1989:

"I finally got an opportunity to answer your letters. I have been very busy at school and work. Some days (especially Thursdays and Fridays), I had to work 16 hours. Straight (8 hours school internship and 8 hours at my job). Thank God that the semester is over at school! I need more rest and time for prayer. In spite of all my burdens—especially my 5 year old son's kidnapping. I have been blessed in many different ways.

After two years of school here in Austin at ACC, I have been able to maintain a GPA of 4.0 and received a great honor. I was nominated a Who's Who in American Junior College.

"I took tears (the cotton ball) with me into the testing center and prayed over all my exams. I truly know that it is not my own intelligence, but God's. And I'm so aware of this, that sometimes I feel I know nothing, since He told me everything on my exams. For instance, I took a 240 question comprehensive final exam this past week. As I was answering my test, I skipped many questions I did not know. Then I asked the Mother of God to ask God for the answers and I went back over them. I could clearly hear her saying 'don't change this one, or the answer is...' After I finished I was still very confused and unsure of the answers. I counted about 30 that I could possibly have answered wrong, but I was very impressed when I found out that I had only missed 13 (a grade of 95). Isn't this marvelous? If you were to ask me the answers to those questions I thought I would get wrong, I would probably tell you, 'Ask The Mother of God, for she told me the answers. I myself don't know them.'

"Also I have been blessed at work. After 6 months I was given a 19% salary increase. Although still not a lot (maybe so I don't get boastful), I am very thankful. At least I have money to pay my rent, bills, and meals.

"I am glad to tell you that I also received a great healing through the Mother of God's tears. This happened several months ago. (About 3 weeks after I visited the Monastery and received a cotton ball with her holy tears). I had an infection on the right upper gum which was getting worse as time went by. I had been to the dentist three times and he could not see anything on the X rays, but he could see a big bloody lump on my gum. He gave me antibiotics, but nothing worked. So I finally gave up and did nothing for almost a year. I had no money to visit another dentist, and was getting worried. When I received the cotton ball, I rubbed my gum with my finger, which had touched the Myrrh. It was not until two or three days later that I realized the big bloody lump was gone. I now have a little scar left, but the lump is gone.

"A friend of mine from work, Mary, who visited the Monastery after I told her, also received a healing. She had very bad foot pain for several months. After she anointed herself with the holy Tears, the pain went away.

"All this, Father Benedict, more than a healing has meant an increase in my faith. I really think that we can do all things through Christ, if we have faith. I want you to know that it is out of love and faith that I have been donating money to the Monastery and to other places. My generosity could not be within me, if God wasn't working on me. I really think He is doing it. He makes me to want to! Your prayers and your love are enough for me. God is doing the rest, believe me. He is transforming me and consoling me so much.

"You cannot imagine how much I desire to visit the Mother of God again. I received my prayer rope in the mail made by Sister Sara, and I would like it blessed with her Tears before I use it. I know I can find God anywhere in my church, house or even on the streets, but I especially like sitting on those chairs under the trees at the Monastery and praying for a while. It gives me so much peace, you know!! My dream is one day to be able to sit under a tree like this one, but up on a hill far from the coming of the Pilgrims. Alone with Jesus!"

ICON WEEPING

From Oklahoma, the Monastery received a report written by B. J. on March 23, 1988:

"I had the Icon of Our All Holy Lady you had mailed to me. Last week I decided to mail it to one of my grandsons. He is 20 years old, without a job, etc, and living alone.

"He appreciates religious pictures, etc., so I mailed it to him. Last Monday his mother and I went by to take him some groceries and see about him. She also had some bad news for him. A job he had been interviewed twice for was given to someone else! He doesn't have a telephone and had been depressed, the last time she saw him. (It's close to 40 miles in distance.)

"He seemed to be in a fairly good mood. A friend was there and they were discussing doing yard work in that area. He needs prayers, and more prayers to help him! No telephone or a car and looking for a job in Tulsa is very hard. He has a bicycle that he rode in college, but he dropped out in the second semester.

"Now for the miracle. His postcard was so faded, it looked like he had put it in the wash. I said "What did you do?" He said nothing. But his Mother and I looked at each other. When you held the card up, the Mother of God seemed to be crying. The tears were running down the card. I felt such a feeling. I could not hold it, and just laid it back down.

"We left and when we got in my car, I said to my daughter. 'What do you think?' She said the tears were for R. I said 'Yes, and for all of us.' Four of us saw this and I feel it has a deep meaning.

"R. has been involved in a lot of things. Drug use, and he paid for the abortion of a girl friend a year ago. No wonder for the tears! He thinks I don't know all this; especially about the girl. So it has affected all of us, too. I had written you about my problems so many times.

"I don't understand exactly what this means for me. I have felt better physically and mentally since this happened.

"The youngest boy is 16 years and in jail for a crime of robbery and shooting. How horrible! He says he is innocent, but evidence points to him. I'm sure it is drug related. His mother had him in a private institution for emotionally disturbed teenagers. When he was arrested it was the first week in February. The crime was on the 16th of December, but an arrest was not made then. There was supposed to be an eye witness, too. That part seems odd and of course it's hard to believe for me that my grandson could do such a thing.

"The same as it was hard to realize he was being sent to the State mental hospital for evaluation. The report after one week (unable to stand trial and assist in his defense)! What the outcome will be, I haven't anyway of knowing. Only God can save that child. I believe He will. What good will 30 years in the pen do? Coming out at 46, no education or training. What would he do? All this is a torment to the older boy, R., because he knows more than I do, I'm sure. He wrote a letter to C. saying he was sorry he had set such an example.

"I have cried and prayed some nights, all night. Constantly as I walk around at my job I pray. I need your prayers and the entire Monastery to remember these boys. I just had to tell you about this happening, and ask for your prayers. Hope your health is better each day, I love you all in Christ and know you do good works."

HEALING OF LEG

Mrs. Catherine Hullinghorst of Metairie, Louisiana, wrote on November 11, 1987, to thank Father Benedict for the Tears of the Mother of God. She recounted that she had anointed a friend's leg after surgery. He was quickly healed and was to be married soon.

MIRACLE OF SAINT SERAPHIM

Bernice Glodo of Chicago, Illinois, wrote on August 17, 1987:

"(We received a miracle) by praying to St. Seraphim of Sarov. So please pray especially for my son's health and that he will quit smoking, Also for my daughter Jane. May the Lord help her physically and financially, and sister Wanda who is very sick. Could you offer my petitions (before) the Icon of Mother of God, please."

RETURN TO CHURCH

Mrs. J. H. of Rich Hill, Missouri, wrote on January 14, 1988:

"Please rush me one of the cotton balls with the Myrrh from the Weeping Icon. I also wish to report a miracle of using it on my granddaughter. She had left the church nine years ago and I had prayed constantly for her. I held her in my arms and anointed her and about two months later, she called and told me she had gone and talked with the Priest and went to Confession. However she is still having difficulty with her marriage. So keep me and my family in your prayers."

HEALING OF ANEMIA

Helen Malgetis of Brisbane, Australia wrote on December 2, 1988:

"Thank you for notifying me of Father Benedict's surgery. The children and I have been to the throne of grace every day and in our prayer cell group. I trust that the operation has been successful and he is well on the way to recovery. When one is continually afflicted as Father Benedict is, there must be a lot of unseen warfare going on.

"I read somewhere that our lives are like a piece of tapestry: on one side there is a mass of tangled threads, but on the other side there is a beautiful picture.

"Now I have some good news for you! Recent blood tests show that I am no longer anemic. My hemoglobin is up to 13.1 which is middle of the range and an absolute miracle. For almost 7 years it has been below the range. Thanks be to God and to all those at the Monastery for your prayers and fasting. I no longer feel tired and depressed. I know that you truly care.

"Bretos still has not got a permanent full–time position, but the Lord has kept him in work with a lot of temporary jobs. He has been tutoring, lecturing, working on a computer at the conservatorium. Presenting music courses to the government for re-accreditation at Musica Nova Concerts. Though this is all fragmented work it is all experience and provides for our daily bread. At the moment, he has applied for a Concert Manager position. Please pray that he gets it, if it is God's will.

"Theodora is enjoying the job where she works as a district receiving officer. At the moment, she is at West End which is densely Greek populated. It is good practice for her Greek, which is limited. Both Bretos and she thank you for the opportunity of doing something for their father. We just loved the photo Father Vasili sent of you all at the building site of the Chapel. Would you be so kind as to thank him for me. At the time I was too sick to reply.

"Now I must ask you another favor. Would you please pray for Bretos and Theodora's inheritance? They have been summoned to the Supreme Court in Sydney by their paternal Grandmother, who seeks to break the will and take half of their house, that has been left to them. She and her daughter are just so wicked. They have persecuted us for years. Although we have not repaid evil for evil and continued to pray for their repentance and salvation. I have asked the Lord to plead for the fatherless and I believe that the Lord will avenge us after all these years."

HEALING OF SKIN IRRITATION

Jane and Buddy McBride of San Antonio, Texas, wrote to Fr. Pangratios on January 15, 1990:

"Recently we made a visit to the Monastery. You were most gracious in showing us around.

"After visiting the Icon of the Mother of God, I had a healing of skin irritation on both of my upper arms. It was gone two days after our visit. The visit to the Icon was also instrumental in lifting a chronic depression my husband has experienced quite often, especially in the morning."

CURE FROM ALCOHOLISM

On April 29, 1989, V. G. of San José, California, wrote:

"I am sorry I delayed writing to you. So much has happened. I couldn't let you know till now. First of all I thank you for not forgetting me and my family in your prayers. Remember you mailed me the picture of the Weeping Icon last year. I asked you to send me one for here. You also told me about a mother that was having a problem with her son. He does not live with her. You told me you sent this mother a copy of the Weeping Virgin. She did a miracle, her son changed from the way he was living. I am a mother that went through the same with Irene. A week after Easter, Irene, my daughter, almost took her life. She lost control and hit bottom. She phoned me with a cry for help and hung up.

"A lady friend of hers phoned me and told me: 'Virginia, Irene looks bad.' I couldn't do much for her, just pray to our Weeping Virgin and our Lord that she would go for help had no way of going to her and putting my arms around her.

"So what happened was that she phoned her younger brother, John, for help. 'Please help me,' she cried to her brother. Irene phoned her daughter. 'Hurry please help me now.' She was about to end her life.

Her daughter lives across the street from Irene. She lives with a family, she just could not take it living with her mother. So her daughter ran to control Irene. My son, John, when Irene called for help, called different places to get help for Irene.

"He called A.A., that is a place where they go for meetings to talk about their drinking problems. Irene has been going to these meetings and they give her books to read and it's helping her.

"People with the same problem pick up Irene and take her to the meetings to stop them from the harm they are doing to themselves and help them to get their lives together. It is an illness, but it is up to them to get well.

"Again Irene almost did away with herself. Right after Easter she was so bad I couldn't even talk to her on the phone. I went to my bedroom, where I have my little corner with our Lord and the Saints, and our Weeping Virgin. I prayed to the Mother of God to please help Irene. On my knees I cried 'please save her from this illness.' Oh, I cried for her.

"Irene has changed. She tells me, 'Mother, I should have paid attention when you told me to go for help.' I told her to keep faith and pray to our Weeping Virgin. We gave Irene a lot of support. She is doing just fine now. The All–Holy Virgin saved her from killing herself.

"Irene saw the light, and our Weeping Virgin is helping. We talk and laugh and she always did go to Church. A day before she almost did away with herself, she did not go to the Church, because she was not feeling good that Sunday. She told me, she almost killed herself. She just could not control the drinking. She was going crazy. To make things worse, at the same time she lost her job. That did not help, but she kept looking for work. I kept praying almost a month, no job. To her surprise on the 23rd day she got a phone call. She is going to start next week. A steady job.

"I have been through a lot of worries over Irene. She looks good now; your praying has helped her a lot. Thank you for sending me our Weeping Virgin. I gave one to Irene.

"The prayers you send me are so beautiful. It's all true, the prayers really make a person stop to think. Irene was suffering, she is not totally cured. But the people will help her. There are so many people that take Irene to different places, where they have meetings.

WEEPING ICON IN CHICAGO

Madelyn Maestranzi wrote on October 10, 1988, from Niles, Illinois:

"Have seen the Weeping Icon here in Chicago, at St. Nicholas Albanian Orthodox Church. Narragansett & Diversay Avenues, Chicago. It has been weeping from December 6, 1986. I have been very moved and blessed.

"Please put my petitions for my daughter, sons, and grandchildren under 'Her Care.'"

HEALING THROUGH USE OF HOLY WATER

On October 10, 1987, Doris Gilchrist wrote from Brooklyn, New York:

"I received your letter with the Holy Water. I am doing as you instructed. I say Thanks.

"After my first drink of water, I sure feel better. Whatever it is inside my stomach, I pray and hope it goes away. Please continue to pray for me. ...Again I say thank you and I am also praying for you and Father Benedict's continuous help."

RELIEF OF MENTAL ILLNESS

The following two letters are from T. P. of Waco, Texas. The first was written on October 22, 1988, and the second, along with the enclosed letter she wrote to her sister, on December 13 of the same year.

"Thank you very much for your prayers for my sister, Catherine, who is very sick with mental illness.

"I received your letters and am deeply moved by the miracles of the Mother of God.

"(After God,) She is the only resort we can turn to. I and my sister Catherine are praying to the Mother of God, who shed tears from the Icon in your church at New Sarov, Blanco, Texas. You mentioned in your letter that you would send a cotton ball with tear from the Mother of God. It will be a great honor if you can send us a tear from the Mother of God.

"My sister and I are desperately praying for the miracles from Mother of God who shed her tears on the Icon, for the cure of mental illness. She has experienced relief just through Prayer to the Mother of God."

—Second Letter—

"I would like to thank you for your kindness and hospitality you extended to us when we visited your Monastery on October 23.

"I was deeply moved by visiting and venerating the Mother of God in the small Chapel. I wrote down my feelings and personal experiences after viewing the Myrrh-Weeping Icon, in the letter to my sister Catherine Hong.

"I thought that you might be interested in reading the copy of the letter. I will pray for your success in carrying out God's wonderful work."

—Letter to Her Sister—

"Dearest C.,

"Thank you for the birthday card. It was the best birthday present.

"I read many times the stories you wrote on my birthday card. You wrote me that you could not sleep with troubling thoughts of death, threat and fear, and you felt that you were stuck in the deep hole immobilized by the threat of death. Then, you talked to your self 'let me endure this hardship and just wait a little longer, help is on the way—Theresa said that she will send me a cotton ball soaked with tears from Blessed Mother from a mountaintop Monastery in Blanco, Texas. The Blessed Mother will not throw me away, she will help me and cure me and love me.'

"You said that a strange thing happened; all that impending threat of death disappeared. Then you were filled with peace and went to sleep. The next day, you were peaceful and felt happy and strong. Then you had a strength of looking into newspaper ads and found a full time job at a first interview. You mentioned throughout your letter that this was a miracle, which I believe.

"Ever since, I received mail from Christ of the Hills Monastery describing the miracles of the Myrrh Weeping Icon, and learning of the thousands of miracles which have already happened—cures of cancer, leukemia, blindness, mental illness—I wanted to visit the Monastery. I was putting off the visit until this time, because Shim was reluctant to go there with me. Shim said 'I don't believe in miracles. There is a scientific explanation of tears flowing down from eyes of the picture of Blessed Mother.'

"I had written earlier to Father Benedict asking him to send me tears from the Mother of God. Since his letter said that he would send one to those who requested it. I told this to Mother from whom you heard about the story...just even thinking about it helped.

"I agree with you—when I read your letter, I decided to go. I would carry your letter and lay it down in front of Blessed Mother's picture and beg for cure of your mental illness.

"Felicia was coming home for one week on her vacation from October 22 to October 29. We were planning to bring Felicia down to San Antonio...."

"The Monastery where The Weeping Icon is in Blanco, Texas, is about 30 miles north of San Antonio.

"I asked Shim if we could stop in Blanco on the way to San Antonio. I described your letter and I wanted very much to go there.

"Shim agreed to go, but he would wait outside in the car, since he does not believe in miracles. I would have to go in myself. After our plans of the Blanco visit were confirmed, I called Father Benedict on Friday night. I told him that I have a chance to go to San Antonio with my husband and daughter, and on the way we would like to stop at the Monastery to pray in front of the Icon for my mentally ill sister. I told him I had written him earlier. I identified myself. I also told him that I am a Roman Catholic and asked him if he would accept me. Father Benedict said that I am very much welcome. God blesses everybody. I also told him about your letter, Catherine.

"Saturday morning October 22nd, we picked up Felicia at DFW Airport at 10:00 a.m., then we went straight to Galleria Shopping Mall in Dallas and shopped all afternoon. I was carrying your letter and I wanted a Xerox copy before I gave it to Father Benedict. Did you know that the shopping center is one of the hardest places to find a (photocopy) machine? I went to (a store's) bookkeeping dept. and asked if she would make a copy of your letter. She flatly refused. I tried the hotel downstairs lobby at a reservation desk, where I was successful in obtaining two copies of your letter. There is always a kind soul among worldly indifference.

"After we finished shopping and eating dinner, the three of us came home at 11:30 p.m. from Dallas.

"We were to get up at 5:00 next morning to drive to Blanco, Texas, to reach there a little before 10:00. Father Benedict told me, that at 10:00 a.m. there will be a beautiful Sunday Service—one of the Monks died, the service will be special and more beautiful. He had told us to come into the Service when we arrive.'

"I did not want to stay for the whole service. I just wanted to see the Icon and pray before it and come out. That's why we wanted to leave a little early to get there before the service started.

"As I told you, when we unpacked all the shopping bags, it was 12:30 a.m. and here I was, still had not translated your letter. I sat down alone, while Shim and Felicia went to sleep, and translated your letter and attached it to your Korean letter. I also made a note of our visit and put it in an envelope addressed to Father Benedict. I was going to leave the envelope in case I did not get to talk to him in person. I had a little sleep that night.

"We all got up at 5:15 a.m. and left the house at 5:45 a.m. It was dark when we left Waco, but saw the day break near Austin. Shim kept yawning and we decided to stop at Denny's and have coffee and breakfast. After breakfast, I took over and drove from Austin to Johnson City then to Blanco. The highway 290 West which I took from Austin to Johnson City, gave us a spectacular view of the beautiful Texas Hill Country. All over the place, there is nothing but green hills with unusual small trees and greenery.

"I prepared Felicia and Shim, (telling them) that the service, we may have to attend is a long liturgy service. If possible, we will just look at the Icon and may then leave early.

"Despite of the fact that I was going to a service for the dead with a body in the unfamiliar church, I was strangely filled with happiness and peace, thinking I was going to see the Mother of God. Time to time, I kept pushing the gas pedal more to get nearer and nearer to Her soon.

"At Johnson City, I got lost and drove around town to find highway 281, south to Blanco toward San Antonio. We saw signs of LBJ historical building and Johnson school. The town was surprisingly so small and ordinary. The road to Blanco from Johnson City was more hilly and there were many mountains (small) all around.

"At Blanco, I let Shim take over. We stopped at a restaurant and learned direction from a waitress how to get to the Christ of the Hills Monastery.

"There was a beautiful Blanco State Park along the Blanco River. Shim drove along the curvy road following the Blanco River. The winding road Shim kept driving did not give us the sight of a church nearby. We finally had to stop at a small store and learned we missed a small country road. We retraced and found a small unpaved road which led us to the Monastery. One had to look real hard to find such a small unpaved road leading down to the bridge underneath. Shim followed this very narrow white road wondering what would happen if there is another oncoming car. The winding road eventually took us to the mountain top where Christ of the Hills Monastery is located.

"At the final climb, passing through the gate of the Monastery, Shim said that our new car will be blessed. The black bumper sticker was all covered with white limestone dust. Felicia later called it holy dust. Because we got lost on the way and had stopped for breakfast, it was about 10:40 a.m. and the service was already in progress.

"After signing the register and trying to find another entrance to enter the church, we saw Father Benedict approaching us outside. He is a huge, all-around big man. Garbed in black clergy cloth and hat. He reminded me of Father Keating in New Haven, who married us. Later Shim told me that he thought about Father Keating also. Surprisingly, he was rather young, maybe 40 to 50 and very friendly. He led us to a small Chapel where the Icon was located. Father Benedict told me the Icon was weeping today. He said: 'when I checked a few hours ago, it was weeping.' I was struck by that comment, since, I had previously read the history of Icon—'On May 7, 1985, an Icon of the Mother of God was discovered weeping

Myrrh by one of the Monks in a small Chapel at Christ of the hills Monastery. The Icon wept continuously from May until October, 1985, and continues to weep intermittently even to this day. Often she seems to weep when a soul comes into her presence who particularly needs her healing love.' I fleetingly thought about the strange happy feeling I felt, driving that hill coming here. I felt the Blessed Mother was waiting for me.

"Inside the Chapel, there was an Icon, rather new, brilliantly colored picture of the Blessed Mother—holding child Christ encased in a glass box. The box was tilted at about a 30 degree angle and placed on a stand about 4 feet tall. (I knelt down and kissed the ground and asked the Blessed Mother to cure Catherine). Father Benedict told us that it is still weeping. You cannot see it well by looking directly, but if you look from the side you can see it. We peeked sideways. Sure enough, there were streams of shiny myrrh flowing down to several cotton balls placed under the stream.

"I asked Father Benedict for a cotton ball, to anoint my sister Catherine. He took out a cotton ball and anointed my forehead, then Shim, and Felicia. There was a strong smell of perfume—like odor and yellowish liquid was soaked in that cotton ball. Later I touched that cotton ball, which was very wet, and I could see lots of Tears on my finger. I rubbed my wet finger on my cheeks, then Shim, and Felicia. Father Benedict carefully wrapped this cotton ball in foil and gave it to me to send to Catherine.

"I have put this cotton ball in foil by Father Benedict,...in a plastic bag to prevent evaporation. I am enclosing this cotton ball with this letter. Please keep this carefully.

"Let us pray hard Catherine, you and I, asking the Blessed Mother to cure your mental illness, relieving your agony and fears continuously in the future as she once relieved your pain. I gave your letter and translation to Father Benedict. He asked me where you were. I pointed to the address on the envelope in which you mailed my birthday card with your letter.

"Before I came out of the Chapel, I prayed a rosary in front of the Weeping Icon, asking her to cure your mental illness. I kissed the top of the glass, asking one more time for help. It was a beautiful day. Sun was shining, temperature was cool, sky was blue. Standing on top of the mountain on (the) Monastery grounds, we could see (a) panorama of hills and green trees all underneath.

"There was a cemetery and a new church was being built with white limestone. I thought that it would be nice if I could be buried there when I die.

"We left the Monastery, Felicia and Shim took turns driving down to San Antonio. It was 12:30 when we reached San Antonio. We enjoyed the shopping at the Market Square, then visited Sea World. We had plenty of time to see almost all the shows and take many pictures of Felicia in her Mexican dress.

"On the way back, Shim drove first and then Felicia drove all the way home. Father and daughter were discussing music, Felicia was interpreting every sound of (each) different instrument and its meaning and Shim listening very impressed with her musical knowledge. Listening to a compact disk in new Mazda 929 is a great joy for Shim these days.

"I decided to catch up (on) some lost sleep in the back seat, by lying down with my head on a pillow. I decided to pray (my) rosary. My thought returned to the earlier visit of Icon in (the) Monastery, in a small Chapel sitting on top of the mountain in Blanco. I thought about the message of the miracle, the Weeping Icon, repentance, prayer, fasting and change of life. According to the Monks, the message of fasting, I (reckon) that it does not only mean strictly not eating foods, but means any self–denial from what I naturally like to do. I went over my daily activity and found there are certain things that may not be pleasing to the Blessed Mother. I thought about steps to change these things. It may not be easy, but I will try one at a time.

"Also I wanted to become a more caring person and spend the rest of my life becoming a better Christian. I felt that visiting the Weeping Icon was a turning point in my life. I am also enclosing a picture of the Icon for Catherine, together with the cotton ball I mentioned earlier.

"Please take good care of yourself. I will continue to pray with you, Catherine, asking Blessed Mother to cure your illness. May God Bless you and keep you in Peace."

HEALING OF HEMORRHOIDS

Madalene Ponce of San José, California, wrote on March 25, 1989:

"Praise to the Lord and His All–Holy Mother!

"We received your letter long before St. Patrick's Day. We also received a letter from Father Vasili before your letter, and our response has been long overdue. We apologize for our late response.

"Our eldest daughter and her family were able to buy an old house and we helped them renovate it in a way suitable for the family. We removed the carpet, (and) the 3-ply wall paper in the kitchen and bathrooms. After that we painted the inside of the house, we helped them move from our house to their house. It was such a big job. A mover was too expensive, they could not afford it.

"This is how we go about our family. We still have to help our children until they are able to go by them-

selves. We pray that God will always guide us through in our small endeavors, until He calls us to Heaven.

"Sorry to say we were not able to reach you before you started the Pilgrimage. However, our thoughts were with you and we prayed for your safe voyage. We hope to see you in your Monastery.

"This is also to express our thanks to the Mother of God. The tears you sent us, I used it for my hemorrhoids and I am glad to tell that the bleeding stopped. I followed the instructions you gave me faithfully and after two weeks using, I noticed the bleeding is gone. Thank you for your prayers. I had this predicament for the last 30 years. I was operated twice, yet it was cured only after using the tears you sent me.

"Father Benedict, thank you so much for sending us the tears of the Mother of God."

MULTIPLE HEALINGS

From Catherine Sopchak on February 16, 1989, came the following report:

"I felt such joy when I received your letter containing the tear of our Lady, the Mother of God. My own tears fell. Thank you!

"I immediately went to see my young friend who is dying of liver cancer. Her name is Madonna Haag and she has three young children. She was very grateful for the anointing and I went back the following week and again blessed her. I will let you know what happens with her. She was already at peace and resigned to God's Will, but I was so anxious to bless her with the tear. She thanked me profusely and has the Icon print by her bed.

"I am going to list the names of those I blessed, their problems, and effect of the anointing:

"Timothy Simmone: infant grandson born with seizures, slight swelling on the right side of brain and possible viral infection in the blood. His soft spot on top of his head has not been visible because of problems. He has been on medication since January 16th. On Wednesday, February 1st, I anointed him with the tear and that night his mother called to tell me his soft spot was normal (first time) and has been ever since.

"Bill Ropchak: husband. He has diabetes and has had a bad leg since February of 1987 when it got sunburned. It was badly swollen and discolored when I blessed him with the tear on Wed. February 1st. He went to doctor on Friday 3rd. Had dye injected into his vein showing no blood clots or serious problems. And the leg has since been less swollen and coloring improved. I really thought he would lose his leg.

"Rosemary Machey—Friend—upset emotionally, many problems. I saw her a week later and she seemed more relaxed.

"Emily Ballery—friend—felt great peace when blessed.

"Bill Sopchak—son, felt a sense of peacefulness all over him. That everything would be all right. He has family problems. He left here full of joy.

"Jane Culican—friend, in hospital with infection in the blood stream. She is very sick, around 70 years old. She also felt full of peace after anointing.

"Bethorny Sopchak—granddaughter, 4 1/2 years old, she has asthma and came over Tuesday morning February 14, all tight and wheezy. I blessed her with the tear and nothing developed. Her breathing cleared and the coughing stopped. She is fine today.

"So far these are the ones I have anointed, including myself. I have tried to be discriminating and not ask help on trivial matters. A friend of mine, who is (named) Francisica, has asked me to bless her, which I will. I did not have the holy tear on my person at the time.

"Also if you would be able to send another tear of our Lady, I will give it to the sister I spoke of. She visits many people who could use the Lady's Blessing. I treasure the tear you sent me and am grateful my name fell into your hands, so I could become acquainted with this miraculous event. I will continue to pray for you. Thank you for your goodness and your prayers."

GAZING UPON A WEEPING IMAGE OF THE MOTHER OF GOD

LaVenta T. Walker sent the following meditation on February 21, 1989:

"Thank you for your letter informing me that prints of the Icon of our Blessed Mother are weeping.

"May the ransomed of the Lord return and come to Zion with songs and everlasting joy upon their hearts. May we obtain joy and gladness. Please Dear Father...May sorrow and sighing flee away.

"May God Bless and enfold us in the Holy Mother's arms as her tears fall on the wounds that are our own very selves."

RETURN OF WALLET

On August 14, 1989, Elia C. Davila of Houston, Texas, wrote:

"The day we went to visit the Weeping Icon, I lost my wallet with money and my credit cards and identification. We stopped at every place we thought of, even went back to the Monastery. We started praying and asking our Lady for her intercession. We told her that our day had been blessed many a way, and that we knew she would intercede for our needs.

"When we arrived in Houston, my daughter was waiting with the news that a lady in New Braunfels had found the wallet. She sent it UPS, not a penny or a card missing! Her name is T.N. and I would appreciate if you would put her in your prayers.

"If you would send me more cotton balls, I would appreciate it. The more we give of them, the more it smells. Thank you for sharing this with us."

CURE FROM A CONCUSSION

M.L. of Spencer, Washington, wrote on June 22, 1989:

"I want to report that my husband Edward was suffering from a concussion after a fall last spring. At that time I received the ball of cotton saturated with myrrh from the picture of our Lady and anointed him with it and as soon as he was anointed he began to get well and is himself again.

"Please send me another ball, so that I can anoint my son Roger, who is suffering from mental depression. So that he can continue his work, which requires a lot of figuring, as he is a cabinet maker."

HEALING OF SCIATIC NERVE

From Wichita, Kansas, Sister Mary Vitalis wrote on May 30, 1989:

"I keep the wooden Icon before me on my desk, plus the larger and the smaller photo, and Mary has made my private bedroom a sanctuary.

"Thus far I have with great trust respected the anointing prayers with the holy tear on my right thigh and back (sciatic nerve), which gives me small relief day and night, even when I awaken.

"I will have opportunity tomorrow to anoint an older Sister who fell and broke her arm in two places. Our Lady will be asked for more favors through the Myrrh Weeping Icon's tear, and I shall be happy to report any miracles or favors received of the Most Holy Mother and Ever Virgin Mary Mother of God at Christ of the Hills Monastery at Blanco, Texas.

"I hope, good Father, your health has improved. My prayers, feeble though they may be, shall include you, as well, as the Monks and Nuns of your Monastery. Your place of residence must be like a piece of Heaven with the All–Holy Virgin's miraculous shedding of holy tears. God bless you all. Do keep us in mind at times."

RELIEF OF ABDOMINAL ILLNESS

Sophia Healy of San Antonio, Texas, wrote on January 12, 1990, to say that, "When the Monk touched my abdomen with the cotton ball with Myrrh on it, it eased an illness I have."

COLON CANCER HEALED

Evangeline Joseph wrote from Bay St. Louis, Mississippi, on June 17, 1989:

"I want you to say a special prayer for me. I am going into the hospital soon to have my gallstones removed. Please pray that my operation will be successful.

"Father Benedict, I wish I was able to come and visit you, but right now I don't have any money to do so. Maybe someday in the future, if God wills, He will see fit to let me make the trip....

"Father Benedict, this picture I am sending you, it is my younger daughter and her family. The husband you see in the picture is Thadeleus, who was so sick with colon cancer last year. He was to die and you sent me a tear drop of the Mother of God, also the Holy Oil and Holy Water. I anointed him in the hospital and he is walking around, driving his car and working in his garden. Thanks to the Lord Jesus Christ and His Holy Mother, he has recovered....

"Well, Dear Father, I don't want to burden you with my troubles, so I will close now. Write when you can, and please thank all the Nuns and Monks for praying for me. May God Bless You and keep you in His care."

PRINT OF ICON WEEPS

Mrs. Leroy Melancon wrote from Eunice, Louisiana, on April 20, 1989 to say:

"My husband has a disease called Alzheimer's disease. He is now in a nursing home since January 25, 1989. My daughter taped the picture, which I have included, to his bed. A few days after, I glanced at the picture, and it seems like the Mother in the picture had wept.

"I am sending the picture, so you may tell me what you think of it."

Note: The Icon indeed appears to have wept.

WEEPING ICON

Mrs. Marie Hofsis wrote from Riverhead, New York, wrote:

"Hoping this note and special card finds you in the best of health. Well, over the past month's you sent to Fred and I several small pictures, and one 5 x 7 mounted Icon of the Weeping Icon. I would like to know in sending out these pictures to family and dear friends if anyone reported of the picture weeping?

"I am asking because since I received the 5 x 7 picture, of the Icon which I had in the bedroom, and now in the living room, I have found it weeping!

"I don't know if its because of the nightmare that Fred and I are facing at the present time.

"You see, as mobile home owners, our present landlord has sold the mobile park, and Fred and I, plus 47 families may become homeless with no place to go. At present all parks for this type of living (are) filled up, plus this is no land zoned for mobile home parks.

"So you see we are facing a nightmare. Fred and I, plus our neighbors need your prayers."

Marie's husband, Fred Hofsis continues:

"I hope this short note finds you in better health. My prayers go out to you so that you will get better.

"I have been having my tribulations with where I live here in Riverhead. I don't know if I mentioned to you that I live in a modular home at this address. This mobile home park where I live is up for sale and the tenants living here are trying to buy it and make it into a co-op. Our backs are literally against the walls here. If we don't buy this property, we all could be evicted and no place to go to put our mobile homes.

"We have contacted New York State and town boards, legislators, etc. for help. We have until May 8, 1989, to come up with $80,000 for the down payment with the state helping us with the balance. It will cost each family here approximately $35,000. We have 47 families living here.

"Please pray about our predicament. There is a picture of the Icon that I took with a Polaroid camera. As you can see the left hand side of the picture, the grayish part, feels like chalk. I would appreciate knowing if this is happening elsewhere? We have the smaller copies but they do not show this. Also the picture was taped to a bedroom wall. As far as I know, I can not locate any water dropping on it.

"Also a friend of our son Peter Bopp of Levittown, New York, was one of the sailors who lost his life in the battleship Iowa. Please pray for him."

Note: The photo indeed shows that the print appeared to be weeping.

LEUKEMIA PATIENT RECEIVES SPIRITUAL BLESSINGS

Sister Barbara Pritchard wrote on February 2, 1990:

"Thank you so much for sending me some of the Holy Mother's tears. I have been anointing so many of our sick—myself after Christmas, as I was down with the flu. A mild case, thank God. Every Sunday I am anointing a young man in our Parish, who has leukemia. He is only 40 years old. He was so touched by the heavenly fragrance—has reported a spiritual lift each time I've anointed him. So I would be grateful if from time to time you could send me some more tears. I find hearts touched, as I tell the story of the Weeping Icon."

RELIEF FROM PAINFUL KNEE

Leona C. Jurado wrote from Vallejo, California, on April 30, 1989:

"Peace be with you all.... Good that I was able to baby sit, even if my knee is painful I could not walk before. I applied the tears of our Mother, the Weeping Icon, three times. Now I could walk slowly, but better since (then. I) could not walk at all before."

CURE OF ARTHRITIS AND CHRONIC BLADDER DISORDER

Ramiro and Maria Esquivel of San Antonio, Texas, wrote on November 12, 1989:

"This is our third visit to this Monastery.

"Our first visit was three weeks ago and we came more out of curiosity than anything else. During the service at the temple everything changed so drastically that it was almost unreal. I felt so clean and so holy inside my heart and soul that it was a beautiful feeling. Towards the end of the service while we took of the blessed bread, my wife and I started to walk outside and she grabbed my arm.

"When we walked outside she confirmed to me almost crying that she had felt her toes and feet 'crossed' under her to the point that she felt that she could not walk. So she had to grab my arm to walk out of the Temple.

"This experience was happening on a Sunday morning at the same time that my wife's mother was getting well in San Antonio after being sick with arthritis for over two years and having to take pain pills daily and seeing a number of doctors without any relief. We think that this is sort of a small miracle, that my mother-in-law was well because my wife was praying so hard to the Holy Virgin for her health.

"This same day my wife experienced chills most of the day that we were at the Monastery and at one moment while we were outside on the way to the book store, my wife felt like she was being engulfed in a cloud of fragrance which smelled like myrrh.

"During the following week after our first visit, we felt that we wanted to go back again. So the following

Sunday we again attended services...and this time my wife experienced another miracle on her person. My wife had suffered from a bladder problem for over two years, which was gradually getting worse. She didn't have any control of her bladder and every time she would cough, sneeze or make any kind of abdominal pressure, she would get wet like an infant. She had been to the doctor several times and she was told the only answer to her problem was surgery to her bladder. Again, after praying to the Virgin at the Monastery, she experienced a complete relief of her bladder problem. She does not have any more problems and she feels normal again.

"Another experience that my wife had, happened at home after our second visit. My wife was sweeping the front porch of the house one morning and she felt suddenly a very strong smell of Myrrh, which seemed to surround her for a few seconds. She got scared and walked back inside the house and later opened the door again, but the smell was gone.

"One other thing happened to us during this second week after our visit .... Our oldest son, who is married, had gone around with an eye infection for about a week, without us knowing about it, since he lives with his wife in his own place.

"The day that he went to visit us, my wife was shocked at the way his eyes looked. One of his eyes had what seemed like broken blood vessels.

"My wife proceeded to take some Holy Water, which we brought home from the Monastery and she anointed my son's eyes and head. That night she prayed (before) the Icon of the Virgin which we have at home also. The next day my son's eyes were clear and without any blood or infection of any kind. Everybody at work commented to ask him how it happened. He looked well and they wondered if he had gone to an eye specialist the day before.

"We gave thanks to the Lord and the All Holy Virgin and wonder whether we can attribute these experiences as miracles. We think they are."

CURE OF ALCOHOLISM

Eugenia Llanos wrote:

"Here I am enclosing two pictures (to place before) The Mother of God, The Weeping Icon. One of the pictures is my sister, C.R. I brought her to visit and ask the Weeping Icon to help her drink no more. Because she used to drink day and night and didn't eat. She was an alcoholic. Now she has changed her life. She is now going to church. I anointed her with the Holy tears of the Myrrh–Weeping Icon. This is one of the miracles which I have seen. I am so happy for her. I just want to thank the Myrrh Weeping Icon. She has answered my Prayers.

"The other picture is my nephew Tony Martinez. He was in a car accident on 10-15-89. As you can see on the picture he has no where to put his feet and the steering wheel was on his neck. They had to call fire department to come to take him out. I started praying for Tony to be all right, but then I stopped and started asking and praying to the Mother of God, and God wanted us to...God wanted us to see that miracles do happen. When we got to the hospital they said he had a broken leg and was going to be paralyzed. But I started praying to the (Mother of God in her) Myrrh Weeping Icon to let Tony not have a broken leg and (be) paralyzed. And I also gave my holy tear to my sister-in-law to anoint him. When my niece went in to see him, the doctor said he was lucky, he didn't have any broken bones. He said it was a miracle. I just wanted to thank the Myrrh Weeping Icon and God for this Miracle, because he has made a lot of people believe.

"Last week I couldn't pray or sing (a) song to God, all I could think was, Thank God for letting Tony be reborn. It was a Miracle. He only had a few stitches on his nose. I already told him that I was going to bring him to come and give thanks and visit the Myrrh Weeping Icon.

"Can you send me a holy tear of the Myrrh Weeping Icon?

"After my first visit to the Weeping Icon, I had a dream that a Priest started ringing the bell that a miracle had happened. I was there with him. These are my two miracles."

Note: From the photographs, it is obviously a miracle that Tony lived.

ANOTHER WEEPING ICON AT PALOS VERDES, CALIFORNIA

On Thursday, January 26, 1989, a telephone call from Mary Aughinbaugh of Palos Verdes, California, came during the day for Father Benedict, who was not in. Father Pangratios received the call. Mrs. Aughinbaugh explained that she had received a small Icon print of the Weeping Icon of the Mother of God from us in the mail, as she had requested. She was calling because the print was weeping.

As soon as Father Benedict returned home he telephoned Mrs. Aughinbaugh, who told him that she had received the card and telephoned at once. After that, she wiped the tears off and they reappeared. She took the card to friends, who removed the tears again and the Icon continued to weep. She brought it to her Priest and to her church and the Icon continued to weep all day. Father Benedict informed her that there had been two other reports of prints of the Icon weeping.

Mrs. Aughinbaugh expressed great wonder at the weeping of the Icon and promised to build a church dedicated to the Mother of God on her property in California. Father Benedict explained to her that the Icon was a call to repentance, prayer, fasting, and a transformation of life. Mrs. Aughinbaugh understood the message of the Icon and pledged to spread the word. She also asked that Icon prints be sent to two friends and relatives of hers, whose names and addresses she gave to Father Benedict. All at the Monastery were stunned by the revelation of another print of the Icon weeping. The Monks and Nuns see this as a call to deepen their prayer life and to seek Christ in an even deeper life of repentance and asceticism.

PEACE OF MIND

Charlotte Kensik wrote to say:

"I received the miracle of peace of mind two weeks ago from our blessed Lord Himself. I saw Him in a dream/vision and He said to me, 'My peace I give you, My peace I leave you. As I left my peace to my disciples at the Last Supper.' Since that time I have experienced this profound sense of peace despite much chaos in my family and work situation.

"This evening I received your literature from a friend who made a Pilgrimage to your Monastery just two weeks ago. Upon reading the literature the words 'many have received the gift of peace of mind' just jumped out of me and I realized the common ground of the events and that my 'peace of mind' came from the intercession of the Mother of God through my friends' prayers for me.

"I have anointed my children and myself and I plan to anoint my friends and relatives who visit me this coming year."

CANCER IN REMISSION

Mrs. Joyce N. Tucker wrote from Baton Rouge, Louisiana on March 20, 1989:

"Thank you so much for the tear of our Dear Mother. I applied it to my husband, who has cancer, and already he is feeling better. He has become more active in the last few days. His cancer is in remission and hopefully it will remain (so) for many years.

"He is undergoing many tests at the moment and I pray that the Holy Mother of God will hear our prayers that all is well."

CURE OF STOMACH PROBLEMS

Frances Clements of San Antonio, Texas, wrote:

"U. Clements, my daughter, was very ill with stomach problems. I brought her to see the Icon to make a promise, that if she would cure her of her constant pain and vomiting, that I would bring her back in two weeks. Within those two weeks she is 100% better."

CURE OF THE FLU

Claudette Henley wrote from Orange, New Jersey, on March 16, 1989:

"I would like to tell you that during this week I had a very bad case of the flu and I put my picture of the Icon on me and felt much better.... Thank you."

CURE OF CANCER

Hattie Saldena wrote the following while on a Pilgrimage at the Monastery:

"Mrs. Dora Saldena was diagnosed with cancer July 23, 1989. The prognosis was very poor with a poor chance of recovery. On this January 7, 1990, she is here giving thanks to the Holy Mother for a Miracle cure.

"At this time, she is eating and feeling much better. She is also gaining her weight back. Mrs. Saldena lives in Austin, Texas. The Holy Mother has granted this miracle to her, her family, and friends."

SPIRITUAL INSPIRATION

Louis Lowenten wrote on July 21, 1989:

"How are you? I hope everyone at the Monastery is well and I send my very best wishes to all.

"I just wanted to share with you my thoughts after my latest retreat at the Monastery. Although I always carry away with me a feeling of restored balance, both physically and spiritually, I was especially aware this time of the value of the unique environment. The hills, the trees, the stream beds, the wildlife, and the opportunity to walk and explore such a quiet, yet varied and stimulating place. While I'm sure that for many, there is a great benefit in reading, studying, conversing, or meditating on religious topics, for me (there) is a special inspiration in the solitude of nature and the chance to wander without the distraction of the business of daily human activities. Here I find God.

"The space and variety of terrain at Christ of the Hills Monastery provides perfect context within which I can relax the inhibitions of my mind and my thoughts and gain greater understanding of my experiences—including those difficult to resolve personal dilemmas, brought on by the rush of life in the city. To be able to spend an entire day in solitude without being constrained by a limited space and especially at a place whose very existence is based on inner growth and exploration is of great personal value to me.

"Thanks again for offering this unique opportunity to anyone who is in need. And again my very best wishes for your health and well-being and that of the permanent residents of the Monastery.

"PS: Every time I return from a retreat I find a greater ease and enjoyment of the sometimes tense work of being a symphony musician. Both me and my cello thank you."

BROKEN FINGERS HEALED

Sr. Mary Moran wrote from the Convent of the Holy Spirit on August 3, 1989:

"I am one of the Holy Spirit Sisters who visited your Monastery on Sunday afternoon and evening. We were all deeply impressed at what we saw and heard. You told us about the Weeping Icon of the Mother of God. We visited the Chapel and saw the beauty of the Altar.

"We admired the picture of our Mother of Perpetual Help at the back. I think you called it a different name, Father.

"Shortly before our leaving, Father, I saw you using the precious tears on blessing a baby and parents, I think. As I was passing by, I said, 'Father will you bless these two fingers on my left hand, which I broke accidentally last spring?' You blessed the fingers back and front and also my left eye. The bone specialist told me those fingers would not fully heal, until I would be able to bend them down to the palm of my hand, just like the finger on my other hand, which I could easily bend.

"I have worked on these two fingers all summer, but could never get them within an inch of the palm. On Monday morning, July 31, I tried it. The two fingers bent down to the palm!! I said to myself the tears of our Dear Blessed Mother must have been with me. I pushed the fingers back and forth and I could do it.

"As far as my eye is concerned, nothing has happened. I couldn't read one word before nor one word after. I concluded that our Blessed Mother wants me to get the cataract removed. I was to get it out last March, but I got the flu and then broke my fingers.

"Pray, Father, that Sister Nurse here will contact Dr. Sam Martin, the eye surgeon, who is anxious to get out this cataract. I hope early in August. We start our missionary work in September. We go to the nursing homes and hospitals, as volunteers.

"The Blessed Mother and the Saints are so good to me. Of course all comes from the source—The Eternal Father.

"One of my friends, Sister Joan, on seeing my hand cured said, 'Sister, I wonder if one would have to go to the Shrine to get blessed by the tears of Blessed Mother?' She was thinking of her Sister in Maryland who suffers terribly from one of her knees, but can have no more surgery, because of heart trouble. Sister was wondering if a piece of cloth could be touched to the tears? If so, could you send it to Sister Joan of Arc, at my same address?

"Sister Joan herself has had much sickness. Some years back, she had one of her legs amputated above the knee. Never got any satisfactory legs she could walk on. So she gets around In a wheel chair. She had trouble with her eyes and ears too, but she is always such a lovely, joyful person. She is 85 years (old).

"On Sunday I had the pleasure of meeting you, Father Benedict. I came from Ireland in 1928 to our Mother house in San Antonio. For many years I wanted to go to Africa, but my Mother did not agree.

"In the summer of 1928 I got material regarding the work of the Holy Ghost Sisters. When I read they did not exclude from their Charity, any class or race of persons but pictured a special donation for the poor .... I saw the Holy Spirit directing me to this work. Through the influence of one of the Priests in our Parish, my mother consented to let me go. Another girl came with me. We will celebrate 60 years of our First Profession next June 1990."

MIRACULOUS HEALING OF PHYSICAL WEAKNESS AND PAIN

Father Mateus, a visiting Priest, wrote from the Monastery itself on Pascha, 1989:

"On the afternoon of Holy Pascha, as I was meditating on the meaning of Divine Liturgy, and rejoicing in the Resurrection of our Lord, I was walking about the Monastery. On impulse, I picked some wild flowers, as a gift to our Holy Lady. I went to the Chapel of the Weeping Icon, laid my gift of flowers at the Icon and sat down to pray. I had been concerned because of physical weakness and pain that I was experiencing.

"Glancing up from my prayer, I was expecting to see the Icon Weeping, but to my surprise and joy, she was not weeping, but smiling, encouragingly.

"Then I had my answers to my prayers and I knew that the cancer was gone for good and that other problems would soon be solved."

RELIEF FROM DEMONIC POSSESSION

M. A. R. wrote from Kaumakani, Kauai, Hawaii, on April 24, 1989:

"I received the tear of the Weeping Icon and although I wanted it most for my healing, a triple blessing overcame me. I anointed my forehead and I prayed for healing.... I felt peace of heart and assurance and thank the Mother of God for interceding for me.

"Later I felt (like) Mary Magdeline, out of whom five devils had been cast. For in fact, I know the lust of the eye, the lust of the flesh, the pride of life, a vain heart and a proud mind were my huge sins, drawn out of me with the miraculous myrrh tear of the Mother of God.

"I used to explain my bad breath due to medication, which I had taken for 20 years. However, when I awoke my mouth felt fresh, as if deep within me an evil thing had been drawn out. I pray the Troparion and the Kontakion every day for thanksgiving.

"The Mother of God has sure been good to me. Although not a Satanist, I had allowed the devil to get a firm hold in my life. So when the snake (demon) came out of me, I felt joyous, full of great pride for God's goodness. Grateful to Mary.

"I requested another myrrh tear, which I hope to help my alcoholic boyfriend with. I hope you will oblige. Our need is great."

MULTIPLE BLESSINGS

Ramona Ramierz wrote to Father Benedict on September 22, 1989, from Austin, Texas:

"I can't explain the joy I experienced when I received your letter—especially the tear from the Holy Mother of God. I feel I've been chosen from our Heavenly Father to do this honor to the Holy Mother. As soon as I received your letter, I immediately blessed myself with the Holy Mother's tear. I felt a lot of peace within myself. I had also felt a lot of mixed feeling in my mind. I was not at peace with myself. After blessing myself everything left me and I felt peace within myself.

"I have felt a lot of peace in my home. As for one our sons, (Joe) he did not have a job. My youngest daughter, Elizabeth, had an increase in pay. Also had a transfer in the store. She is now working in the pharmacy section. Louis also did not have a job. He's been laid off. He has not been called back to his job. I've been praying for his job return.

"I was able to get my Clinic Medical Card, without any problem. I also blessed my husband—he is 80 years old—with our Blessed Mother's tear. He says he feels better and I have noticed a peaceful change. He looks good too. Thanks to God and the Holy Mother.

PERSONS I BLESSED WITH OUR BLESSED MOTHER'S TEARS:

"Angie Gonzales; She had been in pain from her shoulder and the doctors couldn't find anything wrong with her. She was in a lot of pain. As soon as I blessed her with our Blessed Mother's tear, she felt relieved. She felt a lot of peace.

"Josie Montoya: She had a lot of mixed feelings. As soon as I blessed her, she felt peace within herself. As of now, five days later, she is still at peace.

"Veronique Montoya: An eight year old child. She is a much happier child."

HEAVENLY AROMA

Lawerence LeLeux wrote from Houston, Texas, on November 15, 1989:

"I visited your Monastery on November 9, to pray to our All–Holy Lady in the spirit of thanksgiving and supplication. Whereupon I had a profound religious experience. I truly felt her presence, as a young Monk blessed me with the holy myrrh. It was a beautiful event in my life, that I shall not soon forget.

"After leaving, I drove the four hour trip to my home in prayer, contemplating this holy event. As the sweet perfume of our Mother's tear filled my auto. I can only say that this holy experience has produced 'good fruit' in my life.

"I will return in December with my family and other persons of my church parish, who are eager to witness this holy event."

THE WOMAN WITH THE ISSUE OF BLOOD

Guadalupe Flores of Eagle Pass, Texas, wrote on March 23, 1990:

"Many thanks and much love to all of the Brethren at the Monastery. As I told you a couple of days ago, it felt like 'Coming home,' as I returned from a second visit.

"I wish to share with you, as witness to what the Lord has done in my life through the intercession of our Blessed Mother here at the Monastery.

"On December 12, 1989, my father, 79 years old and a victim of Parkinson's disease, fell on the concrete floor of our bathroom. The next morning he was taken to the hospital for a checkup, and for a possible broken hip. Thank God, no such (injury). They only found some badly bruised muscles. As my sister and I were returning him home, we were getting ready to pull/push his wheelchair up onto the front porch at home. My sister was pulling from the handles, as I was pushing from the front, but she missed a step and fell sitting on the upper step (of three). I tried holding on to the chair, so both Dad and the chair would not fall on her. At that moment, I felt a sharp pain in my abdominal area and back. I urged my sister (to) pull out from under and we managed to take our father to his room, where our mom was waiting.

"For the next two days I struggled to get myself to work and was in constant pain, but said nothing to my family. On Friday, December 15 (the second day) at 8:30 a.m., I checked out after only an hour at the office, drove in a daze to the hospital emergency room. I had started to hemorrhage. The E.R. doctor called my personal physician, and both ordered further tests. At the end of the day and only after several hours of treatment, they allowed me to go home, with orders to stay in bed. The hospital was full to capacity with flu patients. Medication was prescribed and on the 18th I was to return to the doctor's office. At this time I was informed that they had found a hernia in my abdominal area, as well as an ovarian cyst, (the size of a grapefruit). They recommended surgery. But the problem was that I'm allergic to multiple drugs.

"Of course, I was scared! All I could do at the moment was say, 'Praise God,' as my only form of prayer. There was no anger or question. All I said was 'Lord, just grant me Your Grace to see these kids through.' (The two little nieces I mentioned to you.)

"On January 7th , I went to visit a homeopathic physician (after having checked with my regular doctor). He started me on oral medication, which slowed down the bleeding. Later on February 7th , I attended a church service, and was prayed over. That night during the prayer, deep within, I asked the Lord to grant me the Scripture reading of the woman with the hemorrhage, and He did. The bleeding did not stop then, but I felt so very sure that He had heard my prayer.

"While the bleeding was less, it still continued and I felt drained.

"On February 16th , my oldest niece (12 years old) and I came to San Antonio to visit a friend. Only an hour after our arrival at her home, she handed me a brochure of our Lady. 'Will you come with me to Blanco, and visit the Weeping Icon of our Lady?' she asked. There were no second thoughts or doubts in me. 'Yes,' I answered. My niece merely answered, 'OK,' but was not enthused at the idea.

"The next day we arrived here around 3:30 p.m., for the first time. And while I'd been looking forward being here, something happened to me. As I stood before the Icon of our Lady (moments before Father opened the case), I have to confess: as I saw the 'strings' on the sides of the Icon *(for hanging medals from)*, to me they looked like 'wires', a thought flashed into my mind, 'this is rigged.' Immediately another thought countered the first. 'Someone wants you to doubt.' I felt ashamed.

"At this very moment Father opened the case and I could see clearly. They were visible witnesses of Miracles! I felt choked up. As I asked for forgiveness, there came over my entire abdominal area a tremendous surge of heat. Since then the bleeding stopped. I feel more alive now.

"I've shared this lovely experience with many friends, far and near, for the Glory of God.

"As for my little niece, she was impressed.... Her own behavior has changed and is more open to our Holy Mother's calling.

"Father, much needs to be healed in our family life, but I'm sure that if we start with what our Blessed Lady asks, gradually things will change in our life.

"Please keep us in your prayers, and likewise. God Bless You."

CURE OF WARTS

From Bertram, Texas, Theodora Sandoval writes on March 29, 1990:

"My four year old grandson, Jesse William Salazar, had warts all over his hands. He had been to the doctor several times. She prescribed (for) him some medicine, but if you forgot to put it on one day, the warts would double in size. He had a little more than sixteen warts, big and small ones.

"Then Father Pangratios gave me a cotton ball, that had some tears from our Blessed Mary. Later, I anointed my grandchild on his hands. Then one day, he no longer had them, except for maybe one or two. My daughter, his mother, was going to have to take him to a dermatologist to get them frozen off. But now, Thanks to our Holy Virgin Mary, he won't have to get them frozen off. And for that I am forever grateful."

ICON WEEPING

Gloria Delgado wrote on March 27, 1990, from Selma, Texas:

"I purchased an Icon print the second week of February 1990. Two weeks later it began to weep. It has wept two other times in the evening."

HEALING OF EPILEPSY

On March 31, 1990, the following was written:

"My name is Mary Anita Bongiorno, I am forty years old and currently reside in Austin, Texas.

"I have had a seizure disorder since I was twenty years old. The older I got the worse my epilepsy became. Recently my seizures became so bad, I could not work. Doctors had me taking a drug called Mcyline, which converts to phenoliarhtral. The drug is also addictive. Side effects are almost as bad as the seizures it stops. In my case, the different drugs available to prevent epilepsy did not work. Even at maximum dosage I experienced seizures. My doctor tried all the available combinations. Yet I still had three and four seizures a day. After my last trip to the doctor, I was out of hope. I came home and said the rosary. I said, 'God, they gave it their best, but cannot help me. You are all I have to turn to. If it is Your will that I suffer this, of course I will—except that I'm so tired and not a smiling person. If You could heal me, I would be better I think at living than I am at suffering.'

"I had a vision of the Holy Virgin Mary. She just smiled, then somewhere above my head a soft feminine voice said, 'Do my work.' I then came back to being aware of my rosary and continued saying it.

"That night my seizures became very hard and my husband took me to Brackenridge Hospital. The next day somewhere inside, I felt a sort of firm determination growing. I had read of Christ of the Hills Monastery. I told my husband to drive me there. On the way I said my rosary and told the Mother of God I had to get well, before I could do anything. When we arrived and entered the tiny Chapel, one of the Monks anointed my forehead, hands, and feet with one of the tears of the Mother of God. I felt a calm warm feeling spread throughout my body, also a vibrant energy.

"The energy itself was a miracle. For I have been filled with it ever since. I quit taking the medicine and have had no more seizures. Just quitting the medicine should have made me have a seizure. Epileptics are warned by neurologists not to discontinue medication. The drugs are barbiturates, and withdrawal without medical supervision will cause a grand mal seizure.

"It has been two months now. Not only have I had no seizures, but I'm full of that wonderful energy. I have not taken medication since my miracle on the little mountain in Blanco, Texas."

HEALING OF OVARIAN CANCER

From San Antonio, Texas, Valli Thompsen wrote on April 14, 1990:

"I just had my third operation of ovarian cancer. All the tests and checking and everything came back negative. NO CANCER.

"I have been praying and looking at the Icon as you suggested, and she has answered all my prayers.

"Due to nerve damage from drugs, my writing is not very good.

"A very dear friend, a sister in Christ and servant of God, has a small Icon of the most precious Myrrh-Weeping Mother and Christ Child. She got it at Christ of the Hills Monastery. Bev, my friend, myself, and two others at different times, noticed the Blessed Mother had been weeping! This was two weeks before the Resurrection. My friend lives and breathes God every moment. She has opened herself, so that God can work through her, and He does. It did not surprise me, that the Icon wept in the home of His humble servant. For 'with God all things are possible.' "

CURE OF LUNG CANCER

Thelma M. Piña wrote from Alice, Texas:

"In March, 1990, we were at Christ of the Hills Monastery in Blanco, Texas. When we left, we took with us some tears of the Virgin Mother of God.

"A few days after, we were advised that my Aunt, who had lung cancer, was worsening—the cancer was spreading and they had to operate. I took the tear to her and anointed her, making prayer and asking the Virgin for her intercession before God and her son Jesus. My Aunt later explained to us that, beginning in her head, she felt a peace and tranquillity indescribable enter her, and after (that) she felt something leave her body through her feet.

"When the doctors operated, they found the only sign of possible cancer was a small tumor, which was miniscule, (and) was nothing like they had diagnosed. (They) further stated (that) she needed no further therapy, because the cancer was gone. They said they could offer no scientific explanation.

"All the family considers this a miracle, attributed to the intercession of the Holy Virgin and her Son, our Lord Jesus Christ."

HEALING OF BRAIN STEM INJURY

From Orrtanna, Pennsylvania, Ruth Kane wrote to Fr. Benedict on April 8, 1990:

"I pray that your health has improved and want to thank you for the message from the Monastery.

"I have been wanting to write to you about a miracle, and have been delaying it—thinking I would not do it well, but with the Virgin Mary's help I will tell you of a young friend.

"Eight months ago, Margaret was driving her car near Gettysburg, Pennsylvania. A driver did not stop at an intersection and struck her car at the driver's seat. Margaret was taken to a trauma unit at a local hospital. She was in a deep coma. Families and friends prayed constantly for her. Churches of all denominations included her in their prayers for the sick, with no improvement in her condition. The doctors finally told her parents they expected no improvement, it was an injury to the brain stem and Margaret would not improve.

"I spoke to her mother and told her about my cotton ball with the tears from the Weeping Icon, and asked her if she would like to bless Margaret with it. She took the cotton with her and blessed her. I also gave her a picture of the Icon to leave at her bedside.

"The next evening Margaret seemed to be even deeper in the coma. The following evening (48 hours after the blessing) when the parents entered her room, Margaret was sitting in a chair and recognized her family. She was able to speak, and called her family members by name.

"A week later she was sent to a rehabilitation center, where she continued to improve. She is now back in her own home and with some direction is keeping house. She continues to improve and anyone that is not aware of her accident would never see her as anything but a normal young woman.

"One of the doctors, seeing her at the rehabilitation center, told her mother that they could not explain it. Not only did she have an injury to the brain stem, but the entire brain had been traumatized due to the severity of the blow. None of the doctors working with her had any hope of improvement. It was truly a miracle.

"I felt the cotton ball must be very precious to the family, so I could not accept it, when the mother offered to return it to me. Many times I wished for the myrrh. Would it be possible for me to have a replacement? We have a little grand-daughter with cerebral palsy and I (would) like to bless her. Please pray for our little Anna.

"I pray someday I may visit your Monastery and be near the Mother of God Icon."

DISAPPEARANCE OF DEMONS

On April 22, 1990, Alfonso Holguin wrote to Fr. Benedict from Laredo, Texas:

"I am sending you these few words to let you know that we are doing fine. Thanks be to God. We are saddened by your Father's death and we will keep him in our prayers every day. Father Benedict, as you know, just today I came out from the hospital, where I (had) spent ten days for a very delicate surgery. But all seems to be fine, thanks be to God. I need three months for the operation to heal completely, for it is going to heal from inside out. The surgery is open so it can drain and will close little by little, God willing.

"Father, remember the girl I talked to you about last time I visited the Monastery? The one that came to some sort of trance and started drawing demons and said that she saw demons in her room. Without her knowing, well, I started praying for her with the cotton ball with the Virgin Mary's tear and gave her the Holy Water to drink. I then made the Sign of the Cross with the holy tears and made a special prayer that her life come back to normal. She is a good girl, goes to church, and told me when I asked her if her dreams were still bothering her. She said no. Thank the God Almighty, and the tear of the Virgin Mother of God and to all of you Brothers and Fathers for your prayers.

"I don't have words to express myself, but from the very first day we visited your Monastery, our lives changed for the better. Something happened since that day; it's beautiful. Also when I came out from surgery, I thought about you all and I called upon you with my mind and asked you to pray for me. I was in terrible pain. I thought and asked the Holy Virgin Mary to give me strength, and my pain and suffering were gone. I had four operations in one week, and just gave up hope. I did not want to go through another one. But when I was there it came to me that this was nothing compared to what our Lord Jesus Christ suffered. That mine was just a little pain compared to the ones (He) suffered, and I felt the need to keep on, that God loves me and that I will pull through for the fourth operation, which was a success. Thank the good Lord and thank you all for keeping up with your prayers for the world. God bless you all."

LUMP IN BREAST REDUCED

On April 9, 1990, Maggie Benip wrote from Corpus Christi, Texas:

"Prayer granted: the lump in my breast reduced greatly in size. Thank you, Blessed Mother of God. The prayer was answered after a visit to your Shrine and using the tears of Most Holy Mother of God."

WISDOM

Mary Kathleen K. R. wrote from San Marcos, Texas, on April 16, 1990, to the Monks:

"This is just a note to let you know that I have received Baptism and Chrismation on Saturday of Great Week at St. Elias Orthodox Church. Thanks be unto God and to you.

"At the Icon of the Most Blessed and Ever-Virgin Mary and Theotokos, I prayed for wisdom and the knowledge of where God wanted me to be. My prayer has been answered.

"The Lord gives wisdom: from His mouth come knowledge and understanding. (This is my miracle). I have found The Church."

PEACE

Jaime Vidal, Professor of Theology, wrote from Seton Hall University on March 14, 1990:

"Through the good offices of my friend, Ed Shirley, Theology Professor, of St. Edward's University, in Austin, Texas, I received a tear of your Weeping Icon of the Theotokos, as well as a picture and some literature on it. These arrived in the mail together with a letter full of hate from a student of mine, which causes me much pain, and yet, when I looked at the small Icon and placed the tear on top of the letter, I was able to find peace and forgive the person who wrote to me, and to pray that he might be healed of his anger and hate. So I, too, have felt her gift of peace and love upon first meeting her! I have placed the tear in the small room which I use for a Chapel to say the Divine Office, together with some Relics of Saints which I have, and have resolved to honor it, especially on every feast of the Theotokos. Since it is the closest thing we can have to a Relic of one whose blessed body is no longer on this earth.

"I also intend to anoint with it the father of one of my students, who has metastasized cancer all over his inner organs; If God should grant him health through His Blessed Mother, I will not omit to let you know for the greater glory of both.

"Please keep me in your prayers, both my earthly needs, especially a secure job, and my spiritual needs."

MULTIPLE MIRACLES

Fred Morin wrote from Buffalo Narrows, Canada, on April 8, 1990:

"These are some of the other miracles that have occurred.

"Diane's Dad, Isdore Laliberti was in the hospital for a bypass heart operation after he was anointed. The doctors checked him up. Then could not find anything wrong with him. They checked and rechecked, (but) still could not find anything wrong. He is home now with his family, doing just great.

"This all happened after Diane phoned you, and asked you to pray for her Dad. Thanks to the intercession of our Mother of God, and the tears.

"Another miracle happened to us. One day Diane was visiting her Mom, while I was at work. Diane has a history of stomach problems, very bad ones. She phoned me from her Mom's place shaking and unable to talk on the phone. She asked me to pick her up. So I did. On our way home from picking her up, I asked her if she would like to stop at the hospital to see a doctor? Her response was 'no.' So I took her in the trailer where I work. We began to say some prayers. And I rubbed the holy tear on her. Then immediately the pain just left her. Since then she hasn't had any stomach problems. Thanks once again to our Mother of God, and for your prayers.

"Another miracle that has occurred was one evening our adopted son's nose was bleeding terribly.

Not realizing this, we told him to be quiet and go to bed. Then we decided to check him up. Sure enough, his pillow was just full of blood. He had a nose bleed. Diane tried everything to stop the bleeding. It was getting worse; nothing helped. So we immediately reached for the tear. We always keep it handy. We began praying and I rubbed my son with the holy tear. Just like that, the bleeding stopped. He doesn't get them anymore.

"Thanks to the Mother of God for her prayers for us. Praised be our Lord Jesus Christ. Miracles happen to us every day, I just cannot explain. It sure is beautiful for you people interceding for us to the Mother of God and her holy tears, and the beautiful fragrance. Beautiful heavenly smell of myrrh. Thank you once again."

HEALING EYE INFECTION

Wanda Hijek wrote from Lynwood, Washington, on March 14, 1990:

"I had a severe eye infection for over four months, which did not respond to medication.

"In desperation I started rubbing the Blessed John oil you sent me on my eyelid and experienced a great improvement in a few days."

CANCER CURE

The Monastery received the following letter from Marie Stefana Pimilia of Austin, Texas, on May 9, 1990:

"In 1954 my mother was given a drug called DES to prevent miscarriage. I was born. Then in 1978 it was discovered that my uterus had cancerous cells. I began going to the DES Clinic at the University of Baylor in Houston, Texas. This is the world authority on DES Centers headed by Dr. Haffman. In 1983, I came to see St. Seraphim's Relics and asked for healing, for a cure, because the doctor had told me that they had to operate immediately, that it was that serious.

"I began praying to St. Seraphim and touching the cloth to me that had touched the Relic. Then I began a spiritual path to seek God and to look at my character defects and I began to change.

"When the Icon of the Mother of God started weeping, I came to pray and ask for healing and forgiveness.

"This year, in 1990, Dr. Simon at Baylor told me that the condition had much improved and was getting better. This means that the cell structure is changing. The cancer cells are becoming healthy cells. I am healing my emotions and my physical body is changing. Thanks to the Mother of God.

"I am grateful for Christ of the Hills Monastery."

GLAUCOMA IMPROVEMENT

Sophie Brown of Victoria, Texas, wrote to Fr. Benedict on May 12, 1990:

"I received your most welcome letter with the tear of the Mother of God from her Myrrh-Weeping Icon. I have used the tear every day and it has helped my weak glaucoma eye. I would like to have another tear, since I have prayed on the one you sent me so many times, that it is almost worn out. Will you be so kind and send me another?

"I went to have a checkup with the doctor and everything proved positive. Thanks to the Icon's tear. I feel great."

MIRACULOUS HEALING OF THE PLACENTA

The following testimony was given at Christ of the Hills Monastery by Dody O'Sullivan from The Woodlands, Texas, on May 18, 1990:

"While blessing a pregnant woman with the Mother of God's tear, in the hospital, who was bleeding with a placenta separation, she felt warmth and something move up. The bleeding stopped and she was allowed to go home. She has not bled since the blessing. We are hoping she can keep the baby in her womb until it will be eight months—June 1st.

"I gave most of the cotton ball with the tears away. I had only a small piece left. I opened the envelope to bless some one and there was a stain of oil on the blue leaflet, larger than the size of a quarter. It continued to produce more tears for a month or so. Almost all people were moved to tears while being blessed with it.

"I blessed a woman with severe arthritis. She had not knelt for years and went up to a kneeler and knelt down with no hesitation."

PILGRIM'S GRATITUDE

Roosevelt and Theresa Morales write from Palacios, Texas, on May 23, 1990:

"Thank you for letting us know of your needs. You and all who share in God's work are always in our prayers.

"We encourage you to persevere in your service to the Pilgrims, because we are witnessing the fruit of your work here in our community, as people are growing in their prayer life and holiness. People are praying, fasting, and loving their brethren. By their fruits you shall know them.

"We hope to visit you this summer, God willing."

THREE SPECIAL MIRACLES FROM PHARR, TEXAS

From McAllen, Texas, Maria Nela S. Sanchez wrote on May 21, 1990:

"It is with great joy that I convey to you three special miracles granted fellow-worker's families from Pharr, Texas.

"Mrs. L. L., a school counselor had been suffering from lysis disease for many years. She is a Baptist. She requested a tear from our Weeping Mother of God with great faith. The next day after anointing her with the tear, she said she felt much better and did not have to take any medication that day for the first time in many years. Then the Monday after Easter, she came into the classroom and hugged me crying joyfully, because she had gone for a check up with the doctor, after not experiencing any more pain. Her doctor was astonished to find out that the lysis was gone. She and her husband and family are very grateful and plan to go to Blanco after school is out.

"Another fellow-worker Mrs. S., a school teacher, also reported to me that her mother had Alzheimer's disease and could not recognize anyone for the last five years. After she was anointed with the tear she started calling her family by name and the family was very amazed about this incredible miracle from the Blessed Mother of God.

"The school nurse, Mrs. M., requested a tear to anoint her old bachelor uncle who was in a coma at the Nursing Home. She cried joyfully when she told me, that after she anointed him with the tear, he woke up and was already walking and talking and is back home, fully recovered. She told me her uncle had told her he experienced the healing with great heat in his body.

"Thank you very much for the Weeping Icon tears. God Bless you and the Monks and Nuns."

TWO MIRACLES IN ONE FAMILY

The following testimony was given by Jaime and Fred Molina of San Antonio, Texas, at the Monastery on May 29, 1990:

"Fred was to have surgery on his right foot. Through prayer, faith, and the anointing of the tear of the Blessed Mother of God in Blanco, Texas, Mr. Molina was healed by the Blessed Mother.

"A grandson was having severe problems being trained to go from diapers (the child is 5 and one-half years old, and still in diapers). Upon anointing, he was completely healed."

PEACE AND HOLINESS

Tish Burnham of Austin, Texas, wrote the following on May 30, 1990:

"...I visited the Monastery and viewed the Icon last Saturday afternoon. I was by myself: my motives were mixed. Principally, I was on a Pilgrimage. My interest was more in making the visit than in seeing an Icon weep, if that makes any sense.

"So what happened? Externally, nothing much. I suffered physically a good deal. I hate the Texas heat (I'm from Boston), so there was that. And standing for the long service was excruciating to my back and legs. So there was that. I saw the Icon in a hurry, couldn't see any tears and wasn't even certain I smelled anything.

"So the question then is, did anything happen? Was my visit a waste of time? My response to that is emphatically not. What does one see and experience when one visits a Monastery out in the wilderness?—solitude, prayerfulness, nature in a pure state, people who dedicate their lives to the service of God and Mary. Virtues in action: hard work, humility, chastity, generosity of heart, hospitality, truthfulness, piety, zeal for souls, special affection for children. That's worth going there for, all in itself.

"Do I believe in the miraculous Icon? Yes. Why, since I personally did not see anything? Basically, because Father Pangratios said so. I asked him how the discovery was made initially and who made it. He told me. I believe him. It's as simple as that. She cries. We all know why. I went down to see her—not to see her cry necessarily, just to see her. She was there. I got to participate in a chanting prayer (Akathist) to her which to me was the high point of the trip.

"It's not something that can be dramatized, but it's proof. It's what happens in the individual soul that counts the most. That after all is the purpose of her weeping.

"Thank you for being there. Thank all of you for dedicating your lives to the service and glory of the Lord. May your place be high in heaven! My special thanks to Father Pangratios, our guide. And I hope Father Vasili's back is better. Greetings to the disabled Nun who has the face of an Angel and chants so sweetly."

HEALING OF KIDNEY STONES

Fr. Benedict received the following letter from Dr. Ed Shirley, Professor of Theology at St. Edward's University, Austin, Texas, written June 4, 1990:

"I evidently did not keep a copy of my testimony concerning the Weeping Icon on my computer, so I have reconstructed the events leading to my healing.

"On Wednesday, September 27, 1989, I noticed a slight pain in my lower back when I awoke. Having had two cases of kidney stones the previous year, I recognized the symptoms immediately, and drove to the doctor's office. Tests confirmed that I did, indeed, have stones, and the doctor prescribed an antibiotic and a pain reliever. The pain got worse through the day, and for the next two days, would come and go. Then, on Friday, the pain seemed to disappear.

"Meanwhile, I was feeling rather burnt out at work, and had been needing to get away for a mini-retreat, and so on Sunday, October 1, I drove out to Christ of the Hills Monastery to pray before the Weeping Icon. I have visited the Monastery several times since 1986, and each time experienced the grace which flows through the Icon. I had never seen the Icon weeping, however.

"When I arrived at the Monastery, I went to the Icon's Chapel and sat to pray. Soon, however, Fr. Pangratios brought a small group of Pilgrims through for a tour. I listened again to the story of the Icon. Fr. Pangratios said that she had been weeping that very morning. This was very exciting for me, for it seemed that on my previous visits, she 'was weeping just yesterday', or 'three days ago.' This was the closest I had come to actually seeing her weep. We all went forward to reverence the Icon, and I noticed the wood was still wet with the tears. Fr. Pangratios anointed us and gave us each a cotton swab with the myrrh. I was thrilled, for as many times as I had visited, and as often as I wanted to, I had never asked for either anointing or some of the tears.

"Afterwards, I wandered around the grounds of the Monastery for a while, spending some silent time with the Lord. I decided to pray before the Icon again before leaving. Part of me was thinking, 'It would be very nice if she were weeping when I got there.' When I entered the Chapel, Fr. Pangratios was there with another group. He motioned me forward and pointed toward the Icon. The Blessed Mother was weeping. The precious tears were flowing in a thick and heavy stream. I was so touched. Everyone was anointed (myself for the second time that day). After some more private prayer, I left the Monastery to return home.

"Everything seemed fine until October 4. It was not to be a tranquil day, however. I woke up with a pain in my back and abdomen, and knew that the kidney stones had not passed after all. The pain continued for the next two days, so on Friday, I was X-rayed and referred to a urologist. He said the stones were too far down in my system to do ultra-sound treatment, and simply advised me to take pain pills and wait. However, the pain kept coming and going through the week-end, and each time it returned, it seemed to be worse.

"Finally, on Monday, October 9, the pain became intense. The next day, I called my doctor and the urologist and told them that the pain was becoming very intense. I was told that if it continued with that intensity, to call back and I would be placed in the hospital. I had to teach a class for the diocesan adult religious education program at 7:30 that night, and did not want to be interrupted by the pain.

"It was then that it struck me that I should turn the matter over to our Blessed Mother. This was around 5:00 p.m. I took the cotton swab with the myrrh out of the foil and blessed myself with the Sign of Cross. Then I anointed myself on the forehead, lower back and abdomen with the Sign of the Cross. I had the sensation of something shifting within me at that very moment. I went to get some dinner, and an hour later I passed the stone, well in time for my class.

"This is not, perhaps, the most amazing healing ever to take place. After all, my life was not threatened, and the stone probably would have eventually passed even without aid from the doctors. But I am convinced that I was healed through the intercession of the Most Holy Mother of God, through the grace of the Weeping Icon.

"I also got your letter about Father's Day. Please remember my father in your prayers that day. He died in October 1984. I will also remember to pray for your father as well.

RELIEF OF STRESS AND UNCERTAINTY

Father Pangratios received the following letter from Rosemary Rotolo of Goodlettsville, Tennessee, written June 2, 1990:

"I was so happy to read in Father Benedict's note that the Pilgrims are coming in increasing numbers. I know how dedicated you are in bringing the message of our Lady to all you meet.

"...The Lady is very strong and very powerful. How my life has suddenly been pulled together, and things fallen into place after years of stress and uncertainty, is a miracle in itself. It is the first time I have known real peace.

"...I enjoy receiving Father Benedict's notes. He writes with such warmth and sincerity."

RELIEF OF COLD SYMPTOMS

Dolores Quevedo wrote from Montbello, California on May 31, 1990:

"I am writing this letter as an act of thanksgiving to the Blessed Mother of God. On May 21st, I came down with a terrible cold—cough, chills, fever etc. On top of it all, I lost my voice. And I was to give one of the keynote conferences and activities at a retreat.

"On May 24th, my friend Rose anointed me with our Lady's tears. I felt so sick that all I could do was look at the little holy Icon with her picture on it. I prayed and believed that she could make me well. My colds usually run a two week course and this one was, or seemed, worse.

"On Friday morning, May 25th, I still had very little voice and a blossoming cold. I was to call my doctor at 10:00 a.m., but when I called he was away on an emergency and I was to call back at 1:00 p.m.

"I went about my work organizing for the retreat. As I was writing I didn't realize that I began singing. I really don't know when she—our Lady, that is—cured me. All I know is that I went to use the phone and I felt perfectly well. I realized that my voice was fully restored. I praised Her Son and I thank Her for the miracle. I didn't make the call.

"I am also a writer of books and I am asking you to help me ask our Lady for a strengthening of my eyes as well as for a complete healing of my feet. I need to have stronger health since I travel.

"Thank you for taking time to read this lengthy epistle,...our Lady had to be honored and thanked.

"Hope to spend a day of prayer when I visit San Antonio, Texas, this summer. Many prayers and blessings on your work and in spreading our Lady's devotion.

LOVE

Hierodeacon Pangratios writes the following:

"On June 25, 1990 Thomas and Betty Ley Hoffman of Phoenix, Arizona, came on a Pilgrimage to see the Weeping Icon. When we walked into the Chapel (this was around 1:15 in the afternoon), we found the Icon had just begun to weep. The streams of tears had not even reached the bottom of the Icon yet. When I mentioned the sweet aroma from the myrrh, Mrs. Hoffman said 'I can't smell.' Several minutes later, Mrs. Hoffman cried out with tears in her eyes, 'I can smell it, I can smell it!' Mr. Hoffman placed his hand on her shoulder and said, 'You can smell it?' Then he turned around to me and said 'She hasn't been able to smell for 15 years.' We spent some time praising God and thanking Him and the Most Holy Theotokos for this great mercy. Then I anointed them both with the myrrh from the Icon."

"Later that day, Mrs. Hoffman wrote the following:

" 'My expression of what happened to me as I viewed the Weeping Icon is the feeling I experienced. Our beautiful Mother made me cry, because I felt the pain she may have suffered, as she watched her Son, our Lord, being crucified on that terrible Cross. The terrible sins of the world today are the suffering she is going through at this time of our earthly life. The hope of our future lies in that little boy that she is holding in her arms. How He clings to His mother. This is how we all must cling to her. She brings us to her Son, Our Salvation. God is so good! He allowed His Son to be born into our world. Thank you, Holy Virgin Mary, for saying yes to God! Oh how we are blessed! God is so good! Thank You, Lord Jesus, for all the graces You bring us. Thank You for dying for us. Oh, I am so sorry I sinned against You. Please forgive me for all my sins. Thank You, God, for bringing us to this place. Thank you, Most Holy Virgin Mary for giving birth to our Lord Jesus. I love you so much! I am eternally grateful for your love for all of us. How I wish I could do something to show you the love I have for you.

" 'Oh, Dear Mother Mary, are you crying because of me? I feel so fortunate to see this miracle happening right in front of me, but please don't feel so sad. I hope and pray that I shall never, ever do anything to make you cry for me. My tears are of the JOY I feel to be in the presence of our Lord. I know He is here. I know how much you love me. Thank you, Lord Jesus. Thank you, Most Holy Virgin Mary. Thank you, Father, for bringing us here. O my Lord, I cannot thank You enough for all the goodness You have brought into my life.

" 'I love You with all my heart, my soul, and my body. I wish everybody could feel the love You give us so generously.

" 'PS: I have been unable to smell since an accident in 1976. Today, Glory To God, I was able to smell a sweet odor of our Lady's' tears. Thank God!'"

WOUNDED FEET HEALED

In July, 1990, Lovedes S. V. Jalavda of West Covina, California, wrote the following:

"It was with great joy that I received a call from my sister in the Philippines telling me that my father's long–time wounds on both feet are now completely healed through the miracle of the myrrh from the Icon of the weeping Madonna of New Sarov. Thank you so much for your prayers.

"Everyday while my sister and my father were praying to the Mother of God, the Icon with the myrrh taped at the back was placed on my father's forehead. Every day the wounds diminished in size. At the same time the cotton also diminished in size. When the wounds disappeared, the cotton with the tears also disappeared. Thanks be to God and the Blessed Mother of God."

BRAIN TUMOR DISAPPEARS

Memorandum prepared at Christ of the Hills Monastery June 4, 1988:

"In March of 1988, John Dente was diagnosed as having a blocked cartoid artery on the right side of his neck. Doctors at the Veterans Administration diagnosed this ailment and urged Mr. Dente to quickly have surgery for it. In the process of preparing him for the surgery a number of tests were done. During the course of this it was discovered that Mr. Dente had a severe aneurysm of the aorta going into the left ventricle of his heart. It was, they said, the size of a cantaloupe and they urged him to immediately enter the hospital that moment. Mr. Dente had to go to Denver, Colorado, and therefore declined admission to the hospital. On returning from Denver, Mr. Dente obtained a second opinion from an arterial surgeon in San Antonio, who urged him to get into an ambulance and go to the hospital that moment. Again, Mr. Dente declined due to the upcoming celebration of Pascha (Easter).

During the third week of April, Mr. Dente underwent further tests and during the fourth week of April, 1988, Mr. Dente entered the Audie Murphey Veteran's Hospital in San Antonio, Texas. It was planned that as soon as his condition was stabilized and all pre-surgical testing was done that he would have surgery for the aneurysm. In the course of preparing for the surgery of the aneurysm, certain symptoms began to appear that concerned the doctors. Therefore, they ordered electroencephalograms and CAT scans of Mr. Dente's brain.

In the first week of May, 1988, the doctors discovered a brain tumor in Mr. Dente's brain. A number of CAT scans were taken over the next few weeks and it was observed that the tumor was invasive and rapidly increasing. Also, Mr. Dente, began to exhibit symptoms of paralysis in part of his body, then slurring of his speech, and then finally the inability to write even his name or to dial a telephone. He got so bad he could not walk. Father Benedict noticed that Mr. Dente missed things he reached for by six or seven inches during this time. Seriously concerned about his health, the Fathers brought tears of the Mother of God from the Myrrh-Weeping Icon to anoint Mr. Dente with the week before the surgery, which was scheduled for May 26.

The night before the surgery, Wednesday, May 25, Father Benedict went to hear Mr. Dente's Confession, bring him Holy Communion, and again anoint him. They had already shaved Mr. Dente's head. They took him immediately after his reception of the Sacrament and anointing to Bexar County Medical Center to have his head marked where the surgery would enter his cranium. After marking his head, one of the doctors wanted to take another CAT scan to make sure they had marked his head correctly. When they took the CAT scan they were amazed to discover that they could not see any tumor. Since they had observed this tumor and its growth in numerous previous tests they knew it had to be there. They took yet another CAT scan and other tests to confirm their new finding. The doctors could find no traces of a brain tumor. Also, Mr. Dente's symptoms of paralysis, slurred speech, lack of coordination, etc., described above, disappeared.

The doctors themselves are perplexed by this finding. Those who have some understanding of the ways of the Heavenly Realm, however, give glory to God, Who is indeed wondrous in His works, and are thankful to His Holy Mother, through whose intercession countless miracles have occurred as a result of anointing with tears of her Myrrh-Weeping Icon."

RETURN OF SIGHT IN LEFT EYE

From Elias Boyd of Austin, Texas, came the following on September 23, 1990:

"I, Elias (Gerald) Boyd, had an operation on my left eye, and the eye—due to severe hemorrhage—was damaged beyond repair. The eye was injected with gas after the operation and I lost the sight of the left eye. Believing in God's power to heal, but never really being convinced of this fact was at times very depressing. One day it was suggested to me to visit Christ of the Hills Monastery. So being free at this time because of ill health to travel, I came to the Monastery, not knowing of the Weeping Icon. While there I was anointed with the tears of the Mother of God.

"I went back to Austin and while at my brother-in-law's service station, I began to see sparks in my left eye. I realized it was car lights passing and then the images of my nephew began to focus and I began to see out of nothing. I called Father James and told him that I could see and I still do.

"Praise to God, it saved my sight and also my soul was saved to tell of God's great love and miracles through a doubting Thomas."

BIRTH OF NORMAL BABY

Rita Rubio of McAllen, Texas, gave the following testimonial at the Monastery on September 9, 1990:

"On July 29th, 1990, my family and I were traveling home after a long, hard two month stay in El Paso, Texas. We went there hoping for a new beginning; we returned with bad news: my husband lost his job.

"My daughter of four months with child was told her baby may be born with Down's syndrome. Every test the doctor took showed she had two decisions to make. One would be to terminate the pregnancy or live with an ill child.

"We then went to Blanco, Texas, on the way home reading of her great miracles. We prayed with all our faith, leaving everything in her hands.

"On August 3rd, 1990, my daughter was told her baby girl will be born healthy and beautiful.

"Here we are August 11th, 1990, visiting her again for the wonderful miracle she has done for us. Giving her thanks."

CHANGE OF HEART

On January 18, 1991, Oliva Salinas wrote thanking the Monks and Nuns.

"I wrote you a long, long letter yesterday thanking you for my son, M. The miracle that our weeping Virgin

Mary did for him, the change that has come upon him. I blessed him this morning hoping and praying he will keep on the right track. Please pray for him to be a healthy man and find a good job for him. He loves to work. He works in the Steak House kitchen. He is a cook."

Mrs. Salinas asks for prayers for her other son who is in basic training in the Army.

ICON WEEPING

Aurora M. Guerrero wrote on January 9, 1991, from Lewisville, Texas:

"A picture from the Shrine of the Blessed Virgin Mary, that I bought in the month of November, started crying the 29th day of November, three days before I went to Los Angeles, California.

"I went to California to visit my family but as soon as I took her with me she stopped crying. She hasn't cried. At night it started crying, and the smell of the myrrh was there. I started praying for hours until I fell asleep praying and the myrrh was hitting me straight on my face and put me to sleep. I am back home here in Lewisville, Texas, and that's why I am writing to you."

HELP IN AN ADDICTION

On July 12, 1990, L. V. wrote from Weslaco, Texas:

"I would like to thank our All Holy Mother for healing my son, R., of the marijuana habit and of many little things R. was in bondage to. When he smelled the tears of our All-Holy Mother, something came over him (and changed him inside). He would smell the myrrh tears many times, because he would feel healing going through him every time he smelled the myrrh tears of our All Holy Mother. He is not able to smoke that stuff any more. Praise the Lord! His life has changed tremendously. His wife is expecting their first baby and my first grandchild. I thank our Lord and His Blessed Mother for answering our prayers. Thank you for your prayers, all of you."

RELIEF FROM PAIN AFTER AMPUTATION

Herminia Llanos writes from Martindale, Texas:

"...I am writing you these few lines to thank you for a miracle. On November 17, 1989, I was in the hospital because they cut off part of my right leg. I was in a lot of pain. Then I asked the Mother of God (through her) Icon to help with the pain, and I put the Icon of the Mother of God on my leg. That's when a lady walked in, whom I had never seen before, and told me to ask her with faith, so that it would be my last pain or my last healing that she would do for me. (At that moment) the doctor walked in and took the cast off my foot. That's when I started to feel that my pains were melting and peeling off my leg. I felt the presence of the Mother of God, that she was the one that healed my pain. I know this was a miracle because right then and there the pain was gone."

CHILD IN NEED OF A LIVER TRANSPLANT

Father Benedict related the following:

"On the 18th of February, 1991, I received a letter from Elizabeth Mohler of Fort Worth, Texas. In the letter she reminded me of my earlier conversation with her. She had brought her daughter Kayla to the Monastery when she was 4 months old. The baby needed a liver transplant and was completely covered with hair. The doctors had little or no hope for her and she was awaiting a transplant and was on a transplant list. The child was anointed with the tears of the Mother of God. Now, two years later, the child is no longer on an active list and is well, has grown normally, and does not appear to be covered with the excessive hair that she once had. Her mother attributes this miracle to the prayers of the Mother of God and of the people here at the Monastery and of others who have prayed for this baby's miraculous cure.

"Certain incurable liver diseases can only be treated by removing the diseased liver and transplanting another liver in the child. It is dangerous surgery at best. There are never enough donors. And there is a rejection factor. This child avoided all of this through the intercessions of the Theotokos and her mother writes:

" 'Thank you, once again, for those precious moments in Blanco, Texas, when Kayla was only four months old. See how far she has come! Thank you for your prayers and the prayers of your people. My people. Our people.'"

SAFE RETURN FROM THE PERSIAN GULF

On April 22, 1991, San Juanita Guerra wrote from San Antonio, Texas:

"In gratitude to our Lord, interceded by our Weeping Icon Mother of God, my son is in the U.S.A. We went to visit the Monastery on April 11, 1991, at about 2:00 p.m. The Mother of God did weep for us! A beautiful and amazing scene; she was showing us her love and care as we were in great need of love, understanding and healing.

"By Friday morning, April 12, 1991, my son called and said he was out of Kuwait City and safe in Saudi Arabia, and that he would be in the States in two weeks. On April 22, 1991, he called from North Carolina.

"The Weeping Icon Mother of God heard our prayers. I will keep on going to visit our friends at the Christ of the Hills Monastery."

HEALING OF A NEWBORN'S FOOT

Cathy Garcia, of Austin, Texas, writes:

"I am writing to let you know that the miraculous tear has healed the foot of my beautiful niece, Claudia Ibarra. Her foot was turned in at birth (April 25, 1989). I anointed her in June of 1990. She now has a straight foot! Hail, Holy Mary Mother of God!! Thank you for letting me share this experience."

PRAYERS FOR HEALING FROM CANCER

On December 30, 1990, Vicky Garza of San Antonio, wrote that she had received a letter from the Monastery with a tear from the Weeping Icon and had taken it to her sister who has cancer.

"I've been praying for her with the cotton, 'In the name of the Father and of the Son and of the Holy Spirit, and in the name of the Mother of God, heal me.' Father, when I prayed this with her the first time she said it felt beautiful. I was rubbing her back with the cotton and repeating the prayer. She said she didn't feel any pain at the moment, only something beautiful. The second and third time I've prayed for her with the cotton saying this prayer, she said she saw our Lady coming toward her with hands outstretched, telling her she going to get well. She cries and prays and laughs with happiness, because she can see our Blessed Mother in those moments. I feel what she's feeling and I know she really sees her. I'm no charismatic. I don't speak in tongues, Father, but I do pray. I shall pray more. I've a family of eight: two married, six still living at home, and my husband. Thank God, for the past week we've been getting the family together and praying. My husband and I always pray the rosary by ourselves or with a group of six couples. We get together and pray rosaries at houses where people want a rosary. I thank God we're saying the rosary together, because it is getting them (the family) away from TV and phone....

"This sister I have that has lung cancer is 53, her name is Carmen Guerrero. We've always been real close, not (just) because she's my sister, but (because) she's the most beautiful person in the world. No matter what it was, I could always talk to her. She would be the only one that could tell me I was wrong about something or other. Right now, she feels apprehensive. She's scared, she's nervous about her illness. I understand but I pray to God that she can accept this illness. I know she has a lot of faith. I have a lot of faith that God is going to heal her if it is His will.

"Father, I'm sending a small donation. Can you please send me cotton with tears from our Lady? I would like to take (them) to my older sister; her name is Lupe Hernandez. She suffered some strokes two years ago and is in a wheelchair, but she's doing real good. She even takes care of her granddaughter. I know it's because she prays a lot. That's where she gets her strength.

"Thank you, Father. Please pray for us and I'll be praying for you. God bless you."

REPENTANCE

On January 10, 1991, Hortencia Flores wrote:

"Happy New Year to all of you down at the Monastery. Wishing you all a good year. And many blessings. This is Mrs. Flores again. Sorry I haven't written to you all. A couple of months ago I wrote to you all about this boy.

"Well, thanks to your prayers offered (before) our Weeping Icon, this young man is having second thoughts about this mess. His mother, Olivia, is so grateful to our sweet, loving Mother (in her) Weeping Icon.... She wants you to keep praying for her son, Moses. She also has a son in the Marines in San Diego, California. His name is David. She wants you to ask our loving, caring Blessed Virgin to help keep her son from going into Saudi Arabia. Dear Nuns and Monks, may God's blessing be upon all of you. Pray for me and my husband, Abel. Also pray for Connie who is in the hospital. Mrs. Allen, Ester and also Nellie who are in the hospital. Please pray for their recovery, hoping in our Lord Christ and His wonderful Mother to keep answering our prayers. I keep all of you in my prayers too."

RECOVERY FROM A HEART ATTACK

On January 3, 1991, David Wong wrote from Davis, California:

"A month ago, my 27 year-old son suffered a severe heart attack, which in turn caused a minor stroke. For three days, he lay in the hospital under intensive care, and I really wasn't sure if he was going to live. One of the first things I did was to anoint him with the blessed tear you sent me and some water I had brought back from London many years ago. After three days, my son's recovery was so swift that he was discharged from the hospital. His doctor thinks that the heart attack was brought on by a virus attack and that he should recover 100% in the very near future. All tests now show that he is normal. The crisis has brought my whole family closer together and to God. May Jesus be praised forever and ever."

PEACE OF MIND AND RELIEF FROM ARTHRITIS

From Detroit Lakes, Minnesota, Peter and Martha Bauer wrote on December 15, 1990:

"In September of 1990, we were very fortunate, finding a pamphlet in our motel describing the Weeping Icon at Christ of the Hills Monastery. Upon arriving there I realized this would be a place where our Blessed Mother would choose to meet her people and heal them. Standing before the Weeping Icon, I cannot find words to say how I felt.

"My request was to receive peace of mind and for relief of my arthritic stiffness. I am unworthy to say, I have received answers to both of my requests. I do have peace of mind, and my stiffness has disappeared and has not returned. I never forget to thank the Mother of God for what she has done for me."

BLESSINGS ON FAMILY LIFE

Father Pangratios received the following letter dated January 14, 1990, from Margaret and Jerry Gerard:

"Thank you so much for the extra brochures and tears on the cotton. We visited you this fall and can't begin to tell you how blessed we were and are. My son is coming back to church, and marrying a pious girl. My husband and I have a new, more peaceful relationship as a result of Mary's intercession and tears, and somehow, more and more, Mary is working in our lives.

"We have 13 children between us (second marriage) and 33 grandchildren.

"God bless you for your wonderful works! We pray for you and send our love and blessings. We have a prayer ministry of 'Inner Healing' in our home on Thursday evenings. Would you pray for us at that time? Thank you again."

HEALING OF ARTHRITIS

Christine Schulze of Johnson City, Texas, wrote the following:

"In January 1990, I, my daughter and two grandsons visited the Monastery. We went on the tour of the church and then the Chapel with the Weeping Icon. The Icon was not weeping while we were here. We were disappointed, but were anointed and listened to the Monk in charge. After we left and arrived home I noticed I felt a great 'high and happiness' and also much energy. I told my daughter and husband who were both skeptical. I said that even my back (arthritis in hips) didn't hurt and I started bending up and down. I had a pinched nerve in my back and had to do back exercises each day so I could sleep without pain in my hip and knee. This pain ceased on this day and I no longer do exercises. However, the arthritis pain in my hips still comes and goes. Hopefully, on my next anointing, it will be gone forever also.

A CHANGING LIFE

January 17, 1991, O. S. wrote to tell the Monks and Nuns of a miraculous change in her son's life. He had told her some time ago that he was homosexual. She had been praying for him to the Mother of God and now she was seeing great changes in his way of life. In the same letter she begged prayers for several other very difficult family situations.

PEACE AND PHYSICAL HEALING

September 2, 1990, Onecinio and Lucinda Chavez wrote from Albuquerque, New Mexico:

"We just want you to know about the visit we made to your Monastery and our Mother, the Mother of God. The tear of our Blessed Mother helped us so much. We are so glad we made this trip. We are more peaceful. I wish I had a tear to bless my daughter, Angelina, when she comes home. She is in need of prayer now.

"I want you to know we feel better, we have been healed physically also. We thank you all for being so nice to us."

PEACE OF MIND

Cheryl Adkinson wrote on July 27, 1990, from Austin, Texas:

"I really enjoyed my visit to your church last weekend. It was a very beautiful experience. I feel very blessed, having received the gift of peace of mind, among many others.

"For a long time now I was having spiritual problems. I felt unprotected and open to negative influences. Now I feel a loving presence around me and I know I am protected.

"Thank you for sharing your precious gift with the public. I will carry the message to all my friends and family with the hopes that they will turn to the love of Christ and the Mother of God for comfort and healing."

PEACE OF MIND

On November 8, 1990, Olivia E. Leces wrote from Laredo, Texas, to tell Father Benedict that, "since my cousin took me to see the Mother of God I have had the most peace of mind I have ever had. Everything has been falling in order. I now have my grandson, Juan Mortin Leces Jr., living with me and getting ready to have my granddaughter live with me also. Grandchildren are a blessing to the grandparents. Please pray for financial matters. Enclosed is a little gift as the last time I sent you a little gift I received a bigger gift from the Mother of God."

HEALING OF LOWER BACK PAIN

Paula Brown from Lake St. Louis, Missouri, wrote on October 15,1990:

"I would like to report to you an instant healing I received after being anointed and prayed upon with the cotton that had absorbed the tears from the Myrrh-Weeping Icon.

"July 6, 1990,.... I was experiencing unexplained pains in my lower back earlier that week, which would shoot through my hip joint and at the base of my spine where my tail bone is. If I would have to bend slightly it would hurt. I had never had lower back trouble like this before. It left me walking like a cripple—very slowly and limping. I was walking this way,...carrying my little toddler, who was a little fussy, back to our car to go home. My niece Cara called after me, 'Aunt Paula, come quick and see Mary's tears!'... A woman was anointing people with a cotton ball of the Myrrh-Weeping Icon and telling everyone about her trip to see the Icon. I asked her if she would anoint me too, and when she did she prayed 'In the name of the Father, Son and Holy Spirit, through the intercession of the Mother of God, be healed.' I remember praying to myself, 'Dear God, I know You can do anything. I believe I could be healed of this back problem if it is Your will.' I didn't feel anything out of the ordinary as I prayed, but when I went back to the car I realized I was walking easier. Then when I bent to put my daughter in her car seat I experienced no shooting pain. When I got home I showed my husband how I could bend over with ease. There was no trace of the discomfort I had felt earlier that night.

"I credit our Lady with this healing because it was so obviously instant. I was feeling so bad that week I was ready to go to a doctor to find out what could be causing it. It lasted four to five days, and then healed by itself after I had been anointed and prayed over. I've heard of things healing slowly after rest and taking it easy, but this happened instantly following the anointing and prayer.

"My mother, sister, husband and children were witnesses to my back problem and they call it a miraculous healing. (My husband is usually a skeptic, but because of the instant recovery, even he believes it was our Lady.)

"I hope this may help to spread the message of our weeping Mother! This is not the first time our Lady has interceded in my life. She truly loves us all.

"P.S. Could I have a cotton ball sent to me, as I know someone with cancer."

RELIEF OF DEPRESSION

Sophia Rutledge, of Carrollton, Texas, wrote:

"The same day I received your letter with the tear of the Myrrh-Weeping Icon I felt a warmth throughout my entire body. Since then my anxieties and post-partum depression have almost all disappeared. Thank God and His Blessed Mother!"

GOOD RECOVERY FROM AN OPERATION

On July 27, 1990, Eva O. Martinez wrote (giving thanks) for the prayers that were answered on her behalf in her husband's recent operation. She writes that her husband "has had a clean slate of health in all his subsequent treatments and examinations.

"All my prayers have been fruitful and my husband has had a clean slate of health in all his subsequent treatments and examinations. Again, thank God that through you I have been heard."

HEALING OF HEART DISEASE

On August 23, 1990, Joseph Meineke wrote from Milford, Ohio:

"You will be happy to learn of a recent miracle that took place through the intercession of the Mother of God via a tear that was brought back from a visit to your Monastery. This woman has had heart trouble and has been taking medicine for the last fifteen years of her life—she is now the "owner" of a perfectly healthy heart. Praise God!! She is no longer in need of any medicine.

"I am a member of a Catholic book publishing company.... I was the one who visited your Monastery and returned with the tear—not that I had anything to do with the healing, just so that you know. After having told my fellow employees about my visit, they were anxious to learn if it were possible for them to receive a tear from the Mother of God—hence my request, as I speak on behalf of them. Would you please, if possible, send each of us a tear? Our total number is ten. I realize that this is a large number of tears but I am absolutely sure that each and every one of them will be used, respected and cherished in a very special way."

TWO HEALINGS

From Miami, Florida, Eva Ballesteros wrote in July of 1990:

"To the people of the Christ of the Hills Monastery. I want to thank you for the tears you sent me. We sent the tears to Peru. It had been already passed to the girl in Peru and to a man that was in very bad condition in the hospital a problem with the kidneys.... Thanks to all the prayers, the man is feeling better and is recovering, now he is in his home; thanks to the Virgin. About the girl, we don't know yet of any changes but we know she is feeling fine."

RECOVERY FROM SURGERY

Mrs. Ann Slevko wrote from East Chicago, Indiana, on July 12, 1990:

"My husband had severe surgery to his left leg and large toe. I blessed him with the wet cotton and I'm sure a miracle was done. Three weeks ago I thought I would lose him—today he is doing fine slowly (but good) and I know the Blessed Mother of God helped him and myself. Please continue to pray for both of us as we are retirees and ailing. Without God's help—nothing can be done, and I love my Faith."

HEALING OF EPILEPSY

Carlos M. Ruiz of Kansas City, Kansas, wrote on November 10, 1990:

"Today as I sit here writing this letter all my thoughts are in our recent trip to Blanco, to see our Mother.

"My girlfriend, her mother and I made the trip from Kansas City because we all have been going through rough times in our lives, and yes the hardest may be yet to come, but I now know, that our Mother will always be there to guide us.

"I know that she has shown herself to us, by curing my girlfriend (Beatrice Arle) of her epilepsy. And by healing my cuts, on my first visit to Blanco.

"As we were making the trip we knew that changes had to be made in our lives. And we must not be afraid to accept our Mother into our hearts. If we had remained the same as we were, we would fail to grow closer to our Mother and God, but if we grow, pray and live our lives as Jesus, we will have a love that is known by very few."

BREAKING THE SMOKING HABIT

November 28, 1990, Maria Theresa Reyna wrote from Corpus Christi, Texas:

"I am writing to let you know of the miracles of our Mother for the people that I have brought here. I don't know if you remember me, I'm the lady that brought a blue bus full of people in March of this year. Any way my name is Maria Teresa Reyna and I have been trying to get people back to the Lord. So when I heard about the Mother weeping there in Blanco, I rented a bus and got 33 persons over there. Then in June I got another bus full of people. In the first bus there were two miracles. The first one was a man that had smoked for 40 years. He was 14 years-old when he started smoking. He came and asked our Mother here to cure him of this. By the time we got back on the bus to return home that same day our Mother had cured him of smoking. Today is November 28, 1990, and since March 18, 1990, he still doesn't smoke.

"Another one is about a lady that has kidney disorder, she has to go to a machine every other day. Well, she has improved a little bit. And she wants to come again."

CHANGED LIVES

On November 27, 1990, H. C. wrote:

"I'll start from the beginning. On October 26, 1990 we visited the Monastery especially (to see) the (Icon of the Virgin). We were three couples and my granddaughter. I was touched by the presence of the sad and weeping Icon: I came home and since then I have been calling on the Icon (of the) Virgin.

I wrote you about my daughter, G. A., (who is) living with J. G. She is a beautiful daughter and a very good teacher. She has two daughters and they and J. were living together for a year. He is a wonderful, caring man. He loved G. and her girls. But me and my husband didn't approve of the way she was living. So I asked a petition of the Virgin, that through the help of our Lord Jesus Christ my daughter and (the man) would get married. So again I wrote to you for your prayer and asked again the Virgin what I wanted—for my daughter to get married.

On Saturday, November 17, 1990, my daughter and her boyfriend surprised me and my husband, (by saying) that they were getting married on Saturday, November 24, 1990. I started crying for happiness. I went to my room and (prayed) to God and to the Virgin that my prayer and yours were answered, and I had said a second petition that week. My daughter said, 'Mother, I couldn't believe it when he said we were getting married....' (My daughter) said, '(there were) days I couldn't sleep because he had never talked about when we would get married.' So I give thanks to God and the Blessed Virgin. I told her how you and the Monks and Nuns have been praying that (they) would get married. Thanks to God and the Weeping Icon, (they) had a beautiful wedding with her two daughters and his little (son). They were their witnesses for them.

"On my next letter I will send a picture of my son-in-law and my daughter. They are so happy now. (The husband) tells me that he doesn't know how he (got the idea) to get married...something came over him, all of a sudden, to get married right away. O Thanks for your prayers. I also will pray for you. My husband and I are so happy.

"I would like for you to pray for two boys that are in jail. People sometimes also come to me for prayer. I tell them what to pray and have faith in God and the Blessed Virgin. So this lady came in yesterday to pray for her nephews that were innocent of the crime they had been accused of. So please present this case to the Weeping Icon.

"My love to all of you. May God bless you, the Monks and the Nuns, for a beautiful way of serving God and the Icon (of the) Blessed Virgin."

EPILEPSY HEALED

Ms. Mary Andrede wrote from Corpus Christi, Texas, on July 28, 1990.

"Just writing to let you know my prayers have been answered.... On February 2nd, you anointed my daughter, Blanche. My daughter had epilepsy. The last time she got sick was February 2nd. This has been the longest time she hasn't been ill. She use to get it two to three times daily. Again, thank you. I'm waiting for the next opportunity to go there again. Please keep us in your prayers."

RECOVERY FROM APPARENT HEART ATTACK

On September 6, 1990, Mabel Manninghoff wrote:

"I took tears of Mary and anointed the sick Marion Vitatoe, who lives at Milford, Ohio. I anointed her with tears. A month ago they rushed her to hospital. They thought she had a heart attack. So her doctor told a heart surgeon to take over, that it most likely was clogged arteries. So he had tests done and said, 'Nothing is wrong with your heart...you have arteries like a young person. So I want you to stop taking heart medicine and you don't need me.' She said, 'Why, that's like a miracle.' He said, 'You can say that.' Marion told me that she thought it was healing from Mary's tears and also our Priest's prayers and anointing with oil. Marion is on oxygen and has bad lungs. I felt like Marion really believed and was healed, so pray for her healing of lungs."

HEALING OF INJURED FOOT

Luisa Vela wrote on July 12, 1990, from Weslaco, Texas:

"This is a little note to thank our Blessed Mother for healing my sister, Pat. Pat came over from Dallas to visit me. She told me she had stuck a needle in her foot and it was hurting very bad. It had been two weeks and the pain was getting worse. I told her about the cotton that smells like myrrh and that they were the tears from the Weeping Icon of the Blessed Mother. I told her about Rudy, my son, and the change in his life. I told her to smell the cotton and I prayed with her and anointed her in the area that was hurting with the tears. This we did at night. The next morning, when she woke up she told me, 'The Blessed Mother healed me. I don't have any more pain and I can walk right.'"

PREVENTION OF A FALL

In October, 1990, Ruth Greene of Arvoda, Colorado, wrote:

"I've good news to report concerning one of your tears. Two weeks ago Monday, while getting off a Senior Van I took one step, felt a little dizzy and sat down hard on the floor. The driver was reaching to take hold of my hand. I carry a bag with sewing or crocheting material, and this time I had a jacket and my cane. He helped me up and inside and called a lady to help me to my apartment.

"I was paining. I called a daughter-in-law and she came and took me to my doctor where I was X-rayed four times. No broken bones and no bruises, all internal. My left foot also pained on the side, so that was X-rayed also. I've much rheumatoid arthritis all through my body.

"Doctor prescribed pain pills and to take it easy and if it was still paining in two weeks to come back. At times it is worse than others, right now as I sit writing at 4:25 a.m. There is no pain, only a soreness.

"This past Sunday (I had the tear with me) and as I was cleaning my kitchen floor I felt a little faint and felt myself falling but I was caught in mid-air on the knob of the cupboard beneath the sink, there's a small tear in my slacks. I scraped my elbow in two places and got a nasty bruise behind my left knee but thanks to the Blessed Mother's tear my fall was broken. (It's hard telling what would have happened if I'd sat down hard the second time in two weeks. I got unhooked and scooted across my small kitchen to the rug and crept on my hands and knees to the door, reached up to door knob and pulled myself up to standing position and I stood and praised the Lord and His Blessed Mother."

RESTORATION OF EYESIGHT

On July 16, 1990, Dorothy Harris of Lake Charles, Louisiana, wrote:

"This is to let you know that Mary Katherine Preis of Orange, Texas, had her eyesight mostly restored when she was anointed with a tear of our Holy Mother which was brought from your Monastery and given to me. My friend, Mary Katherine, only needs eye glasses for close reading—agate sized type used in newspaper classified advertising. She has a pulmonary disorder and has been bed-ridden and on oxygen for some time now. I had hoped our Lady would ask our Lord to heal her lungs. She is so pleased with her miracle and I am too. She wants to pack up her oxygen and come see you all. However, many blood clots went into her lungs and she was in a critical state about three weeks ago. She loves our Lady dearly. She is home and is healing now. I apologize for having lost your letter and being unable to address you by name. I hope one day we can pay a visit to your Shrine there."

RESCUE FROM DANGER AND HEALING OF ASTHMA

Father Pangratios received the following letter on December 2, 1990, from Julian and Vidala V. Treviño of Victoria, Texas:

"Dear Father Pangratios,

"I am so excited and wish to share my miracles with you, which have occurred since my visit to view the Weeping Icon of the Blessed Virgin Mary on November 24, 1990. I have been speaking of it to all and any one who will listen!

"When we entered the Chapel, my nose was assailed with the smell of fresh roses. I worried that I would be unable to stay because I have inhalant allergies and I have suffered for many years. As I stood near the Icon I saw the many fresh roses surround the altar upon which the Weeping Icon rests. My nose itched and my eyes watered. My husband too saw and smelled the roses.

"You spoke of the Icon and allowed us a moment of prayer. While praying I was still distracted by the fresh roses. You said we would smell the scent of myrrh when we got near the Icon. You opened the case and my face was showered with an intense wave of heat and the smell of the myrrh overpowered the aroma of the fresh roses! You may recall me now; I was sobbing profusely! I could not stop. I could not control it!

"On our way home, we stopped in San Antonio for dinner. It was dark when we started back home. My husband and I talked of the Icon and of the Monks and Nuns of the Monastery. I must have dozed off. My husband was praying to the Mother of God. I was dreaming of the Monastery and suddenly I saw your face, Father, and you said "open your eyes!" I did so immediately to find my husband asleep at the wheel and on the wrong side of the highway! I gently spoke to him and told him he was on the wrong side of the road. He woke suddenly and swerved towards the right side of the road. He said he was just looking down! There came, upon that instant that he swerved the car, another vehicle at great speed! We were safely on our side of the road by then. I drove safely home and my husband snored all the way!

"I have suffered with asthma for many years. I have been receiving treatment with pills and sprays. Since my return home after the November 24, 1990 visit, I have attempted to use my spray medication only once. I thought I should use it as the physician prescribed it several years ago. I was surprised to find myself choking and gasping for air when I used it! I have not used it since; I do not need to, since I have not had an asthma attack since!

"I returned to Christ of the Hills Monastery with my sister and nieces on December 1, 1990. You can well imagine my surprise to find the same roses surrounding the altar of the Weeping Icon only to see that they are artificial! And no sweet odor of fresh roses! When anointed with the Virgin Mary's tears, I was at great peace and felt very blessed by my Holy Mother.

"My husband and I have been very blessed since we started praying to the Mother of God together daily for several months now. We encouraged our family to join together once a week at each other's home respectively to pray to the Mother of God. Everyone has received a blessing since that time.

"...We pray for the strength to continue with our daily life and we dedicate ourselves and all our work for the glory of God.

"My husband and I shall continue to visit the Monastery with our nieces, nephews and brothers and sisters. We support you and Christ of the Hills Monastery in all your endeavors."

HEALING FROM CANCER

On May 3, 1994, Edward and Rose Micara wrote from Ossining, New York:

"In October 1990, we visited Texas to see a Navy buddy of my husband's. We learned at that time that he had cancer and his time was limited. My husband was inconsolable. In the lobby of our hotel, I found your pamphlet 'Shrine of the Blessed Virgin Mary.' I said to my Husband, "Let's go for George." When we arrived it was so peaceful and quiet and the Monks were wonderful to us. One Monk took us on a tour and then to see the Virgin.

"When we reached the Weeping Icon, I couldn't believe the overwhelming feelings I had in such a tiny Chapel. I felt as though I was a very small child and my mother had just wrapped her arms around me and poured forth all the love and protection a mother could possibly bestow on one little child. I felt that she had given it all to me. 'O, dear Mother of God, save some for everyone else,' I thought. Then as the Monk anointed us with the tears of the Icon, I wept and felt so very loved and (that) everything would indeed be fine.

"Before we left, the Monk gave us some tears of the Icon to take to our friend George. His wife anointed him and he went for his operation. Afterwards he was pronounced cancer free and doing very, very well today.

"We recently phoned the Monastery to ask for tears of the Icon for my uncle (Joseph DeAngelis) who is very sick also with cancer. They received the tears and my aunt anointed my uncle. She says he feels stronger and he even looks better.

"May God always bless the Monks of Christ of the Hills Monastery and through her tears may the Blessed Virgin always love and protect them! Please remember you are all in our prayers."

HEALING OF A BABY'S EAR

Anne S. Connell of Birmingham, Alabama, wrote on October 2, 1994:

"My grandson was told that even with medication, it was doubtful that surgery and a possible hearing loss could be avoided. We blessed him each day he was on the medication. In fact he wanted to anoint himself at age 3 and a half. At the end of the medicine he was checked and of course didn't need surgery. You and I know it was the tears of the Mother of God that healed him.

"I myself have financial needs. Please pray that we may find solutions."

HEALING OF ASTHMA AND IMMUNE DISORDER

Martha Klein wrote from Dallas, Texas, on August 9, 1994:

"I first visited the Monastery a little over a year ago. I went home with a cotton ball soaked with the tears of the Icon of the Holy Mother. Having it in my possession was rather distressing. My Priest suggested the next time my son Christopher was acutely ill, I anoint him with the tear.

"Christopher has been hospitalized many times. I stopped counting at 35 when he was three. His medical diagnoses include severe asthma, a primary immune deficiency and an unspecified bowel motility disorder. Christopher's asthma and immune deficiency were reasonably well controlled with a very intense and rigid medical regime. The bowel motility was a severe problem. Periodically his bowel simply shut down, resulting in an apparent obstruction—and hospitalization.

"This happened again (on) September 30, 1993. This time I anointed him with the tears and continued to do so each day until the cotton ball had dried up the second week of November. On October 2, Christopher had started taking a new medication that had just become available in the United States. We had been waiting several years for it. The improvement in Christopher's condition was dramatic. However, the third week of November he started to decline again. We increased his medication with little improvement.

"On the Sunday after Thanksgiving my parish Priest gave me two more of the cotton balls. I began anointing Christopher again. Again the improvement was dramatic. Only this time I knew it was not the medication, but rather the blessing of the Holy Lady. I have continued to anoint him daily. We made another Pilgrimage to the Monastery on December 28, 1993—with Christopher. Today he is free of medication and healthier than I every though he would be."

RELIEF OF PARKINSON'S SYMPTOMS

Markella Alotzas wrote from Baltimore, Maryland, on September 9, 1994, that her husband has Parkinson's Disease. He has especial difficulty with his bowels, and it gives him much pain. Through prayer, blessing with Holy Oil and the intercession of St. John (Maximovitch) he has been able to get relief. She asks prayers for her family, especially her grandson who is young and has just been diagnosed diabetic.

RESTORATION OF A BROKEN MARRIAGE

On September 12, 1994, Larry D. Brown of Carrollton, Texas, wrote:

"I visited your Monastery with a friend on August 27.

"About six months ago my wife of ten years left me and moved to Iowa with our children. During this time I have had almost no communication with her or our children. I couldn't understand why she had left or why she wouldn't talk.

"Shortly after she left I went to church to pray by myself. I also visit the church regularly and light a candle for my wife and children and then pray under a statue of the Virgin Mary holding the baby Jesus.

"When Vera told me about a friend of hers who had seen the Icon I knew we had to go. I told her I felt it was very important that I see this prior to a divorce hearing which was scheduled to decide temporary custody of our children. My wife had told me that she would not even try to reconcile, calling it a 'permanently dead issue.' I felt my wife had led a very troubled life and that since she left I knew I understood her better than ever before. I had begun to see ways my own behavior was contributing to this. I wanted very badly to have a chance to make her understand this, and be given a chance to make it up to her. I somehow knew that seeing this miracle would help.

"I don't know how to describe the feeling I had upon seeing the Icon. I'm not even sure I felt anything. I do know that afterwards I felt much better about myself and was more confident that everything was going to work out for the better. It was a tremendous experience and I plan on making a return trip someday. (Maybe even with my wife and kids.)

"The day before the court hearing I picked up Vera at the airport after she had visited her boyfriend. We went to a restaurant for a coke and we were sitting outside talking about the hearing and our trip to Blanco. We both have things going on in our lives that we have been doing a lot of praying about. We were both hoping for a miracle to help us out. Vera has been a tremendous friend to both my wife and me during our separation, and during our talk she proved it again. She started praying and asked God that if she was to receive a miracle, to give it to me. I think the only thing in my life that has touched me more than that prayer was the birth of my children. The next day I received that miracle.

"At the temporary hearing my wife offered to talk to me alone to discuss things. We ended up talking the whole day and she finally agreed to try marital counseling. I have no other explanation for her turning-around other than that God was in the room with us, guiding our actions. I know that if we can make the counseling work it will be better for the children and us. I have been praying that God would find a way to put our family back together and now He has given us that opportunity. I truly have received a miracle.

"I don't know how things will work out from here, but I know that God is looking out for all of us and He will do what is best for my family.

"God bless all of you!"

HEALING FROM A LIFE-THREATENING BACTERIAL INFECTION

Father Pangratios received the following on September 23, 1993, from Bishop Chrysostomos:

"May the Lord bless you.

"I am much indebted to the prayers of your Brotherhood before the miraculous Icon of the Mother of God.

"Just before the midnight Liturgy which we celebrated at our Monastery in honor of the Theotokos several days ago, I passed out momentarily near my cell. A severe diabetic, I attributed this to an insulin reaction and immediately ingested glucose.

"Following the Liturgy, I went to bed and began, during the night, to feel seriously ill. All of my bodily systems had shut down, a condition which can easily and quickly lead to renal failure in a diabetic. My blood sugar readings were four times the normal reading, having reached a very dangerous level. I experienced, indeed, a curious phenomenon, similar to phenomena described in near-death experiences, though at no time did I feel as though I were 'outside' my body. This feeling of being near death clearly demonstrates the ferocity of the bacterial infection that had invaded my body.

"I resisted efforts to hospitalize me and began taking antibiotic drugs for the treatment of my infection. So severe were my nausea and malaise, that I phoned my spiritual Father, Metropolitan Cyprian, a number of my spiritual children, and the Christ of the Hills Monastery for prayers. Father Benedict agreed to light a candle in front of the Weeping Icon of the Mother of God. And indeed, shortly after he made this promise, I began to improve. By the next morning, I was able to sit up comfortably and urine samples showed a decrease in leukocytes (a sign that the massive infection was waning) and blood sugar levels. I am not, at this writing, fully recovered, but I have no doubt that the prayers of my Spiritual Father and others and the intercessions of the Mother of God, through your Icon, helped me avoid what was very close to being a life-threatening condition.

"I cannot say that my beliefs are evidence of a miracle, but I can attest to the fact that my recovery has been abnormally rapid and that it has corresponded to the prayers offered for me, including those before the Weeping Icon of the Theotokos at your Monastery."

ICON PRINT REPORTED WEEPING

Colleen Smith wrote from Raleigh, North Carolina, to Fr. Pangratios to report that a small print she had had of the Weeping Icon since 1988 or 1989 showed signs of having wept. She did not know when it had begun, but she writes that the Icon "shows heavily developed tear lines from both eyes…down to the bottom of the print. The tear lines from the right eye are somewhat heavier than the left eye."

LEUKEMIA IN REMISSION

James Dowell Deviller wrote from Lafayette, California, on February 2, 1990, that he "was sick with leukemia and given a 10% (chance of) remission." *He was anointed with the tears from the Weeping Icon and since then he has never been sick and is in complete remission. He has* "never needed blood and was never despondent and in a good frame of mind. April 12, one year of remission, no bone marrow (is needed) for another 6 months. No blood (has been) needed since last April." *He visits the doctor only every three weeks. Chemo is given at home by his wife. He and his wife are very encouraged and are still praying every day for the blessings that God has been so gracious to give them.*

HEALING OF FOOT

Ima Ramirez of Beeville, wrote on November 22, 1991, that she had had some disease in her foot for eighteen months and had seen more than eleven doctors and surgeons. They had been unable to find what was wrong. Then she had visited her sister in Houston. Her sister told her that she had a cotton ball with tears from the Weeping Icon, and she wanted to bless Ima's foot with it. Ima refused because she feared infecting it worse. Her sister blessed her any-

way. The next day Ima's brother asked how her foot was. She took her removable cast off to check, and the foot was healed.

HEALING OF EYES

On June 18, 1992, Father George Collina wrote the following:

"Father Raymond Ball has asked me to write this letter. I have been having problems with my eyesight for about two months due to a congenital problem, which had previously been under control. My doctor was having difficulty in fitting me with special lenses to correct the problem. After several failed pairs of contact lenses had been made, Fr. Raymond Ball brought me a cotton ball dipped in the tears of the Blessed Mother from your Monastery. I prayed for healing and anointed my eyelids with the oil. On two successive visits to the doctor, the problem had disappeared. No new corrective lenses were needed. I told the story to my doctor who agreed that God works in mysterious ways."

HEALING OF SEVERE RASH

Oralia Velez of Friendswood, Texas, wrote to Fr. Gregory on June 6, 1994:

"It is with extreme happiness that I write the following letter to you. I visited the Monastery last Friday with my husband and my son. You were our guide. We were very impressed at the kindness you showed and appreciated how you blessed us and prayed for us. You blessed my son who had a severe rash. By the following day, we had already seen a big improvement in his condition. It has now been three days since our visit and his condition continues to improve.

"After we left the Monastery, we went to San Antonio to visit my brother and no sooner had we entered the house when he told us he wanted to go to confession and to start all over again! This is the biggest miracle I could ever expect. Thank you and the Blessed Mother for your prayers and most of all I thank the Lord for everything going on in our lives."

WALKING RESTORED

Anita Dunson of Vallejo, California, wrote on June 11 of 1994, that her disabled father, who had been unable to walk for four years, was now walking. This was the answer to her prayers before the miracle working Icon.

HEALING OF MARRIAGE AND FROM SEVERE DEPRESSION

From Morrison, Colorado, C. G. wrote on March 4, 1991:

"I am writing to share with you (the) experience I had with the tear from the Mother of God Icon. My family and I visited the Icon on January 10th and 11th of this year. The whole circumstance of how we got there and our experience of being there was extraordinary in itself. We came to be healed as a family and more importantly to have our marriage healed after eight and a half years of abuse, bad times, unemployment and alcoholism. We also had found out in the last few months that my husband has many mental maladies and nonfunctions that directly contributed to our misguided lives. The prognosis for a 'cure' was zero—we could only hope that he would eventually become a self-sufficient adult instead of being completely dependent on me. With the past, present and future holding so much pain and suffering for me, I decided a divorce was the best decision to make, even though I strongly believe in marriage and my vows.

"I received an immense amount of peace and strength from visiting the Icon. The presence of the Blessed Virgin Mary while I was standing there was so strong, that I was able to feel her place her hands on top of my head. Since that time, I have developed a devotion for her that I never had before. For the first time in my life I have direction and am guided daily by God through the intercession of the Mother of God and the Saints. My spirituality and reverence has blossomed and rewarded me with a happiness and joy I never thought possible. It has been eight weeks now. In that amount of time I've done more healing, processing and growing than I have in the four and a half years I've been in therapy. In fact, I will be terminating my treatment (as) soon as God has promised me that I will never have to experience another depression again. I have managed through eight weeks, always knowing I'm being very well taken care of and the strength I was granted at the Monastery will always stay with me to get me through the toughest of life's blows. My life has truly been transformed as I no longer have a fear to live.

"After being back for two weeks, we were all very discouraged that my husband hadn't experienced any blessing or healing like the three of us had. I became very angry and scared that I would have to proceed with the divorce. On the second Sunday after we came back, I blessed my husband on the forehead with the tear. His deep depression was miraculously lifted that day and he was also able to discontinue his antidepressant medication on that same day! What we thought was a 'miracle day' has turned into six weeks of him healing and becoming a walking miracle. The three doctors that are regularly treating him cannot believe his improvement as they didn't see him reaching this point for a long time. Week to week, he continually amazes myself and our children. This was a 35 year old man who was totally shut down emotionally with the mentality and capabilities of a 13 year old just two months ago! I had even checked into the possibility of having him institutionalized. He is now an active, loving member of our family and learns every day new ways to take care of us (physically, emotionally, financially, mentally) instead of him being totally cared for. My children have a Daddy now and I no longer am a single parent. My marriage began on that day and looks like it will grow into something very special and great.

"Our joy in sharing this experience with others is beyond words. At my low points, I continue to be blessed by the presence of the Mother of God, similar to my experience in front of the Weeping Icon.

"P. S. Both of my children received profound healing also, and that is very beautiful to experience each day as their mother."

PROTECTION AND CURE OF CANCER

From Midland, Texas, Mrs. John Frazar wrote on July 23, 1994:

"Recently, after having a mammogram, I was told that I had a dark spot on my right breast. To say that I was upset is an understatement! Fortunately, I had a tear of the Mother of God from the Weeping Icon at Christ of the Hills Monastery. I anointed myself and asked for the Holy Mother's intercession in my healing. The doctor called two weeks later and said that it was just overlapping tissue and nothing to worry about.

"Before this miracle, my sister had sent another little box with our Blessed Mother's tear. We gave it to a young man whose wife was diagnosed with cancer on her spine and it was inoperable. They went back to the doctor (after she was anointed) and her cancer is in remission!"

HEALING OF CANCER ON THE TONGUE

Ann Jeanette Miner of Merritt Island, Florida, wrote on August 8, 1994, that she and her family believe that the anointing with the tear of the Weeping Icon is "responsible for healing my brother's cancer of the tongue."

MANY HEALINGS FROM MOUNT ATHOS MONASTERY

The following letter was received from Hilandar Monastery on Mount Athos, Greece, dated September 14, 1994:

"We received your generous gift of Holy tears and have used your gift to help cure and heal many of our worshippers.

"If you have occasion to enrich our Monastery with more Holy tears your gift would be welcome. We gave one of the tears to a Priest near Belgrade who soaked a tear in Holy Water and gave it to many parishioners who were sick and dying. One of the parishioners who was suffering of cancer was cured. Her husband has come to Hilandar to help with our work.

"Your blessing, your thoughtfulness and your generosity will always be appreciated and remembered."

DEAFNESS CURED

Sergio Yakovlev Agraz gave the following testimony on January 1, 1992:

"Gabriela Yakovlev from Mexico City was cured six months ago by the tear of the Weeping Icon Virgin Mary. She was about to be deaf. She is 13, and is now being told by the doctors she is in perfect condition."

HEALING FROM SEVERE HEADACHES AND NECK INJURY

A letter signed Br. David Talaghinkoff and dated August 10, 1991, from Austin, Texas, says:

"Over two years ago I was involved in an accident which resulted in a 'permanent' lower neck injury. Medical doctors, chiropractors, massage therapists—all told me that the supporting muscles at the base of my neck were injured and spasmed beyond their help, and that all I could do was take painkillers and receive therapy to control the blinding headaches which would rob me of sight and hearing periodically.

"I did follow their advice. I also prayed, fasted and did penance so that my mind and spirit would be strong enough to bear the pain. Soon, though, I was at my wit's end and was only able to function 'half drugged out,' for to even stand would cause almost unbearable nausea, pain and tinnitis.

"The Blessed St. Sergius of Radonezh appeared to me in a dream visitation saying to seek out the Holy Icon—praise unto God—and I would be whole. It wasn't until yesterday, August 9, 1992, that I was able to come to New Sarov. The pain was bearable enough without medication. When being anointed with the Holy tears, a great warmth was felt in my hands, spine, and neck. My pain was gone! The muscles had relaxed, and I was at long last without the constant companions of nausea, tinnitis, and headache. Last evening I could sleep the sleep of peace and comfort.

"All glory, honor and praise be unto our Holy Mother Theotokos!"

HEALINGS OF ANEMIA AND CANCER

Fr. Deacon William Weir of St. Sava Serbian Orthodox Church in Jackson, California, writes:

"On April 2, 1993, the Friday of the Fifth week of Lent, Brother John (of Christ of the Hills Monastery) was tonsured Fr. Jeremiah. (On that day) I visited the Shrine of the Blessed Theotokos at Christ of the Hills Monastery. At the time of my leaving I was given a number of envelopes containing cotton with oil from the Weeping Icon. I took these back to California and distributed them to members of our parish who were ill or otherwise in need. I kept one at home. My wife became afflicted with a condition of significantly reduced iron in the blood. I anointed her at home and her condition gradually improved. The cotton was quite dry and was returned to the reliquary which was given to me by Mother Seraphima and placed on a table where we keep Icons.

"Several months later a friend of mine, Kenneth Klein, was in the hospital for a routine removal of a cyst from behind his left knee. On the day he was supposed to leave the hospital he was told by the doctors who performed the surgery that it was a malignant tumor, that he had chondor sarcoma which had entered the marrow of his bones. At minimum, his left leg would have to be amputated at the hip such that he would probably not be able to be fitted with a prosthetic device. He was scheduled for a bone scan to see how far in his system the cancer had spread through his bone marrow. That Monday evening, my wife and I decided to go visit him and to read prayers for him. As we were leaving the house we both simultaneously thought of taking the reliquary with the dry cotton and anointing him with it. I opened the reliquary and was surprised at the strength of the aroma. I assumed that it was probably attributable to the fact that the reliquary was substantially airtight. We went to the hospital and spent some time chatting with our friend, his wife and other friends. When all but his wife had left, I told him about the Weeping Icon and that it had healed others. I asked if he would mind if I read some prayers and anointed him with the Holy Oil. I read several prayers from the Book of Needs for those who are sick or facing serious surgery. As I took the cotton from the reliquary I noticed two things, first the strong fragrance was still present and it was extremely wet with oil. It was so wet that it left large streaks of oil on my friend's head where he was anointed in the Orthodox way and above and below the area of affliction on his leg. My wife noticed the fragrance, the density and quantity of oil and an obvious change in our friend's breathing.

"The next day he went for the bone scan. It was negative, meaning that there was no spread beyond his left leg and that did not show up. The morning after that he had a blood scan which came back negative for the presence of cancer active in the body. Later that same afternoon he received the results of a second biopsy from Mayo Clinic which showed that the tumors had been removed and the pieces from the other tumors removed for testing were not malignant. This contradicted the earlier tests and visual observations of the physicians. Our friend had held the reliquary in his hand or on his person from the time we gave it to him. All of us with first hand observations of this event have no logical explanation for this dramatic turn-around other than it was a miracle wrought by the intercession of the Theotokos."

HEALING OF FACIAL PARALYSIS

Hieromonk John translated from Spanish the following statement given by Mrs. Martha Duran of Austin, Texas, dated October 28, 1993:

"The right side of her face was paralyzed and unable to move. The doctor said it was a paralyzed nerve and would take about a month to heal. She was given some medicine to take for a week. The day after finishing the medicine there was still no change. She came to the Shrine and was anointed. The next day she noticed movement on the right side of her face and a couple of days later her face was completely back to normal."

HEALING OF BURN

Mary Maiorka of Lockhart, Texas, wrote on October 7, 1991, wrote that Crystal Lynn Maiorka, who is now 3, had been burned on her right leg in August of 1989. It was a second- and third-degree burns, for which she'd had therapy for over three months. The week after she was to go to a specialist to have her leg examined, the doctor wanted to see where they were going to take skin from to cover the scars that would not heal. Mary brought her to the Mother of God at Christ of the Hills Monastery to have her blessed. On the third day after the blessing her leg was healed. She never had to go back to see the specialist. Mary writes that the Icon was weeping at the time of her visit, and that she will never forget this miracle of God.

HEALING OF THROAT CANCER

San Juanita Guerra (Kina) of San Antonio writes:

"Felix, my husband of 34 years is a heavy smoker. About October 1990, Felix developed a severe cold and terrible cough. He went to the doctor and was under medication for two weeks. He went to the doctor (again), as he was worse. Felix was under medication for two more weeks, and was told he should get better.

"At the end of this time no change had happened, so he was sent to an ENT specialist, Dr. Tally. Dr. Tally immediately started laser treatments and at this time a tumor was removed from his voice box and an irritation was discovered on his left vocal cord. Felix had two more laser treatments at two week intervals. By this time cancer was discovered. Felix's voice was hoarse by now, and Dr. Tally suggested radiation treatments to stop the cancer from spreading to the lymph nodes, from which they could spread through the body. Felix refused the radiation.

"I prayed to our Lord and to our Weeping Icon Mother of God to intercede so Felix could accept radiation treatments.

"Felix started going to the Medical Cancer Center for his radiation treatments. At the third treatment his voice was gone completely. By now he was mean, frustrated, rebellious and mad at everybody and especially me. I prayed for his acceptance of his illness and for him to regain his voice and for the cancer to be removed. At his thirty-seventh treatment, Dr. Voight said his throat was clear and assured Felix that he would regain his voice in time.

"In May 1991, our oldest son, Felix Jr., came home safe from Saudi Arabia and on the 24th he and his family came to see us here in San Antonio. Felix started talking clearly on May 27th !

"On May 30th we went to visit our dear friends the Monks at Christ of the Hills. Felix and I wanted to share our miracle with our friends the Fathers and the Nuns. It is a joy to go to this sacred place. I feel calm, joyful and happy when I am at this quiet, serene place. I will visit as often as I can. I'll keep on passing out literature about the Weeping Icon.

"Fathers, keep on with your great way of welcoming us Pilgrims. We go there to find peace of mind and to calm our anxieties."

END OF SEIZURES IN INFANT

Eric and Anna Gill of Bartlesville, Oklahoma, wrote the following on September 28, 1991:

"With thanks to God, our son Peter Michael was healed with the tears from the Weeping Icon.

"He started having seizures at about six months of age. They were terrifying, full-body seizures that were about two weeks apart and all while he slept. He was hospitalized after the first and sent to specialists. Nothing could be found but doctors were suggesting treatment with an anti-seizure medication such as phenobarbital.

"Our daughter's Godmother sent a cotton ball that had been soaked in the tears from the Icon. We already had a copy of the Icon and had had it at the hospital when Peter developed a serious infection after birth.

"I waited several days before anointing him. Late one night I felt a strong need to anoint both my children. Quietly, I entered Peter's room and opened the foil. I had always heard of myrrh's sweet fragrance—suddenly I had no doubt and no fear—God truly was with us. I anointed Peter and Alexandra. Peter had a seizure the next day but there was no fear.

"I anointed him again before the last series of tests. I had had a dream while pregnant with Peter (about) the Archangel Michael.... In the dream I felt a warmth and strength in my hands. When I anointed Peter the second time, I felt the same power in my hand as I held the cotton ball. The tests were normal and no treatment was pursued. Peter has not had a seizure now for seven weeks."

HEALING FROM DRUG ABUSE

G. M. from Roslindale, Massachusetts, on July 29, 1991:

"My daughter, K., was into drugs and prostitution to support her drug habit. This all happened after she lost her son from drowning at the age of two years and five months. Three of her children were put up for adoption by the state. I pray that we will see these children again.

"Now my daughter is married to a wonderful man. They have two children. Your prayers for my daughter have been answered. Her meeting with (her husband) was a very holy miracle. I have my daughter's permission to write to you about this miracle."

CANCER HEALING

J. Richard Avena of San Antonio, Texas, wrote:

"In 1989 I was diagnosed as having a malignant tumor (lipo sarcoma). My family and I came here to pray. About a week later I had major surgery and later received chemotherapy and radiation. I have since gone through CAT scans and X rays, and I am totally clean of any cancer. We still come here to pray and thank God."

CHRONIC COUGHING CURED

Mary Raygoza of San Antonio, Texas, wrote that she visited the Icon in November of 1991. She had been coughing for a year. Doctors took X rays and couldn't find anything wrong and gave her cough medicine. She would cough all night and couldn't get any sleep. After visiting the Shrine on a Saturday in November and being anointed, she went home and went to sleep. The next morning she went to church and later that day her husband noticed she was not coughing and hadn't been. She has not had the chronic cough any more for nine months.

HEALING OF EYES

From Cheryl Martinez of San Antonio, Texas, came the following letter of thanks on October 13, 1992:

"I want to thank you from the bottom of my heart for sending me the tears of the Weeping Icon. These past few days unexpectedly my eyes were giving me some serious problems. I was worried to say the least. The drops the doctor gave me weren't working. I felt scared. When I remembered that you had sent me the blessed tears last week, I immediately put them against both my eyes. Next morning I felt fantastic and my eyes have never been better."

RELIEF OF EYE TROUBLE

Mary C. Leven wrote from Warminster, Pennsylvania, on December 6, 1992:

"About four years ago I had surgery on one eye. Results: awful—no center vision. The other eye was weak and needed a cataract removed. The sight was failing there too.

"Every day I hold the Icon of the Mother of God to my eyes and ask for improvement and I anoint them with the (tears). Praise God there is some improvement. Please send another tear."

THANKS FOR HEALINGS

John Koshinz wrote from Phoenix, Arizona, on December 26, 1992:

"I continue to use regularly the Blessed John Oil I received from the Monastery. It has provided both healing and insight. I had two old tears from the Weeping Icon that I had been keeping in the refrigerator because they had been used up. To my surprise, they 'regenerated' and became moist again after I received the Icon of St. Seraphim and the cloth touched to his Relics from the Monastery. I continue to receive healing from them."

RELIEF OF FEVER

Father Pangratios was told on January 23, 1992, by Randy Tijerina of Austin, Texas, that Randy had had a fever the previous day of 102° and after being anointed by a friend with the myrrh from the Holy Icon, the fever was completely cured in two hours without medication. Randy said that he had immediately felt as though something new had happened—as if he had been cleansed.

HEALING OF INFECTION FROM A SPIDER BITE

Ellen Pugh wrote from Memphis, Tennessee on February 10, 1993:

"A young friend has been battling a brown recluse spider bite on her hip. To complicate matters, her leg is paralyzed and she was treated at first for a bed sore. She has spent the last two years in and out of the hospital and could have died several times. This last time she was so bad that they thought she had gotten an infection in the bone and if so, they might have to amputate her leg.

"I gave the myrrh tear of the Mother of God to my son who took it to the hospital to her. The next day my son called and told me with an exclamation of wonderment that he thought a miracle had happened. She had taken the myrrh with her to the bone biopsy. The test results came back negative. The infection was a simple staph one and very treatable, and not in the bone.

"I praise God for two miracles—a healing and that my son now believes."

CONCEPTION OF CHILD IN BARREN MARRIAGE

Deborah Humanitzki wrote from Valley Stream, New York, on February 8, 1993:

"My new husband and I have been trying to have a child for two years. He was married before for 18 years, and they had had no children, and it was important to him to have a child to love and raise. I am now 42 years old and have had some gynecological complications, but we kept praying that God would grant us a child.

"I anointed myself with the tear of the Mother of God Icon. I also anointed my husband. I would like to tell you that I am now pregnant, and the baby is due in September!"

DISAPPEARANCE OF LUMP ON EYELID

Rose Linskens wrote from Warren, Michigan, on February 6, 1993, that a lump on her eyelid had gradually disappeared after a friend anointed her with the tear from the Weeping Icon of the Mother of God.

TWO HEALINGS

Mary Esther Foreman wrote from Round Rock, Texas, on March 29, 1993:

"I blessed a co-worker who was having female problems and has had two prior surgeries within the past six months. The doctors were preparing for a third. The day after she was blessed, the bleeding stopped and the doctor said she is improving.

"I also gave a cotton ball with the tears to a friend who is suffering from AIDS. He blessed his roommate in a medical facility who had been on a catheter for four months due to lack of bladder control. Two days after he was blessed the catheter was taken out and his bladder was working fine."

PEACEFUL DEATH

Irena Jakus wrote from Fridley, Minnesota, on August 16, 1993, that she gave a cotton ball with the tears of the Mother of God to a friend of hers whose brother was dying. This friend suddenly got word that he was about to die and took the tear with her as she ran out to go to the hospital. She went to his bed and took out the cotton ball and anointed her brother. Then she explained to the people in the room what she was doing. Before she came her brother was very restless, but after being anointed he became peaceful and there was a smile on his lips and it seemed to all present in the room that it was filled with the smell of roses. Several of the people there had been estranged from the Faith, but they all then began to pray.

HELP WITH DIABETES

On August 11, 1993, Markella Alatzas of Baltimore, Maryland, wrote that her husband who is 81 and had Parkinson's was taken off his diabetes medication by his doctor. He had been anointed with the Holy tear and the doctor said he was doing very well.

HEALING OF ACNE

Mrs. R. H. Richmond of Sacramento, California, wrote on May 20, 1993, that she had suffered greatly from severe acne on her face for many years. Since she had anointed herself with the tear of the Mother of God, her acne problems had disappeared.

RECOVERY FROM HEART BYPASS SURGERY

Mrs. Jean Lubreski wrote from Baltimore, Maryland, on March 5, 1993, that her brother had had a quadruple bypass surgery and was dying when she went to the hospital and anointed him. He pulled through and the doctors said it was a miracle.

RELIEF OF PAIN IN ARM

Betty Dotts of Lansing, Michigan, wrote on March 27, 1991, that she had brought a tear home from the Monastery and had anointed her husband with it. He had been having pain in his arm which was either arthritis or bursitis and was not able to be very active. After anointing, his pain went away. (Through anointing with) the myrrh, (God) has blessed her as well with peace and strength when she most needed it.

HEALING OF GALL STONES AND GANGRENE

Georgia Bonney of Greenville, Texas, wrote on March 29, 1991:

"Many thanks and blessings for the prayers offered up during the recent illness of my mother. I called you in my hour of need and your prayers helped us through a very difficult time. Mother is 81 years old and the final diagnosis, which resulted in three hours of surgery, was a gallbladder with over one hundred stones and gangrene. It had infused her whole system. Mother is now out of the hospital and slowly regaining her strength. We all call it a modern day miracle."

HEALING OF LUPUS

Ernest Espindola of Victoria, Texas, wrote on May 3, 1991 that he was healed of lupus at the Monastery a year ago.

MANY BLESSINGS

Flo Hecker wrote the Monastery that through blessing with the holy tears of the Mother of God, her five year old granddaughter had become much less willful and had begun praying.

Her niece had relief from high blood pressure.

Her nephew was drinking less.

A young woman named Samantha had been diagnosed with cancer throughout her body. When the tumor was removed, the doctors could not understand why the original tests had showed the cancer. There was apparently none there now.

GREAT JOY

Tamara Groppel wrote from San Antonio on February 20, 1991:

"My Daughter and I had the privilege of visiting your Monastery and there are no words to describe how deeply I was touched by all of it. I am Russian Orthodox, and although I lived in San Antonio for 20 years, I just found out about your Monastery. When I left, I felt—and still 'till now I feel—like I was in the presence of Jesus Christ Himself and His Holy Mother. I've never had such a feeling before, despite the fact that I attended quite a number of Churches in Shanghai and China, as well as in San Francisco."

HEALING OF INJURED FOOT

Joan Heit of Galveston, Texas, wrote on July 6, 1992:

"The Holy Oil from the Icon of the Mother of God you mailed me a couple of months ago cured my foot. At school we have a Fourth of July Parade in the parking lot with our children on bicycles all decorated with balloons. One little boy couldn't get his bike going, so I walked out to help him. As I was leaving the parking lot, another child ran over my foot. It hurt for a while, but I just rubbed it and continued to watch the children. Going home and taking off my shoe the pain became so great I couldn't walk. I soaked it and wrapped it up and put a pillow under it and stayed in bed. Before going to bed I took the oil and put it on my foot and prayed. I wrapped it again and went to sleep. In the morning when I got up there was no pain and I could walk on it."

HEALING OF BLINDNESS

Lucille Gaona of Austin, Texas, was legally blind when she first visited the Monastery. She had been receiving laser treatments, and was losing her sight because of diabetes. She writes:

"On the first visit I could not see anything well enough to walk alone and had to have someone guide me. I was wearing dark glasses. We visited the Icon and prayed before it before we were anointed. I could hardly see the Icon and it seemed very small. After being anointed, I started looking around the Chapel and I could see a little bit of the Icons on the walls. I had not been able to see them before being anointed.

"I walked out of the Chapel with my family and friends, and one of my family members said, 'Look, Lucy is walking by herself without any help.' That is when I realized that for the first time in several months that I was able to walk without assistance.

"Over the next few months my sight gradually got better. The sight came back quicker to the right eye and about six months ago my sight in the right eye is just about normal."

A MEDITATION

Rita Svjagintsev of Austin, Texas, wrote the following meditation on May 25, 1991:

"Because I am mother, because future generations carry my flesh and blood, I have become intensely conscious of my being personally, intimately and definitely bound to the destiny of mankind.

"Because I am woman I can never be satisfied with abstractions, with the mere vision of meanings. All vision must become enfleshed, must find expression and form in the flesh. Even God, His Word, yearned to become flesh. In the Old Testament the Word of God enters humanity by the pathway of men's minds and hearts and emerges then from the mouth of the prophet. In the New Testament the Word of God becomes flesh in the womb of a woman.

"Woman became Mother of the God-Man. She, the new Eve, is Mother of God and of mankind.

"It seems to me, the longer we walk our spiritual earth journey, so interwoven in everyday life and interknitted in human relationships, the more it dawns on us that we participate in the function and task of this one woman, Mary of Nazareth. All of us who in solitude and silence hear and conceive through the womb of the ear the Word of God, the eternal Christ Child, partake personally and intimately in the events which lead from the girl-mother of Nazareth to the Woman clothed with the Sun. Simply expressed, we are in the process of becoming and being Church.

"Perhaps it is the privilege of the old woman, who has walked a long journey and lived an existence within ordinary joys and sufferings, to dare to give expression to such wondrous divinization of human life.

"Mary, the Mother of Humanity.

"Some weeks ago I awoke in the night. The reason for my awakening was, if I can remember correctly, my concern about my children and grandchildren. I was so keenly aware of my human inadequacy and limitations.

"As I let myself be carried into the images and thoughts of the human interweavings of my life, another thought interspersed itself: It cannot be very long any more that I must die. How would I die? My thoughts wandered into the future. How would it be if (just in case) I were to see the Face of God? Would I be granted the Beatific Vision? I imagined myself to be looking into that Beauty and Truth, into that Light and Love which had lured me to follow it, sometimes subtly, sometimes violently, but with consistency all my life long.

"To my great surprise I did not feel fulfilled and happy at this thought of 'Beatific Vision.' This startled me. Had I not believed that always, in all things, I was seeking the countenance of my God? It occurred to me that The 'Beatific Vision' could make me only happy if I could forget everything and everybody whose lives I had shared and for whom I had cared. Does heaven presuppose amnesia? Would this be happiness? These were my thoughts.

"And then a dialogue with my Lord and God developed. Would it be heaven, I asked, if You would have to knock out of me the memory of those You gave me to love and care for? Is heaven a shrinkage of consciousness?

"Then He asked: What is it that you wish?

"And I said: I desire most of all not to forget but to see! To see all of the universe You created; to look into Your secrets, from the waves of light and atoms to the infinite cosmos. I wish to look into the secrets of the human story.

"And now, in my imagination, I floated through the universe. Then my vision narrowed and I looked first at my children and grandchildren, my husband, my brother, etc.; then, in ever-widening circles I saw all those I care for and love and serve. All humanity circled around me in near and far places. I saw hunger, war, sickness and suffering interspersed with lights of hope and here and there even a glimmer of joy. I began to weep.

"Again I said to my Lord: How could I enjoy looking at You as long as there is a valley of tears, where there is no certainty that they, too, shall enter into the Light of Your Beauty.... Through Your eyes I wish to see Your universe and Your humanity. Share with me Your vision. This should make me happy.

"I then felt that I was gently moved and turned in such a way that I was allowed to look through God's eyes (if one may dare to say it this way) into humanity. As I looked, again I began to weep: gently, compassionately, tenderly, embracingly. I was sorrowful and consoled at the same time.

"It was at this point that a memory slipped into my gaze. It was the Myrrh-Weeping Icon of the Theotokos in the Orthodox Monastery up in the Texas Hill Country. With one gaze I understood why the Mother of God, the Mother of humanity, is weeping tears of myrrh: bitter tears, fragrant tears. She who is taken up into Heaven, crowned with glory, is weeping nonetheless. My purpose as the woman I am would not be disrupted by death. I may hope to complete the meaning of my life in union with Mary, the Mother of God, the Mother of Eve's children.

"It was then that I understood that Mary is weeping the tears of God and that I am weeping Mary's tears; that I am alive in her heart, and she is the heart of the Church; and in that depth the heart of the Church is beating with the pulsating Life of the Holy Trinity. A glance of comprehension was given me by which I know that all love and caring flow into one river. All is geared towards one goal, the completion of humanity in God. All is filled with utter trust and infinite hope. Nothing is wasted. 'All shall be well.' And there is peace of heart.

"I must add that the day before this night of prayerful tears I had made an effort to lay aside the endeavor of my intellect to find meaningful theological answers to the vexing and painful complexities of my conflicts within and outside the ongoings of the busy church around me, from which I am interiorly so strangely removed, which had caused me such great sorrow.

"It seems to me that by the act of putting aside my effort to find human answers for my dilemma I created room for the deeper answer to echo within me. However, I believe the mystery would not have opened up to me if I had avoided the scouring-out process of coming to the limit of my own human effort.

"The answer comes in the silence and solitude of the night as a gift of simplicity in which faith, hope and love merge into one stream of LIFE.

"May the Lord grant me the gift of simplicity as I walk closer to the blessed gate of death."

FORGIVENESS AND PEACE

On November 16, 1989, R. O. of San Antonio, Texas, wrote:

"I would like to share a special experience with you when I was anointed with the tears of our Mother of God. My husband and I are separated and are pursuing a divorce. During my marriage and separation, my husband had committed adultery. When I found out of the incident and that this young girl was pregnant from my husband, I was very hurt and angry with my husband. My brother had invited me to visit the Shrine of the Mother of God in Blanco, Texas. As I was anointed by your Priest, I had felt a tremendous pressure in my chest. After my visit to the Shrine and the anointing, my anger and hurt towards my husband were completely gone. I have no bitterness or hurt toward my husband. I am a much happier person and my faith towards the dear Lord is strong. I forgave my husband and we talk now without any anger or bitterness."

HEALING OF BABY'S HEART TROUBLE

Diana Manoquin, a grandmother, wrote from Weslaco, Texas, on August 11, 1991:

"Baby Tony, one year old, had heart problems. The child was taken to different doctors from San Antonio and Corpus Christi. The child was diagnosed as having a heart problem and heart murmur. I prayed before the Icon of the Mother of God for a miracle and the miracle took place. Now baby Tony is very healthy and has no more heart problems."

A BLESSED DEATH

On April 24, 1994, Karen Peterson of Sioux City, Iowa, wrote the following moving account:

"First, this is Holy Week, and I wish you many blessings as you walk with Christ through His Glorious Passion. I can't imagine how He suffered. I can't even give up a little meat and cheese without grumbling!

"Next, I want to thank you for the book you sent, *The Way of the Pilgrim*. The timing was amazing. I received this shortly after my husband gave me a prayer rope that he had brought back with him from Mt. Athos. And I was thinking that I should dig up my old copy of *The Pilgrim* when yours came in the mail.

"My husband, Gary, was recently on Mt. Athos with our Parish Priest, Fr. Tom Gegley. He and Fr. Tom went to Greece on February 20 and were on the Holy Mountain from the 23rd (of February) through the 2nd of March. They saw many of the Monasteries and visited a Skete as well.

"Father Benedict, the experience was too close to heaven for Gary. He even had a vision of Angels to bless him. It is sad for me to tell you, Father, but on April 4th, one month after coming home, my husband—who took the name of the Apostle Andrew when we converted six years ago—died of a massive heart attack at the age of 47. I find it comforting that he celebrated his last Communion and Liturgy on the Sunday of the Elevation of the Cross, and died early on Monday morning, the day dedicated to the Angels. (I have a special devotion to St. Michael the Archangel, so Mondays are special to me.)

"Gary, or I should now call him Andrew, had a very hard life what with an abusive alcoholic stepfather, and everyone said Andrew would never amount to anything. But with the grace of God, he raised himself out of that pit and made a new life for himself, and later with me and our children. We have two daughters ages 21 and 19, and a little boy—also named Andrew Michael—who will be four this September. Such treasures they are to me! Andrew never really went a day without carrying the pain of his early life with him. And when the day came when he realized he needed a living God in his life and began to embrace the Orthodox Church, a true miracle was made! He truly became a new creation, and though he still had painful memories and 'garbage' to deal with, he had the comfort of a loving Jesus Christ to share the load with him.

"Gary and I were to celebrate our 25th anniversary this August; and to celebrate, we had hoped to make a Pilgrimage to visit at Christ of the Hills Monastery. I would still like to do this and perhaps stay with the Nuns for a few days.

"I thank God for bringing you and the Monastery into our lives. May He continue to bless you all. Have a most blessed Pascha!"

TANGIBLE PRESENCE OF GOD

Bonnie Latiolais wrote on August 25, 1991:

"My husband Rick and I visited the Shrine of the Weeping Icon in late July. We were very moved by the strong presence of God and our Lady at the Monastery. Since we've been back, we've anointed many people with the tears of the Mother of God. Many healings, both spiritual and physical have been reported by people being blessed with the tears. We wish to thank you for making our visit there so enriching.

"I left some petitions for prayer with you while we were there. I am pleased to say that many prayers are being answered through the intercession of the

Mother of God. Thank you for all of your constant prayers for all of us.... His Holy and Blessed Mother is very powerful.

"I was given 200 leaflets on the Shrine when we visited there. We own a religious shop, so I have distributed most of them already. Consequently, many people have already planned Pilgrimages there.

"Please continue to pray for us and be assured of our constant prayers for you."

PROTECTION IN AN AUTO ACCIDENT

Graciela G. Villafranca wrote that her prayers for her son before the Weeping Icon had been answered.

"Six weeks ago Jorge had an automobile accident. He dozed off while leaving work. The truck turned over twice, but Jorge walked away with a bump on his head and a bruise on his back. The Lord God gave my son Jorge this life back and it was a miracle from heaven. Then just six weeks ago, he was on his way to a drilling site to work and a big truck side-swiped him and damaged his new truck, but Jorge was not hurt."

SUCCESSFUL HEART SURGERY

San Juanita Guerra of San Antonio, Texas, wrote:

"Here I am again thanking our lovely Mother of God Weeping Icon for interceding for my in-law Israel Lerma, age 42. He came out of heart surgery—five bypasses—doing just great. He was home three days after surgery and had no side effects or complications."

HEALING OF EAR

From Pauline Valdez the following note was received: "I had an earache. I used the oil you sent us and it went away."

A CHILD'S HEART IRREGULARITY CORRECTED

On March 3, 1995, Mary Muñiz wrote from League City, Texas:

"About three weeks ago my husband Ray, and my three sons and I went to the Monastery. The reason we went is because I had taken our son Benjamin to the doctor due to a bad cough. The cough was not serious but it turned out that the doctor heard his heart beating extra beats. She said it was not common in children and that sometimes a child might be born with a problem and it not show up till later in life. I was told to take him back two weeks later and if she still heard it she would send him to a heart doctor. I was scared and I cried and prayed. I also found a Weeping Icon leaflet I had been saving for months. I told my husband about it and we decided we needed to take Benjamin. We had a very pleasant trip over there and I have to tell you I had never before that day experienced such peacefulness. Even my boys liked it. When you (Father Gregory) took us inside the Shrine I prayed so hard for Benjamin. You also anointed us with tears and we were all blessed by the 94 year old Father (Father Joseph).

"After we got in our vehicle to come back home, I had such a good feeling that everything was going to be OK.

"Well, that was on a Saturday. On Wednesday I took Benjamin back to the doctor and she said she did not hear the extra beats and that everything was normal. We were so happy. We hope to go to visit the Weeping Icon at least once a year. The wonderful experience we all had there will be a memory we will treasure forever. I also bought the book *The Way of the Pilgrim* and I am enjoying it very much."

HEALING AND FAITH

Penny Teal wrote from Orange, Texas, on March 3, 1995:

"With the tears of the Blessed Mother you sent me last year I blessed a man with congenital heart failure. He has till spring to live. After the blessing, he didn't need a nitro pill for 30 days. He (was) agnostic and (is) now interested in God. I also blessed a lady with a malignant tumor with the tears. She is healed. I know these miracles were granted through the intercession of the Mother of God and her tears."

PROTECTION THROUGH CHEMOTHERAPY

From Clarksburg, West Virginia, Pauline Muffler wrote on the third of February, 1995:

"About seven or eight months ago I was having trouble with my throat. I went to the doctor and they told me I had lymphoma and I would have to have chemotherapy. Our dear Priest-friend from Houston comes to your Monastery and has the tears and sent them to me. Before I would go for my treatment, I would anoint myself with the tears. I never once got sick, I ate good all the time, I went to work the next day, and never had any problems. I live my normal life and the doctor just looks at me. I do have to have surgery for another problem, but I feel that the tears took me through the treatments. I want to ask your prayers for my surgery.... Thank you so much for your prayers and I will let you know of my recovery."

PEACEFUL DEATH

Sandy Whitney wrote from Birmingham, Alabama, on January 11, 1995:

"I received some of the tears from a friend in McAllen. A few days later a dear friend named Sara, after heart surgery, went into a coma. Her family, which is Baptist, wanted to do everything they could for her. Her son insisted on doing everything including putting Holy Oil and Holy Water on her. I mentioned I had the tears from the Weeping Icon, and they wanted her anointed with them.

"We anointed Sara and you could smell the roses throughout her room. Sara wasn't healed but her family felt such peace flow through them that they accepted God's will completely. There is such a strong bonding with me and Sara's family to this day. Of course, we all miss Sara but she left us many wonderful blessings with us all."

HEALING FROM END-STAGE RENAL FAILURE

Rusty Camacho wrote from San Antonio, Texas, on April 10, 1994 that he had been diagnosed with clerodema and end-stage renal failure in December of 1989. He had gone through the years searching for inner peace through Christ's love. He had moved from Hawaii in 1991, and to San Antonio in 1992. He then heard of Christ of the Hills Monastery and of the Holy Myrrh-Weeping Icon. He had been drawn to it and he visited in June of 1993. Since then he has given thanks for his blessings every day. He has not been on dialysis for nearly a year now.

NEW HOPE AND FAITH

Renee Holloway wrote to the Monks:

"I visited the Monastery in January of 1994 with my husband and parents. In March of 1994, my mother was diagnosed with colon cancer. She had a large malignant tumor removed and underwent six months of chemotherapy. I admired her for her strength. Two weeks ago, she had her first three-month cancer checkup. Currently she's free and clear of cancer.

"In February of 1994, my father had to retire from employment due to health reasons. The transition was very difficult for him. I find it interesting that he retired just in time to care for my mother when she needed it most.

"One day in late spring of 1994, my husband and I were arguing. I came inside, went to my bedroom and pulled out the envelope from the Monastery. I pulled out the cotton ball and said the prayer according to the instructions on the brochure. I said a few additional prayers also. You should know that I'm not one to attend church every Sunday, but I do believe in God.

"What happened next is difficult to describe. For a split second I felt my heart arch upward as a smile crept across my face. I felt an intense purity that I have never felt in my life. I honestly believe a presence was with me that day. It was the most unusual, weird, wonderful awakening. I call it an awakening because I know there is something beyond this life. I have decided that the God I learned about in 12 years of Catholic education will no longer come off the shelf when I need Him. I have decided to cultivate this relationship everyday.

"Several other incidents have occurred since then. I honestly believe a Higher Being is behind these events. They're unexplainable.... My sister says (that) God is much smarter than we are, so you should not worry about things. She says He knows the plan for us, and that things always work themselves out. Deep down, I believe her.

"Thank you for sharing your Monastery with me, my husband and parents. Someday, I'll be back."

HELP IN LIVING WITH AIDS

T. V. of California wrote to Fr. Benedict on April 7, 1991:

"I want to take this opportunity to express my thanks to you and your religious community for your continued support and devotion to the Icon of the Mother of God. I was first introduced to the Icon by my dear friend M. K. of Austin, Texas.

"She first was anointed with the Blessed tears of the Icon about a year or so ago. She brought me a cotton ball with some of the tears. I was immediately drawn to Blanco, Texas, and the power of the Mother of God. I have been to the Monastery many times since then. I have since moved to California. I am now living with AIDS in my life. I have asked many times for your prayers to the Mother of God for help in dealing with this disease. I am thankful to you for your many prayers on my behalf. I have begun to receive the blessings of your prayers in my life. I now have 'full-blown' AIDS. However, I have begun to experience the blessings that AIDS has brought to my life. I'm now living on disability and cannot work; and yet, because of the AIDS disease, the quality of my life is better than it ever has been or I ever expected it to be. I am now a volunteer (for an AIDS center). I am the food-bank coordinator for the center's attempt at feeding the many people that are affected by AIDS and HIV infection. I have met many people who are living or assisting others living with AIDS. The love and concern that I feel from these people has enriched my life, and the lives of my family.

"My family was drawn together because of my AIDS condition and experienced a closeness that would never have been possible without such a devastating disease touching my life. I feel my great joy and strength has come through my devotion to the Weeping Icon and my cry for your prayers. I have two of the wooden Icons in my house. One is by my bed and the other is in my living room. I have sent the little picture of the Mother of God to many family and friends who were in need of her blessings. I continue to feel her favor and love and her intercession to her Son and God on my behalf.

"I once again ask for your prayers and thoughts. May God continue to touch all of your lives and the lives of the people your prayer and devotion reach."

HEALING FROM DRUG ADDICTION

A man sent the Monastery the following account of the change in his life:

"I had been a drug user for twenty-nine years. A lifestyle that revolved around sex and drugs was exciting. It had its downside—the overdoses, the time spent in hospitals even in the years before there was specialized treatment for alcohol and drugs. In later years I used vacation periods from work to go through drug treatment centers. Narcotics, amphetamines or anything I could get in a needle and get a rush from, I would use. Over the years there were near-fatal overdoses. (There have been times when) I have passed out with a needle in me, and when revived by other addicts, would finish shooting up. One time I was so high I accidentally used some chicken soup to melt my drugs with instead of water, and realizing my mistake shot up the mixture anyway rather than waste the drug.

"All this I considered a price worth paying to use drugs. But the first time I shot up cocaine, the price became too much and I was trapped. The short duration of the rush and the high of cocaine and the overwhelming depression that followed, turned my already difficult life into a nightmare that was unmanageable. These nightmares were real and lasted from 24 to 72 hours, injecting cocaine from 20 to 50 times, attempting to reproduce the first high or just ward off the inevitable depression. The bouts continued until there was no more money, nothing else to pawn or the drug supply ran out. My body would give out in exhaustion and depression. I was totally obsessed with cocaine; it held me in a superhuman grip.

"Constantly sick and looking to my work associates like a man about to have a heart attack, my credit was gone, my job was almost gone and my whole life was a living nightmare that cannot be adequately described. Now my chest had become infected. I injected the drugs in my chest to avoid having track marks on my arms. My chest was swollen and red from the hours of injecting cocaine and I could see that the infection was spreading towards my heart.

"Falling on the carpet of the motel room floor, I begged God to deliver me from this living hell. I knew now that there had to be a personal, supernatural power of good because I was now under the control of a personal, supernatural power of evil that was slowly killing me and destroying my family.

"An educated man in my forties, I had grown up in an upper-class home where we went to Church and read the Bible and went to private religious school because it was the proper thing for a well-bred person to do. Religion was an important part of looking socially acceptable and doing the 'right' thing.

"Now everything had changed. I knew a real demon so I knew there had to be a real God or else every human being would be under demonic control. I recalled a Bible verse from my religious upbringing, 'Whatever you ask for when you pray, believe that you have received it and you will have it.' (St. Mark 11:24.) I asked God to free me from this demon that held me addicted to cocaine against my will, and, since I now believed in a real God, I believed His Word, and believed that because I asked Him, He would free me. I believed that now I must be truly free in spite of my current condition because the Bible also says, 'We walk by faith, not by sight.' (II Corinthians 5:7.)

"I returned to my home very sick, not knowing what to do, but I read another Bible verse that said, 'We make plans, but God directs our steps.' (Proverbs 16:9.) I knew that I needed immediate medical attention so I chose a physician who was an expert in addiction since I knew I could not explain my condition. By now, any doctor would have recognized me as an addict.

"The good doctor I went to told me he would treat my infection and that, if I survived the infection, I would have to follow his treatment approach to addiction or he would inform my employer of my situation. This would have resulted in my termination and since I was very sick and scared anyway, I agreed. He cut open my chest; put me on antibiotics and ordered me to start attending A.A. or N.A. meetings, at least one per day. He also ordered me to report to him every three days for drug testing and direction. Fear kept me off cocaine for ten days, a real miracle I thought, but on the tenth day I told the doctor my craving for cocaine was more than I could stand. I could not sleep more than a few hours at night and my mind constantly raced with wild and uncontrollable thoughts. He took a careful history of me and determined that I had had these symptoms for most of my life. Being well experienced, he believed that I had a manic-depressive condition and put me on the drug, lithium. The overpowering urge for cocaine subsided. I began sleeping more at night and my thoughts did not race out of control. I considered lithium my miracle.

"Yet months went by and I became increasingly depressed. My doctor sent me to a psychiatrist who tried every class of anti-depressant on me without result. At ten months of sobriety on lithium and regular A.A. and N.A. meetings I was suicidally depressed. I saw addicts and alcoholics come into A.A. and N.A. and be in much better shape than I was when they had only 30 days sobriety. The psychiatrists wanted to try, ECT (shock therapy), on me. I was afraid of being made into a zombie and I refused this.

"During my ten months of sobriety, I had read about and become interested in Orthodoxy. I began attending the Orthodox Church to thank God for delivering me from cocaine. But my obsession with dying became worse. My younger brother, who was also my best friend, had committed suicide 12 years ago. I wanted to join him. On the verge of suicide, I went out and used cocaine again, twice. In an almost audible voice God told me that although I was no longer a cocaine addict, the demon He had freed me from could come back into my life if I willed that by my actions.

"At this point God intervened again, even without my asking this time. A friend who knew I was attending the Orthodox Church told me of a nearby Orthodox Monastery of Orthodox Monks who had an Icon of the Blessed Mother that wept myrrh. I was desperate and went to see if this was truly a miracle. I saw for myself the Weeping Icon of the Mother of God and learned that she was causing many other miraculous events throughout the world. I returned to the Monastery after struggling for a few more months with sobriety. There were many curious tourists as well as devout Pilgrims. I had learned of one of the titles of the Mother of God that particularly interested me, "the Scourge of demons." I stood in front of her Icon and asked her to help me with the demons that still haunt me. I felt a great warmth and left the presence of her Icon with a feeling of peace. The desire to kill myself was gone. I felt the need to pray and to start spending time at the Monastery.

"Again my steps were being directed, this time by the Mother of God. I stopped using lithium completely and stopped attending A.A. and N.A. meetings. I stopped seeing psychiatrists and put my trust in the Mother of God.

"Shortly after this, the Abbot of the Monastery gave a sermon that I felt the Mother of God directed at me. He spoke of the importance of having a spiritual director, a person with many years' experience in the spiritual life who could act as a guide. Without this, he said, a newly–saved soul could easily fall into error. He spoke of the need to learn to pray the 'prayer of the heart.' This simple prayer, 'Lord Jesus Christ, Son of God, have mercy on me, a sinner,' was very powerful. After his sermon I asked a Monk of many years' experience to be my spiritual guide. Now, when I go to him upset with my worldly troubles, he listens and then says, 'let us begin the prayer.' Through the intercession of God's Mother, the Holy Spirit transfers from my spiritual director to me, some of his spiritual strength. This process cannot be explained. Herein lies the beauty of Orthodoxy, the emphasis on experiencing God. At the Monastery, all prayer, Services, studies and direction are aimed at obtaining this direct contact with God. It does not involve either emotionalism or intellectuality but an unexplainable direct experience that results in peace in the midst of a chaotic world.

"Jesus and His Mother are alive and real. 'Ask and you will receive, seek and you will find.' (St. Matthew 7:7.) This once lost drug addict found a life so abundant it cannot be explained but must be experienced."

GREATER PEACE

R. W. wrote on August 8, 1991, telling the Monks of his gratitude. He recounted his difficult life history with drug use, mental illness, imprisonment and a motor cycle accident. He then describes the experience of his Pilgrimage to the Monastery. He writes: "We walked around a bit and then the Sister rang the service bell so I went in and watched and listened. Then we went in to pray and I wanted to see the Icon. It was a pleasant feeling but I did not even realize that I had no pains. I bowed to the Icon and put my forehead on the frame and then Fr. Pangratios anointed me and that worked. I really have no pain and I can eat things I couldn't before. The holy attitude of the place influenced me."

RELIEF OF RESPIRATORY DISTRESS

Agnes Hoff of Bellevue, Nebraska, wrote on July 19, 1993:

"I have multiple respiratory problems. One day I just could not breathe, and I anointed myself with the cotton ball of myrrh and I could breathe. I feel it was a miracle from the Icon. Please pray for the healing of my lungs and heart and that I am able to give up smoking."

HEALING OF AN INJURED FOOT

Mrs. Del Carmen Jimenez writes: "I suffered a foot injury when moving a sofa which fell on the big toe of my left foot. It was very painful and there was danger because of my diabetes. A doctor prescribed an ointment and compresses but the wound would not heal for a long time and was very painful. At church I was anointed with the tears of the Blessed Mother from New Sarov and soon the wound on my foot healed. I continued attending the weekly anointings at the church and every time I was anointed I felt a great joy. It made me cry for joy and love. I still cry because, who am I for our All–Holy Virgin Mary to notice me. I ask her forgiveness and give her a thousand thanks!"

HELP WITH HYPOGLYCEMIA

Teresa Thompson wrote from Chihuahua, Mexico:

"After visiting New Sarov I arrived in Chihuahua, Mexico, carrying with me a piece of cotton soaked with the miraculous tears of our Lady, and invited the family member to be anointed. My sister-in-law had suffered hypoglycemia for years and several times had been hospitalized in danger of going into a coma. After being anointed she ceased experiencing low sugar crises and she stopped watching closely her diet. She felt surprisingly well. The last time she was under the doctor's supervision he found that her pancreas is functioning perfectly well and (her doctor) has certified this.

"Later she wrote: In August 1990 my aunt, almost 80 but still driving, had a car collision from which she emerged alive but in a coma and was immediately hospitalized. Her condition was deteriorating, mostly she was unconscious and when she talked at all it was incoherently. Two days later my father (her brother) was on his way to see her. At the airport I put into his pocket a tear from the Weeping Icon which I had previously obtained and said to him: you must anoint her!

"On arrival, at the hospital he was overwhelmed with sorrow at the sight of his sister's poor condition and appearance, but somehow he managed to remember the tear in his pocket and while praying for her healing he anointed her. After a few minutes she opened her eyes, looked at him with recognition and greeted him. From that moment on, her recovery was steady, recognizing friends and relatives and holding small conversations. A week later she was sent home. I saw her again two months later and was amazed at her good condition. She was amazed too. I have no doubt that through the Mother of God's intercession she received a grace of healing."

A BENIGN TUMOR

Yolanda Lozano Lazo de Castellanos wrote on March 27, 1991:

"I wish to give a testimony. On the third of December, 1990, I went to my gynecologist, since for some time I had had pain in my left breast. The doctor gave me alarming results of tests that a tumor of cancerous type had been diagnosed and immediate surgery was recommended. The same day that I told my family the results of the tests and the diagnosis, my mother told me that my cousin knew of a woman who had cotton with tears from an Icon of the Mother of God, and she anointed me with them. Two days later they performed the surgery and to the surprise of everyone—including the doctor—the tumor was large but benign. For this, we give thanks to God."

PEACE OF MIND

R.R. wrote on November 13, 1989, from San Antonio, Texas:

"I recently visited the Shrine of the Mother of God and was given a small wad of cotton with the myrrh tears. While there I returned to the Shrine for a few minutes and asked the Mother of God to please take away the hate and anger I had been feeling over the past few months due to family problems which put my job and my future in jeopardy. I worked out the job problems, but I could not get over the maliciousness of a family member whom I had helped over this past year. As I drove away from the Monastery a sense of peace came over me which remains with me today. It is a small thing in light of so many grave problems people face, but for me it was meaningful."

STRENGTH IN SUFFERINGS

Miss Annie J. Thevis wrote from Crowley, Louisiana, on March 30, of 1989:

"Thank you very much for the Icon of the Myrrh Weeping Mother of God and for the holy tear. I made the Sign of the Cross with it and praying, looked at the

Weeping Icon. I had real pace and I felt very calm and happy and have more strength in my sufferings. Although I have a crippling form of arthritis, pray (that) I may keep on doing good with my pains if it is God's will, and that I may go on without any medication, since some medication that was given me caused an ulcer. I surely hope one day I'll get to Blanco."

HELP FOR THE ELDERLY

Ethel M. Welch wrote from Toledo, Ohio, on May 7, 1984:

"I am writing to let you know that right after I had sent my letter to you with the request, the miracle really happened. I was living in an old folks home that was getting very run down and wondering where I would move to next when out of the blue, as it were, a friend of mine bought this beautiful old mansion in which I now have a lovely apartment.

"Also I want to tell you of another miracle which the Lord did for me. I was almost completely blind at the age of 75, but after two operations, with contact lenses implanted, I now have good vision. I am a firm believer in miracles."

CONSOLATION

D. B. wrote from British Colombia, Canada, on July 29, 1988:

"It is a comfort to know you are being held in prayer by God's people. There is so much power in prayer....I ask for prayer for my loved ones. Thank you for praying for me as well as these others."

Note: A Priest reports that "This man was suicidal just months ago and now has improved 100% and he is very positive."

A PRAYER IN HONOR OF THE MOTHER OF GOD

Mrs. Bertina Milovsky wrote from Wyndmoor, Pennsylvania, on June 9, 1989:

"Enclosed is a check for you. I thank you for all the prayers for me and for the wonderful Icon and the tear of the Mother of God. This is a little prayer I was inspired to write:

" 'Oh, Weeping Icon, fair and sweet, whose heart is torn with pain and strife, bring us by your tears to remorse and sorrow for our sins. Turn, O Queen of heavenly splendor, to us who cry to you. For you who abide with the Father and the Son can plead for us in our time of need.'

"Thank you and God bless you!"

RECOVERY AFTER A DIAGNOSIS OF LUPUS

Angel and Josie Rodriquez wrote on October 9th, 1989:

"Our daughter, Sandra, was diagnosed as having lupus, a crippling and terminal disease. She was in a lot of pain and there wasn't much the doctors could do for her. We brought her to Austin and a well-known internist confirmed the diagnosis. We heard of the blessed Weeping Icon and we brought her here. Father Benedict prayed for her. Meanwhile another test was last and all I can remember is the nurse from the internist's office, telling me to tell Sandra that it was not lupus. By this time my daughter was walking again. All of the swelling is gone and there is no pain! Praise the Lord Jesus Christ!"

SUCCESSFUL REMOVAL OF A LARGE BRAIN TUMOR

Julia Vera wrote on June 29, 1990 from Houston, Texas:

"I am able to write now and tell you of my report of a miraculous occurrence. Our principal at school brought me a holy tear in late March. She anointed me in back of the head and left ear where a large brain tumor was located. I underwent two surgeries (one 14 hours and one 10 hours), but the neurosurgeon was able to remove all of the brain tumor. It was very large and was wrapped around with the left facial nerve. The surgeon was very careful, but the left facial nerve was torn off when he removed this benign tumor. So I had to undergo nerve transplant on the left side of my face to replace the facial nerve. I have to wait about six months for this transplant to work—to restore the movement on the left side of my face. I also lost my hearing in my left ear when the facial nerve was torn. I really need the Monks and Nuns to pray that I receive another miracle and be healed from the paralysis on the left side of my face, eye, and throat, and be healed from the dry eye syndrome and deafness in my left ear. I am grateful that the tumor was benign and I am alive. If you can, will you send me another tear from the Icon?"

CANCER IN REMISSION

On May 12, 1995, Mary Cartledge wrote to Hieromonk Gregory from Virginia Beach, Virginia:

"On May 9th , I visited your Monastery on a Pilgrimage from my home in Virginia. In the course of my visit, I received many blessings for not only myself but my family and friends. I spoke with you about several miracles in the lives of others whom I had given the tears from your Weeping Icon. I have now written these up for you:

"When I first received a tiny piece of cotton soaked in myrrh from your Icon, my first inclination was to share it with as many people as was possible. I called a dear friend to come over. We each blessed ourselves with the myrrh and could feel the presence of God very strongly. When my friend returned to her home she blessed her children with the oil left on her face. For days afterward she could smell the myrrh in her bedroom, even though no one else in her family was able to.

"Days later I sent the cotton ball my sister sent me with a friend who was going to Seattle to visit her son who was seriously ill in the hospital with non-Hodgkin's lymphoma. His was the most aggressive type, Burkett's lymphoma, in which tumors can double in size in 24 hours. Her son was in the second of a series of six chemotherapy treatments when she visited. When he felt well enough, they took the tears of your Icon and the brochure my sister sent and went to the hospital's Chapel. There they prayed and (her son) blessed himself with the Icon's tears. This was his only opportunity to use the tears. Even though my intention was for him to keep them, my friend brought them home with her to Virginia. (Her son) continued with his chemotherapy. However the sixth round of chemotherapy did not make him sick as all the others had. After finishing all his treatments, his doctor performed a spinal tap to check on the status of his lymphoma.

"To everyone's utter amazement, he is in complete remission. His doctor stated that he has never seen anything like this. He is presenting (his) miraculous cure to a symposium of doctors in the Northwest."

HEALING OF SWOLLEN GLANDS

On April 4, 1994, John K. Shryock wrote from Barto, Pennsylvania:

"I am an 80% disabled Veteran of the Vietnam War, and what I have to tell you here is true. I was healed of swollen glands of the neck by using the Holy Oil (from the tomb of St. John Maximovitch) that your Monastery had sent me recently. I had swollen glands of the neck for at least three months. I went to the doctor and he gave me pills to take. The pills did nothing for my neck. My neck was swollen and stiff at times. I put your Holy Oil on my glands and neck and the next morning I was 90% better. That night I put more Holy Oil on my neck and the second morning I was completely healed. It is ten days now since I was healed and there are no problems with my neck. I want to first of all thank God for healing me. And thank God for the Holy Oil you sent. I am very, very poor. Please pray for me."

RELIEF AFTER A HEART ATTACK IN BULGARIA

The Convent of the Protection of the Most Holy Mother of God in Sofia, Bulgaria, wrote to Father Benedict on April 15 (Old Calendar), 1995:

"Christ is risen!

"We would like to greet you, the Very Reverend Abbot of your Holy Monastery, and all the brothers for the greatest Christian Holyday—the Resurrection of our Lord Jesus Christ. We sincerely wish you, as our Saviour has said it, that His joy might remain in you and that your joy might be full. (John 15:11.)

"We thank you for your kind letter and for the precious gift which moved us so much! It may be probably of interest to you to learn that your Weeping Icon of the Holy Mother of God helped an ill Christian here in Bulgaria. This lady is called Nelly Chopova and she is a shop-assistant in our bookstore. Two months ago she suffered a heart attack. She was in a very bad state and she couldn't move her left arm. Then she asked for the tears of the Theotokos to anoint her arm with it. Immediately after that she felt a great relief and she could receive the Holy Communion. Now she is much better and she thanks you from deep in her soul.

"We keep in our hearts the souvenir of your visit in Bulgaria and we pray fervently for all of you. We beg your blessing and your holy prayers."

MANY BLESSINGS

From Canadian, Texas, Leda Smith wrote on July 23, 1992:

"I had the pleasure to visit your Monastery a short time ago, and I received a cotton ball with the tears from the Weeping Icon.

"When I returned home, my husband rubbed the tears on a sore that would not go away for such a long time. The very next day it was gone.

"My husband (excited about his healing) rubbed the tears on his grandmother's bad knee, and she said that her knee was much relieved. I also put it on my mother's eyes. She has a problem on her eyes, and she's had it for ages, for years and years. It helped greatly. I also used it for my aunt who has bone cancer, and she claimed to be in less pain.

"I wanted to express my gratitude for your sharing this miracle with everyone."

HEARING RESTORED

In an undated letter received in 1997, Gwen Clavelle wrote from Lafayette, Louisiana:

"I'm writing to share with you a gift our Most Holy Mother gave to my son. My son had a hearing loss in one of his ears. I made the Sign of the Cross with the cotton ball of tears on his ears and seconds later his hearing was restored. I wanted to thank you for sharing your miracle with the world. If at all possible I would like another cotton ball with tears. I hope to visit your Monastery one day."

CONSOLATION

In another undated letter in 1997, John Rangel of El Centro, California, writes:

"Last summer, I was in the midst of a very beautiful relationship. She was the most beautiful and wonderful companion our Father could place in my life. Our obstacle—was distance. My fiancée and I had been going through a time of trial and difficulties.

"Not long into this new relationship, she began to experience various health problems. Conquering each one with amazing faith and vitality. She was about to undergo her third operation within a year and a half. All operations were due to different causes. She wanted me to be there at her side, but my economic condition at the time would not allow me to be with her. The day of the surgery, a friend shared some tears that she had, and introduced me to the Weeping Icon and told me that the tears would help the two of us through anything: and it did. My friend blessed me with the tears. A peace of mind enveloped me.

"Upon arriving home, I received a phone call from my fiancée's sister—to hurry and travel as soon as possible (350 miles) because my fiancée almost died on the operating table. A path was opened for me to be at my fiancée's side a few hours later. The operation was more complicated than had been expected. Recovery was to be lengthy. We both cried and prayed. It was then that I remembered the tears in my pocket. I blessed her, and she blessed me. The tears began to take effect on her. She was in the hospital only a few days; less than was expected. The incisions healed quickly, the surgery accomplished more than the doctors hoped for. For that we were so grateful.

"In the year that passed, my fiancée became healthier. Her attitude became better in almost all things. She had new hope for herself after encountering a time of despair.

"Slowly but surely, the relationship began to experience rocky times... Finally, in the middle of July of this year, she told me that she did not want to be 'tied down' in a relationship.

"The pain was incredible. My first thought was to pray. In search of my book of prayers, I found your information folder that I had been given long ago. Immediately, I called and asked for some tears. I was so happy to find them in my mail a few days later. Yes, they gave me a respite from my pain. I could see many things clearly afterwards. To realize that from God we receive love from others. That our Holy Mother of God is there to hold us as her own when times are tough.

"As the days passed, I felt lonely. I accepted God's will as my own. His love surpassed most of the loneliness. About a month later, I received a phone call from my 'ex' that her father was in a serious accident near where I lived, and would I go see how he was doing until she arrived. He was taken to the hospital in very serious condition. A Priest friend came and gave him final rites and blessings. The poor man was in intensive care for about three weeks. I went as often as permitted to pray over him and bless him with the Holy Oil and with the tears. Her father recovered quickly from injuries that should have taken at least three months to recover from. The other day, I felt very lonely. Times are a little rough, but there are many worse off than me. I wondered if I would ever find peace and love again.

"Sadness was a part of my life that day. A few hours later, I looked for the remnants of the tears. Perhaps I could have a little rest in prayer. But I had run dry blessing the gentleman I mentioned. To my surprise, there was a great deal of tears in the piece of cotton that was almost dry from a month before! I felt there was a message. So I began to pray. While the sadness has not totally gone away, my prayers were being answered.

"My brothers and sisters, I thank you. I will pray for you and all those who seek your spiritual aid. I hope that you will pray for me. I can attest to the divine power and blessing of the tears. While it is not much, please accept the enclosed offering in thanksgiving. May God bless you in His gracious love."

RELIEF FROM SENILITY

On September 19, 1997, Sallie Ann Radick of Pittsburgh, Pennsylvania wrote to express her gratitude:

"I have written you before and have received from you tears of the Icon. Thank you so very much for sharing the tears.

"My Mother, Mildred G. Radick, just turned eighty years old. The doctors have said that there is deterioration of the brain, which would indicate senility and/or Alzheimer's. I have never accepted either conclusion and just know there is still a lot of life left in my Mother.

"We are Serbian Orthodox, and each night when mother gets into bed, I say the Lord's Prayer with her, and then bless her with the tears of the Icon. The clarity of thought and tranquillity that comes to Mom from doing this is a small miracle and ever so appreciated.

We have our best conversations of the day right after the blessing is done.

"Would it be too much for me to ask that you send me ten of the packets of the tears of the Icon. I use them daily and really do need to have more. It makes such a difference in my life and certainly in my Mother's."

INTERNAL BLEEDING STOPPED

Halina Kacicki wrote on November 9, 1996, from Scottsdale, Arizona:

"I went to my doctor's for a checkup (I had been feeling poorly, faint, very dizzy, in pain from my stomach and heart area). The doctor had come from the lab after taking a second series of tests. A CBC blood count indicated that my blood level was 7 or below. A normal level is 14. I had been bleeding internally for some time and kept pushing myself not to be a wimp. I was rushed to emergency. Prior to going I made a brief stop at home to make arrangements for my pets. My neighbor in the complex had received the tears of the Mother of God from her aunt who had visited your Monastery in Texas. Upon anointing each other and myself again I also made the Sign of the Cross in a clean glass. I added bottled water to the glass and drank it. The bleeding *stopped.* I went home after the next day."

MANY MIRACLES

From Downingtown, Pennsylvania, Julie A. Schomp wrote about her experiences with the tears of the Mother of God. She wrote on November 18, 1996.

"I was given some of the Blessed tears of the Mother of God about three years ago, shortly after the suicide of my sister, which was an event that I shall never forget and I thought I'd never be able to get over.

"Back in 1993, when I was first given the tears, I thanked the friend, a man from my Parish. But, being of limited faith and ignorant of the many miracles being accomplished through the Most Holy Virgin's intercession, I put the tiny packet in my jeans pocket and there they sat for many months. I probably wore them to the barn a zillion times before ever washing them! I had mentioned the packet to a woman in our home school group and she remembered them on some feast of the Mother of God. She asked me to bring them along to our get together to bless the children. This threw me into a panic as I searched to find them. Once found, I was disappointed to find that they were all dried up never having been used. I dutifully brought them along, though, to show my friend my sad state of reverence for the tears that she was so excited about. After looking at them she asked me to at least tell the children (ages 2 to 14) what I knew about them and where they came from. I did the best I could, even though my belief in them was skeptical at best. I was then asked to bless each child on the forehead with the dried out cotton ball. While doing this myself I was shocked to find that they were becoming more and more moist as I blessed each person. Needless to say, my amazement was being quickly transformed into faith and a profound sense of love!

"Since that event, I was asked to bring the tears to another friend's house who had lost her four–year–old son very shortly after my sister's death. Now, not too long after giving the tears to (the bereaved mother) one of the other women found out that her father had a serious ailment and needed surgery. Both of Marge's parents drove out from Northeast Philly to be anointed. The dad was moved to tears himself as we told him the story of the tears as we knew it so far. I could see how frightened he was and how much comfort the tears brought him so I told him to take them with him. He kept them with him until they were wheeling him into the O.R. and his wife took them from him. He went through the surgery fine and is doing well today. But before they were able to return the tears to me, his wife was told that she had a cancerous cyst on her eyebrow. Her dad laid the cotton swab with the tears on the spot and prayed asking for a healing for his wife, too. In the morning the spot was gone. Praising God, they were reluctant to give me back the tears!

"Before that could happen, though, another friend got a phone call that her brother lay near death out in Seattle. She flew out immediately but called me and asked to have the tears mailed to her ASAP. Well, this was Sunday evening before Labor Day, 1995. I couldn't see any way to get them there that quickly as he was not even expected to last through the night.

Marge's dad, however, found a (carrier) and got them there the next day, Labor Day. My friend was relieved to be able to anoint her brother even through the disgruntled remarks of family members. Now this brother has recovered and is serious about his faith.

"The tears returned to the Northeast and to me. In January, another friend was faced with a great trial. Her husband fell off their roof trying to shovel the snow. It was during last year's 30" snowfall and he was concerned about the roof collapsing. The fall resulted in multiple skull fractures. At first, he, too, was not expected to live through the night. Emergency surgery was performed to relieve the swelling by removing a portion of one of the lobes of his brain. When he was still alive the next morning the doctors assured his wife that if he did survive he would be a total vegetable for the remainder of his life. When we heard of the accident we naturally got the tears over to her as quickly as we could. He was anointed and the next day he came out of his coma and within a day or two began talking! He is back at work today with a slight memory loss of the events surrounding the accident. But most importantly, he now joins his wife at Church regularly and has a deepened faith in God and a special tenderness for our Most Holy Lady.

"In the late spring, I brought the tears with me to a Post-Abortion Healing Retreat at which I volunteer. There I met a woman who was dying of breast cancer and was sure the cancer was God's punishment to her for the abortion she had committed ten years earlier. This woman anxiously opened her heart to the Lord, poured out her sorrow and accepted His powerful healing love. I gave the tears to her to take back to her breast cancer support group. She died just three months later but her death was happy.

"I gave the tears away because I felt that our Lady wanted to be in that group. I know that they are still being used and that the Mother of God is still working and praying wherever they are present. I ask that you send me another packet for me to keep with me. I look forward to hearing from you. Pray for me as I will certainly pray for you."

A CHILD'S LIFE SAVED

Maria Kaldis reported the following about the miraculous healing of her son, Christos, when he was two–and–a–half years old:

Her two older children were down with strep throat and the youngest, Christos, was throwing up and diagnosed as probably having the same thing. In less than a week, however, he became very weak. In this condition he slipped from his chair at one point and struck his head behind the right ear. Not long afterward the doctors determined that his blood was clotting, his platelet count was low, and his white blood cell count high. They decided to test him for leukemia, a brief procedure. He turned out not to have leukemia, but his condition worsened and so they decided to check him into the hospital. Paralysis was setting in on his left side. It was only when the doctors performed a CAT scan on Christos that they found an orange-sized blood clot behind his left ear. The second they realized this it seemed as if the whole roomful of doctors and medical personnel went crazy.

The boy's brain had swollen and he was close to bleeding to death. He was in such a state that the doctors could not operate on him. They decided that they could give him two medications to see if they could improve his condition enough for an operation. He had 15 minutes to respond—if he did not, then all they could do would be to try to make him comfortable. Without anyone's knowledge, however, a Priest slipped in and anointed Christos with myrrh from the Weeping Icon. He had hurried from a considerable distance to do this, and somehow arrived just at the right time. This was on January 16, 1998.

Christos responded to the medicine, received a blood transfusion, and was then operated on. Sixty stitches were put in his head. The doctors said afterward that he would undergo months of rehabilitation, experience seizures, and have to have a shunt put in. But the Priest served a paraklesis. Within three weeks the two-year-old Christos was walking, and within a month he had no limp or difficulty getting around. He experienced no seizures and underwent no rehabilitation except what his family did with him at home. The doctors say that they did not do this on their own, that there is no "textbook" reason why Christos should be so healthy.

Maria Kaldis reported this miracle when she came to the Monastery over half a year later to thank the Theotokos for the deliverance of her little son. We (the Monks) saw Christos, now three years old, running about and getting into trouble to the annoyance of his older siblings and the delight of his mother.

AN INFANT'S EYE SPARED

The Monks received the following letter, postmarked December 16, 1997, from Mary Fuentes, in Edinburg, Texas:

"My daughter, Illyana Fuentes, was born on August 20, 1996. She was born two months premature and was kept in the hospital for one month. When she was three weeks old the doctors told us that her eyes did not develop normally and she was blind. After so many doctors and eye exams they found a mass in her right eye. They thought it was a tumor and it would be life–threatening at her age. The doctors didn't think it was a tumor but it was a possibility and they only way they could find out what it is was to remove her eye. This was devastating to us, but we had faith in God and decided to hold off on the operation.

"A friend of the family visited Christ of the Hills Monastery and she brought me some tears of the Mother of God from her Myrrh–Weeping Icon. I would anoint Illyana before she would go to sleep and myself too. My prayers were answered and I was given peace of mind through all our ordeals.

"On December 2, 1997, I took Illyana to her eye doctor for a regular checkup and he gave us good news. Our prayers were answered and a miracle was granted by God through the intercessions of the Mother of God in her Holy Icon. After an eye exam the doctor told us that the mass in her eye that they thought was a tumor had shrunk and now is gone.

"I thank God for His miracle through all our ordeals and anguish. I knew God was always with us and through His love He gave us a miracle. I would appreciate your prayers and I will continue to anoint Illyana with the tears of the Holy Icon. I have faith and hope that through the intercession of the Mother of God we will be granted another miracle for Illyana.

"May God bless you!"

A CHILD SPARED FROM ASTHMA DEATH

The following letter, dated February 8, 1966, came to the Monastery from Mrs. Costas Georghiou, in Doha, Qatar:

"Just a note to thank you for your kindness during our visit to your Monastery over the New Year's holiday. We truly enjoyed this experience.

"I would like to share with you or miracle since this visit. We were about to leave Houston for London and on to Cyprus and then Qatar. Our daughter Chrystalla, age seven years, was feeling poorly for a couple of days. We took her to our pediatrician twice and he told us he felt she could make this trip. However, when we arrived at the ticket counter they called the doctor, and he told them she had a 95% chance of no problem They decided that we must have oxygen on the plane, and we were delayed five hours. My husband was very upset about this matter, we waited for four hours and were about to board the plane when Chrystalla stopped breathing and was rushed to Texas Children's Hospital, with a severe asthma attack.

"Chrystalla stayed in the hospital for eight days, with a severe sinus infection and also pneumonia. We were told that she would not have lived to land if we had boarded the plane. I believe that this was a divine intervention of the Holy Mother. I know that our visit to your holy place and the beautiful crying Icon of the Blessed Mother has changed my life in many ways. But this was truly a blessed miracle. Also I treasure and keep the tear of Mary Mother of God close to us, and when Chrystalla was so ill I blessed her with it. I know in my heart that without the help of God and His Blessed Mother I would not be so blessed.

"Thank you for your prayers, and please continue to pray for my family. Thank you more than I can ever tell you. We plan to return to Houston for good in June, as Costas was offered two positions in Texas. We will look forward to visiting you then."

A BROKEN ANKLE HEALED

A person who requested to remain anonymous wrote on the 17th of September, 1997:

"I fractured my ankle on the last weekend of April. I had emergency surgery. I had a plate put in and stayed a few days in the hospital.

"A month later, the first weekend of May, I had a second surgery. Before I had the second surgery my mother introduced me to our Lady of the Shrine (the Myrrh–Weeping Icon of the Theotokos). I believe wholeheartedly in our Lady, and naturally at this time I prayed to her even more. I could not believe that I had the tears of our Lady in my hands. I was extremely happy and felt comforted by her closeness. I went for X rays before my second surgery and the doctor said I had to have a good amount of screws. Then my miracle began. When he opened my ankle up he said it was unbelievable that I only needed one. You see, my surgery was within twenty-four hours of the X rays.

"Naturally I had inside therapy for my ankle. Then came my other miracle. I had to have outpatient therapy. At the end of my outside therapy I was doing things with it that I wasn't supposed to do until next year in January of 1998. You see I finished my physical therapy in late August of 1997. Our Lady is amazing and she really loves us all and wants us to be close to her Son."

GIFT OF TEARS

Christina Bocanegra wrote from San Benito, Texas, on December 29, 1997:

"Enclosed please find a check to help on the building of more facilities for the Monks in your Monastery.

"I will never forget the day that my husband Victor and I visited Christ of the Hills Monastery and saw the Weeping Icon of New Sarov. Tears started flowing out of my eyes and I couldn't stop them for a while. I felt that our Beloved Mother of God had and has great cause to weep. I felt that she weeps for us all.

"Fr. Benedict, your letters never cease to inspire me. There's always a phrase or two that clings to me and helps me cope with whatever troubles me. I always read your letters with anticipation. I pray to God to inspire more people to give to this great cause so that Christ of the Hills Monastery flourishes in abundance and meets all the needs of the Monks always. It is my hope that your Monastery never will have to move out of Blanco, Texas. May the good Lord in His mercy grant you the wisdom and the strength to administer His works for many years.

"I have no words to express my feelings when you mentioned that more Monks or Novices are coming in even though life is difficult at the Monastery. I think God has a plan for everyone and everything. "

NECK INJURY HEALED

On June 8, 1996, Robert Cook wrote from San Marcos, Texas:

"In January 1985 I was involved in an auto accident which resulted in the fourth through the seventh disk in my neck being ruptured. In February 1993, I was in another accident which aggravated the injury causing less mobility, more pain, and a gradual deterioration of my ability to use my arms. Neurosurgeons had told me that they would only do surgery to relieve the pressure on the nerve branches as a last resort, since the chance of giving me relief was so small (less than 30%).

"By early 1995 I was suffering from migraine headaches three to four times a week, and by mid–summer they had become a constant part of my life. To keep the headaches and the pain and pressure in my neck at a bearable level, I was taking four Advil, two to three times a day every day. By November, 1995, I was losing the ability to straighten out my arms, and they hurt so much when I tried to use them, that I could hardly lift a salt shaker. I also suffer from a form of asthma, caused by a lung infection I suffered a few years ago which makes me cough without ceasing whenever I am around strong scents. (i.e., I can't walk down a detergent aisle in a supermarket, be around perfumes, and even the incense in church makes me cough).

"On January 18, 1996, I had an appointment with my family doctor and he advised me that I now had to have something done to relieve the pressure on the nerves or I would soon lose the use of my arms. An appointment was made with my neurologist in Austin for February 2, 1996, for a review of the options which were available and an evaluation of how to best relieve the pressure.

"On Sunday, January 28, 1996, my wife and I paid a visit to the Shrine of the Blessed Virgin Mary at Christ of the Hills Monastery. Before leaving our home to visit the Shrine I had prayed that if the Blessed Virgin was pleased that we came to visit her that she would show us in some small way.

"Upon arriving we were ushered to the Chapel by an elderly gentleman, and upon entering encountered several people listening to the Monk explaining the history of the Icon. I had suggested that our Blessed Mother could allow us to smell a scent of roses during our visit if she was pleased with our presence when I had prayed earlier. I did not smell incense burning, but the smell of roses gradually got stronger during the time I was in the Chapel. Following the anointing of the people by the Monk, my wife left the Chapel while I remained to light candles and pray for our son, his girlfriend and her family, and my wife's niece. I then left and we visited the gift shop and then returned home.

"While driving back to San Marcos, I asked my wife if she had smelled the roses in the Chapel. Her reply was, 'What roses, all I could smell was burning incense and wondered how you were staying in the Chapel without coughing.' We returned home and that night I didn't take any Advil before going to bed. The next morning I got up and my arms were straight and I went to the kitchen and opened the refrigerator and lifted out a gallon of milk without pain, and told my wife 'look, and it doesn't even hurt, and I don't have a headache either.' She said, 'praise God!' and we offered prayers of thanks.

"Upon keeping my appointment with Dr. Robert Cain on February 2nd I told him I felt foolish since the problems that I had been having were gone. His reply was, 'I hope so, because your neck is a mess that we really don't want to have to get into.'

"To this date I have had no headaches and my arms have not had the pain in the muscles from the pinched nerves, and I'm still able to straighten out my arms. I still have the asthma, and the arthritis in my joints still acts up, but thanks to God and the intercessions of our Blessed Mother I can live a very normal life."

FRAGRANCE OF ROSES

Sister Theodora wrote from Dearborn, Michigan, on July 20, 1996:

"Glory to God for all things! I received your letter of June 20, 1996, explaining the 'Akathist to St. Paraskeva' and your making copies to distribute. Surely, this Saint is well loved of our Lord and performs miracles.

"I was overjoyed to receive the cotton ball of the blessed tears of the Most Holy Theotokos. However, I should tell you that when I went to the post office to get my mail, there as a huge "smell" of roses throughout the whole post office and at first I thought perhaps someone brought roses from their local rose garden for the postal clerks as sometimes they do, but no, it was coming from my box. As I opened it the great odor overwhelmed me. As I opened the letter I could see the large oil stain right through the envelope and everything in it and my box. The plastic broke through and the oil spread everywhere. What a beautiful blessing. Thank you for sending it and all praise, honor, and glory to God and His Saints and His most Holy, most Blessed, most Pure Mother Mary, our never failing Theotokos. There are many more miracles awaiting all of you there at Blanco. Just ask for your needs and they will be supplied.

"It takes eight to ten days for your mail to arrive here. Again thank you for your beautiful, blessed message and the tears and oil of the most Holy Mother of God."

A BLESSED DEATH

Joseph Tucker wrote from Kingsburg, California, on April 11, 1997:

"Thank you for the Holy Oils. I do believe that a miracle was done by our Blessed Mother, and this is why. Letters to and from England take from five to eight days. I sent the tears to my sister in London, England, on a Monday, and she got it on that Thursday morning, a time of only three days. Thelma, my sister, blessed her oldest son Joseph, who had cancer of the liver and pancreas. That afternoon he had a heart attack, I believe from the treatment, which dislodged some plaque, and hence the heart attack. Joseph died a very peaceful death that evening at 6 p.m. He was 51 years old.

"I believe that our Blessed Mother wanted (her tears to) get to Joseph in time, and she did it, moving that letter so fast that he did get it.

"Thank you very much for your help. I have so much love for our Blessed Mother.

"I am going to bless my wife, Yvonne. She does not know it, but she has to go back for another mammogram. I feel very afraid for her, but I know that our Blessed Mother will help her, just as she cured our youngest granddaughter. The hole in her heart closed."

INFANT'S HEART DEFECT HEALED

Joe and Yvonne Tucker wrote from Kingsburg, California, On January 31, 1996:

"Our granddaughter, Aimee Michelle Vallaret, was born on October 14, 1995. Two days later, when she was to be released from the hospital, the pediatrician diagnosed her with a patent ductus arteriosus (a hole in the heart), which the doctor said might require surgical intervention to correct. Children who have a hole in their heart that does not close have a very short life expectancy.

"We had been to your Monastery on August 16, 1995, at which time my daughter was blessed with the sacred tears of Mary while she was pregnant. We returned on November 13th with Aimee who was then one month old, and she was anointed with the tears of our Blessed Mother and blessed by Father Joseph, Father Gregory and two other Priests. We ourselves were anointed at that time. We asked that our Blessed Mother cure Aimee without surgery. We received the blessed tears to take home and Aimee was anointed with them at each bath time.

"On January 2, 1996, her parents took her to see a pediatric cardiologist regarding her heart defect. It was at this visit that the doctor confirmed that the hole had 'closed up' spontaneously and would not require any surgical treatment.

"We returned to your Monastery on January 29, 1996, to give thanks to our Blessed Mother for her help. We were all once again anointed. We left a silver heart medal at the Icon in thanksgiving that no surgical procedure was now required. We thanked our Blessed Mother for her love and intercession and feel that our faith in her divine compassion has given Aimee a whole and healthy heart. When Aimee is six months old, she will be examined again by the pediatric cardiologist to confirm that the hole in the heart is history. Praises and thanks to the Blessed Mother of God!"

ST. SERAPHIM HEALS A WOMAN

In a letter postmarked July 19, 1997, Claudia A'Vant wrote from East Providence, Rhode Island, to one of the Monks:

"I am writing to inform you that through the intercession of St. Seraphim of Sarov I have received numerous cures, physically and spiritually. St. Seraphim has protected me and saved my life in numerous ways. I worked nearly seven years teaching nutrition. Rarely was I ever sick, thank God. But in 1995, when my job was downsized I soon lost my health benefits. I began experiencing extreme pain in my uterus. I received health benefits and was seen by nearly ten physicians. They all made different diagnoses and gave me medications that made the pain worse. There was a time (when) the pain was so unbearable I thought my insides would be torn from me. I can't describe the pain I went through. It was constant attacks that would come and go. My family seemed to abandon me as though I were crazy and making these stories up. One day my sister took me to a used book store. We were going to spend a night in Newport. We decided it was good to take a few books along with us. I selected at least four books and one of the books was one on St. Seraphim. I did not have enough money for all the books. Since I am Roman Catholic I had never heard of St. Seraphim and wasn't sure if I should take his books home with me. I stopped at least fifteen minutes trying to decide and finally I took the St. Seraphim book and put the other book back on the shelf. I did not read the book that weekend. It stayed in my room until one day I was having the worst attack I ever had. I had started reading the St. Seraphim book and started crying. Something in the book related to faith. I said to myself, I don't understand what faith means. If I could, maybe the pain would go away, and I kept crying. The pain seemed to effect my heart and my chest. It was so horrible I couldn't bear a minute longer. And I couldn't go to another doctor. I just knew I was going to die. Suddenly I went to get up from my bed. The pain I felt vanished. I kept walking around my house. I felt incredibly happy, a happiness I never experienced before. St. Seraphim had stopped the pain I had suffered for nearly two years. It was the worst of all the other pains I had experienced since all these problems started.

"I know I have confidence in St. Seraphim that he will guide me up to the hills of Christ of the Hills Monastery. And then I will complete the story of the wonderful St. Seraphim, who has saved my life. Thank you for all your wonderful prayers, and for the myrrh from the Weeping Icon. The Blessed Mother has taken me into her arms because of your prayers."

VARIOUS MIRACLES REPORTED

On November 8, 1995, Eugene Naheim wrote to the Monks:

"Recently I moved from Ohio to be daily in prayer in front of the Weeping Icon. There many miraculous healings took place. In the last two months, since I am here—A lady came to pray for her paralyzed mother, who was at home in a wheelchair. The Priest gave the lady some oil blessed with tears. She went home, anointed her mother and the mother started to walk. Two weeks ago they both came into the church to give thanks. The old lady walks normally. I was telling another lady, who came to pray, about this healing. She said, 'Look what happened to me! I had colon cancer, prayed to the Icon and the cancer disappeared.' A lady from Mexico told me about another lady from Mexico, who was given here a small bottle with oil and tears. At home, when the bottle was empty, over night it was full again. Since then the bottle is always full."

PAIN-FREE RECOVERY FROM SURGERY

The Carl family sent a card they had received from their cousin and an explanation dated December 26, 1996, from Lakeside City, Texas. They had visited the Shrine of the Weeping Icon and had anointed their cousin in the hospital the day before she was to have surgery for peritoneal dialysis. She had had a kidney transplant and the kidney was being rejected. The doctor was amazed that she never asked for any pain medication whey she woke up from surgery.

The woman who underwent the surgery writes:

"What a wonderful gift you gave me. I can't tell you all the different ways the Blessed Mother has touched me through her 'tears.' Dialysis has continued to improve every time. My surgery went so smooth for the peritoneal dialysis. Like I told you on the phone—NO PAIN. I've felt that real sense of *peace* you spoke of. She feels so near all the time."

HEALINGS IN ROMANIA

Toma Stefan wrote from Sibiu, Romania:

"(It) was a great blessing for me to have in my hands, in front of my eyes, the tears of Mother of God." *Toma tells about the Caliu Monastery in Altemia, Romania. There, he writes, is a wonderful Monk, the Abbot, who has the power from God to heal many Christians of their diseases. This Monk is his*

Confessor. The Monks of that Monastery pray constantly for Christ of the Hills Monastery. He encloses a paper Icon print of an Icon of the Mother of God which is at Nicula Monastery in Romania, and has wept for a long time.

Toma then writes about his aunt, a woman of great faith. "When she put a tear from the envelope with the Mother of God's tears on her eye, with which she didn't see so well, after this moment she sees perfectly all the time. She told me this after I came from the Orthodox Theological Seminary."

He then tells about working as a substitute teacher in a school, where he told the pupils about the Weeping Icon, and about their devout attention. He tells how he hopes, "after a few weeks God will help me, to go with (an) envelope with the Mother of God's tears (to) an asylum of old people who are very depressed. This asylum is in my home town, Sibiu." *He writes of his interest in the Saints of America, of whom he had not heard before, and his especial interest in St. John (Maximovitch). He closes with a quote from St. Symeon, the New Theologian about the Saints:* "Saints from every generation form a part of a golden chain, in which each Saint is a separate link, united to the next by faith, works, and love."

BROKEN ANKLE FREED FROM PAIN

Rustica Sarmiento wrote from Houston, Texas, on February 17, 1997:

"I am one of those people who was cured by the tears of our Blessed Virgin Mary. Father, I had an accident three years ago and I have a fractured ankle. I was operated (on) and I suffered a lot of pain even when the cast was removed. I used the tears of our Blessed Virgin Mary and at the end the pain was gone. But as of the last three weeks (since the) accident happened, I forgot that I have a fractured ankle and I walk very fast. At evening time I feel pain in my ankle and I thought of the tears, and I don't have any more. Please send me some of the tears. I am looking forward (to hearing from you) and thank you."

HEALING BY SAINT JOHN OF RILA

Theodore described his experience as a Pilgrim in Bulgaria:

"I accompanied my Spiritual Father and two of his Novices on a Pilgrimage to some of the Holy Places of Orthodoxy last year. On this trip I had an experience that brought home to me the reality of the Church's teaching on the matter of Saints being able to directly intervene in our lives when we pray for their intercession.

"We had taken a short side trip from Athens to Sophia, Bulgaria. There we stayed at the Convent of the Holy Protection, attended an All–Night Vigil and then the next morning, went to a Liturgy at the Church of St. John of Rila. Later that afternoon we were unpredictably taken to a Monastery in the mountains 70 km. away from Sophia. This Monastery was dedicated to St. John the Forerunner. Two Monks had lived as hermits in this abandoned Monastery for years until the breakup of the Soviet Union; but now, at the time of our visit, there were thirty Novices with them. We were also told that we were the first foreigners to visit this Monastery in 100 years. Our visit there was in mid-January and the temperature was well below freezing. A young Novice showed us to our quarters for the night. It was in a building made of stone but without heat (except for a tiny electric space heater in my cell) and most of my warm clothes were still somewhere in my 'lost' luggage.

"We arrived at the Monastery at 5:45 p.m., just in time for another Vigil, which lasted for about three and one half hours and afterwards went into the Trapeza (refectory room) for the evening meal. This was well after the Nativity Fast was over, so they treated us to the yogurts and cheeses made from the Monastery's sheep and goats. Unfortunately, about half way through I had to rush out because of illness, but when with help of Pepto-Bismol, I was able to return to hear some of the fascinating stories about the life of this spiritual community. I found out that St. John of Rila had lived in these mountains in the early 900's after his parents had died and when he had first taken up the hermit life, but before he went to live in the Rila Mountains.

"Our plan for the following morning was that we would attend a very early Liturgy and then be brought back to Sophia, to catch our scheduled flight back to Athens in the early afternoon, thus, we retired early. When I lay down to sleep I was somewhat dismayed that the bed was a piece of plywood with some blankets on it. I decided that I had to sleep in all my clothes including jacket and stocking cap because I was so cold. Even so, with three or four blankets on top of me and two under me I could not seem to get warm. I comforted myself with the Jesus prayer and reflected on how different this life was to my comfortable life in America.

"About one or two in the morning I was awakened by shooting pains in my abdomen. When I was fully awake I also noticed that about every minute or two my body would go through uncontrollable shivering. I was freezing! Immediately, I assumed that I must be getting amoebic dysentery, because it felt so similar to when I had come down with it in Mexico. I remembered how, that time, I had alternated between chills and feverish sweating episodes for three days. I had the thought that I should get up and take some Bactrim that was in my medicine kit. It was there for just such an occasion. However, I was afraid to get out from under my blankets because I might lose the precious little warmth I had. I was terrified that I would have another attack of diarrhea and then have to try and get to the outhouse which was more than 75 yards away from the building I was in. I was also terrified that at any moment I would be breaking into a sweat and then I would surely freeze to death. I can't remember ever feeling so frightened, alone and vulnerable, in all my life even though I had once been stranded on top of a mountain peak in the Tetons over night without water, food or warm clothes. On that climbing trip we had route problems, had run out of daylight and couldn't descend. That night had been brutal and cold and we couldn't fall asleep all night because of the shivering. But now, I was also sick and that made me feel ever so much more vulnerable. I also assumed that now I would be too sick to travel in the morning back to Sophia. Unfortunately, for our flight back to Athens we had non-refundable tickets. Thus, I would be ruining the trip for all of us.

"I started praying: 'Lord Jesus Christ, Son of God, have mercy on me a sinner,' and 'O Most Holy Theotokos, save us,' over and over, going back and forth from one prayer to the other, but without any relief. I laid there cold, shivering, pains shooting throughout my abdomen, helpless and scared for what seemed forever. Eventually my mind flashed to a story that I had heard the previous day, about the cave in the Rila mountains where St. John sometimes slept. I had been told that a person could hardly kneel in that space and that mainly one could just lay there in a fetal position. I now reflected on how I was also laying on my right side, in a fetal position, though on a bed. I thought: 'What kind of people could these hermits have been?' St. John, for example, lived for years without contact with any people, living on herbs and berries, often dwelling in a hollowed out tree. Did he have fires in the winter? Did he have furs to keep him warm? Did he ever get sick? It seemed utterly impossible for a person to live this way all alone. Earlier, on the previous day, Bishop Photius had given each of us an Icon of St. John, and I now retrieved his image on that Icon into my mind's eye. Then I also remembered, that a friend who had recently died, had six months earlier given me an audio tape of a commemorative service for the feast day of St. John of Rila. At that time I had not even heard of this Bulgarian Saint and hesychast. This struck me as so serendipitous and coincidental that I thought, maybe this was somehow a sign. Maybe I should call on St. John, to intercede with God for me, in my desperate plight. So, in addition to my prayers to Christ and to the Theotokos I added: 'St. John of Rila, please pray to God for me.'

"Incredibly, after three to five minutes I started feeling warm, my pain disappeared and instead of anguish and fear in my heart I felt a sense of peace and tranquillity. It was just totally bewildering. I started thinking maybe this was some type of *prelest* or delusion, my condition could not possibly have changed just like that! But, in my heart I felt such a deep gratitude, thinking, 'Glory be to Christ and His Saints.'

"That morning after the Liturgy I spoke to Father Simeon and asked him about my experience. He said, 'St. John visited you last night. This is his territory. He responded to your prayers because of your sincere desperation and because you did not give up, calling on the name of Jesus Christ and His Holy Mother.'

"Earlier, before our trip, I remembered that Father Simeon had said that great blessings often came together with great trials. He had said that our attitude should be to accept such trials for Christ's sake, rather than murmuring against God or feeling sorry for ourselves. This was a tall order that I could not do all by myself. So to succeed at even this, we also needed to call on God and His Saints to help give us this attitude.

"Later, I remembered thinking: 'Why would Christ respond to St. John's prayers for me and not directly to my prayers or to my prayers to the Most Holy Theotokos for her intercession?' But, I guess that's really the wrong question. *All* my desperate praying was calling on the mercy of God for me in my helplessness. Only the sudden timing of my relief had made such an impression on me. Maybe I had to feel and bear my helplessness patiently. Maybe it served to soften my hardened and normally self-sufficient heart to the reality that my life is really in God's hands, and I need to learn to rely on Him alone. Maybe it served to help me accept in faith, the miraculous stories I later heard from other Monks on our trip, about how various other Saints have made themselves known to the faithful in recent times.

"I can tell you that now, when I venerate St. John of Rila's Icon, when I kiss his hand, it is a different sort of experience than before, when I absentmindedly crossed myself and kissed the Icon without even knowing who the Saint was. I now have been given a sense of reverence, attention and respect. May I also approach and venerate the Icons of other Saints with the same reverence. In the name of the Father and the Son and the Holy Spirit. Amen."

HEALING FROM MENTAL ILLNESS

In March of 1996, S. T. wrote from Brownsville, Texas, to the Monastery:

"Greetings to you and all my brothers and sisters in Christ. Thank you all for your prayers. I'm healed completely from all my disease and mental illness.

May the Lord bless you abundantly and richly and use you for His purpose, eternal life in Jesus Christ. May you keep reaching out to those abandoned and lost and keep comforting the needy."

GIFT OF A CHILD

Diane Mulkern wrote to the Monastery from Hyannis, Massachusetts, on July 30, 1996:

"I am writing this letter which is long overdue to thank you and to forward to you the enclosed money which I received as a birthday present in February. I have held onto the money in hope of buying something special for myself and finally came to the conclusion that the special thing that I could do with the money was to send it to you in hope that it would help you to carry on God's work.

"I first became aware of your (Monastery) and the living miracle in your Monastery when my parents returned home to Boston from a visit to my brother in San Antonio. My parents had visited your Monastery and spoke of their personal spiritual experience while visiting. My mother had brought home a cotton swab dipped in the myrrh from our Lady's Icon. I too was moved by their story and their experience.

"My story is this: I am currently 44 years old. My husband and I have been married for four years (never married before) and very much wanted a child. We prayed and asked to be blessed (with a child) but it appeared that it would not happen. At the time that my parents were in Texas I became pregnant. Upon their return I gave them the good news and my father expressed to me that this was the sign made real of his spiritual experience while at the Monastery.

"I used the swab of cotton to anoint myself numerous times during my pregnancy. Finally, I passed it on to my sister-in-law who is also praying for a child....

"My daughter, who is named Victoria Marie, is a healthy, wonderful ten-month-old. She is everything that is beautiful and right with this world and I see heaven in her eyes and my heart is so full of love because of her. She is a miracle.

"Thank you for your gift of serving our Lord and His Mother, for sharing their gift and their message.

OVARIAN MASS DISSOLVED

On January 22, 1996, Dorothy Giosa wrote to thank the Monks for their evlogia (holy objects sent as a blessing). She recounts:

"Six months ago, an MRI showed a mass on my left ovary. On further examination, the doctor decided to wait six months and recheck it. (On) Friday, January 18, the ultrasound was repeated at the hospital. I then went to the post office where your package was waiting for me. I opened the packet, anointed myself and venerated the Icon. Today was my appointment with the doctor. I was so relieved when he told me that the test results showed that the mass has been dissolved. He was happy with the results, and I was greatly relieved."

CANCER DISAPPEARS

John Daugherty wrote from Sacramento, California:

"I recently was diagnosed with cancer. A friend who is a Deacon came to my hospital room and told me of your work and the Weeping Icon. He also anointed me and gave me the tear of the Myrrh-Weeping Icon. My wife anointed me with the tear on numerous occasions.

"The doctor told me he believes the cancer is gone. I firmly and sincerely believe it was the power of prayer and the anointing with the tears of the Mother of God that gave me my recovery."

Mr. Daugherty's friend, the Deacon mentioned above, wrote a note to Fr. Pangratios explaining that the turn around in the cancer occurred the day after he had anointed him, and that his recovery is apparently complete.

RECOVERY FROM LIFE-THREATENING INFECTION

Rosa Maria writes:

"In 1985 I retired from teaching school, a position I held for 31 years. In 1986 I started getting sick off and on. In 1988, I was diagnosed with 'San Juaquin Valley Fever' (a fungus). I was sent to Seton Hospital in Austin for there were no infectious disease doctors in Laredo. I stayed in the hospital for six months, because the fungus traveled all over my body, locating itself in my left knee, where it ate part of the knee bone and the cartilage. It then traveled to my head, making me very disoriented. At this time, meningitis set in. From so much blood being taken out, my veins collapsed, and so they fed me with a tube. After a while the veins in my leg were ruined. I was very, very sick. I didn't know anything that happened to me after that. I was given experimental medicines through a shunt that was planted on top of my head. They removed my gall bladder.

"I have been having to go to Austin for lumbar punctures to test the level of fungus left in my body. Thank God! Everything is all right. But I still have my problems. I can't put my left foot down, for the bone is missing and it makes my knee hurt a lot.

"My daughter came (to the Monastery) to see the Mother of God, and she brought me the tears. I started using them on my ulcerated leg and now I am glad to say that the Mother of God heard my cry and she answered me with a miracle. I almost died, so my doctor told me later. But I told him, 'God still wants me to come home to my family,' and I did. Thank you, and pray for me."

CANCER DISAPPEARS

Bob Southern wrote from Daphne, Alabama, on July 17, 1995, about a woman who had come into church, with her husband, weeping. Mr. Southern and his wife asked the woman what was wrong and she told them,

"I have a very active cancer in my colon. I'm scheduled for surgery in the morning. I want to ask all of you to pray for me."

After they prayed for her, they told her about the Weeping Icon and their visit to the Shrine to the Mother of God at Christ of the Hills Monastery. They invited them to come home with them so that they might anoint the sick woman. After the woman was anointed, they asked her husband to call them following the operation.

"The next morning the husband called and talked to my wife, Louise, and said that his wife was doing well. He said the doctors could not understand it, that there was no cancer present. This was her second operation. I believe they told us that the first operation had revealed the cancer."

MOTHER SPARED IN AUTO ACCIDENT

Sarah Tune wrote from Euless, Texas, in a letter postmarked the 27th of June, 1997:

"My youth group visited the Shrine of the Mother of God on Wednesday, June 18. That day I prayed extra hard for the protection of my family—I didn't know why—when I was about to be blessed with the myrrh. Many of my friends were very moved by our visit, including myself. I cried a little afterward, but I also was very quiet after getting blessed, wondering and feeling so special that I had a gift from God on my hands and head. But then I didn't know what a true gift I had been given. When I got home on Friday, my mother told me, after pointing out the grass on the car and the way it shook at 60m.p.h., that she had been in an accident on Wednesday night on the highway after avoiding hitting an animal. She crashed into the curb and was airborne and then she hit the grass and ground in a ditch. She was fine and the car had very little damage. Normally cars will flip many times with just such an accident. She told me she knew she should have been dead from the accident, but was fine. She knew an Angel had been with her and saved her life. When she told me this I asked her when it had happened, and she told me it was Wednesday. I immediately remembered my visit and burst into tears, so hard that it took me a while to tell her that we went to your Monastery and had visited the Weeping Icon that day. She then also burst into tears and we both cried the whole way home, knowing that my visit and prayer and her life all came for us from God. Even as I was writing this I cried in amazement and thankfulness that God had directed me to your Monastery and spared her life. This has been a wonderful blessing to both of us. I don't know the words for the wonderful feeling I had and have today, but simply in awe of how much God has cared for me and my mother and loves us. I can't seem to stop saying 'Thank You' to God for everything He has done for me. I also thank you."

STIFF KNEE HEALED

Fr. Dominic Elms wrote from St. Bernard, Ohio, on December 28, 1995:

"This Christmas I was given an Icon (of the Mother of God) and the oil from the Weeping Icon. I have had some problems with my left knee and have tried just about everything to correct the problem. It started giving me problems about a month and a half ago. I woke up one morning and I was unable to bend it, it was so stiff. I started to walk with a limp and sometimes I had to sit down for a while because of the pain. I went to a chiropractor and he said that I had runner's knee, and to put ice on it. I tried ointments, then I tried the tear from the Icon, and right away I was able to bend my knee with no problem. I have no pain. All I feel is a warm feeling going through my knee. I walk around my room without a limp, and this happened immediately after I anointed my knee."

BREAST LUMPS DISAPPEAR, GRANDDAUGHTER SPARED SERIOUS INJURY IN AUTO ACCIDENT

Cayetana Rejas wrote from Euless, Texas, on June 19, 1998:

"Last year I took my mammogram and it showed that I had some calcification, so I had to have a biopsy. I was glad that it was not cancer, but the doctor told me to be sure to take my mammograms every year. Around the first of November I went for a mammogram and they also had to do an ultrasound. It showed that

I again had a cyst on the same breast. On the weekend of November 16, my husband and my daughter and a friend of hers and myself went to visit the Icon at Blanco, Texas. I was so glad we went there. I felt a lot of peace of mind. I didn't even want to leave there, it's so peaceful and quiet, and I could really feel her presence there.

"When I went to see the doctor, she examined me and couldn't find any lumps or anything. Thanks to God and to His Mother.

"Please keep on praying for me because I also have glaucoma on both of my eyes. So far I'm doing better. I already had laser surgery on both of them."

In a separate note she wrote:

"My granddaughter came to work here at the Dallas and Forth Worth area from El Paso on June 2, 1998. She had to go to work in Dallas. She doesn't know this area well, and she got lost. Because she was reading the names of the streets, she ran a stop light and another car hit her. Our pickup truck that she was driving was totaled. The door on her side was torn off completely. Almost all of the trim on the side was gone, and even the seat (was damaged). Thanks to God and His Mother, she (had only) a few scratches on her leg. Everybody that sees the pickup says that they don't know how she didn't get hurt. When my daughter and my husband went to clean out the pickup, they found a prayer rope and my daughter says that is what saved her child."

GRATITUDE FOR THE LOVE OF THE MOTHER OF GOD

Esther Bonini wrote on February 2, 1998:

"With all my heart, I thank you for the beautiful gifts you sent us. I pray that someday we may visit you and your tranquil and holy setting. It does sound like heaven on earth.

"The Holy Mother's tears are beyond comprehension. One cannot even look at her sacred tears without feeling great emotion. She stirs the soul with a profound and awesome reality of her presence. And her heavenly fragrance embraces us with her love and compassion for all her children."

CURE OF DIZZY SPELLS

On the 2nd of February, 1998, Shelly Pickler wrote from Mount Vernon, Missouri:

"The weekend of December 14, 1996, my friend Pat Baker and I went to St. Louis, Missouri, to visit her brother; this was Pat's last visit with her brother, as she was dying of cancer. I was to drive her to St. Louis, as she was in quite a bit of pain, fairly weak and on medication. Her vision wasn't very good, and she suffered from occasional migraine headaches which left her temporarily blind. Our trip from Billings to St. Louis would take us approximately four to four and one-half hours.

"Pat's brother had suffered a severe stroke a few years earlier, leaving him in a wheelchair and in intense pain. He was very bitter and news of his only sister's health would only add to his bitterness. Pat's mission in seeing him was to tell him to get his life right with God—get over the bitterness, and love God. Her intent wasn't to tell him she was dying, only to let him know her health wasn't good.

"Now, shifting gears, I'll tell you about me. At the time I was 30. Since I was very young, I'd suffered from dizziness and fainting spells, occasional 'absences' where I would realize I'd gotten myself from point A to point B when driving, and having no recollection of (the time in-between), or I'd 'blank out' when sitting at my computer at work with several minutes elapsing without my being able to account for them. These 'attacks' could be accompanied by shortness of breath, a generally terrifying 'out of control' feeling, headaches, racing heart, loss of memory, etc. The first time I remember fainting was in first grade.

"At the point of my trip with Pat, my struggle with this problem had increased to occurring several times a day. I was terrified to drive, shop, etc. In fact, in June of 1996, my husband and I were expecting our first child. I was shopping one Saturday, started feeling dizzy, fainted, and miscarried our child.

"Over the years I'd been to doctors who'd labeled my problem as hypoglycemia. Then, in November and December of 1996, with the increase of these attacks, I returned to the doctor, who suggested it could be a number of things from heart problems to mini-seizures, to blood pressure problems. So I began a battery of tests to determine exactly what was wrong.

"My friendship with Pat was really one rooted in faith. She had met a man who told her about a miraculous cure his son had received through the intercession of the Most Holy Mother via some tears from her holy Icon (the son had recovered from a coma). Pat sent off for the tears and received two packages of them, one of which she later gave me. She took these tears on our trip to anoint her brother in hopes of its helping either his physical condition or his attitude.

"Very quickly into our trip, I had a dizzy attack and almost had an accident. Pulling the car over, I intended to call my husband to pick us up and postpone the trip until the next weekend, realizing that neither Pat nor I would be fit to get us to St. Louis and back in a one day trip, at this point. Pat was so disappointed, feeling that this would be her last opportunity to see her brother (which it was). How could I let her down? She suggested my using the tears, but I declined, feeling I was unworthy and preferring an anointing when I could do so with my husband. Finally, she begged me to let her drive! Although the thought of her driving terrified me, how could I refuse her one of her last wishes?

"Pat was convinced that she was up to driving, and I was miserably dizzy, to the point of nearly (being) sick. Pat's driving us was the only way we'd get there that day.

"I certainly had feelings of guilt—feeling responsible for safely transporting my friend for such a worthy mission. Now, she was behind the wheel. And I was the one complaining of my temporary infirmity, while she was the one that would soon die.

"When we arrived at her brother's, Pat was weak and I was incredibly miserable. Her driving hadn't helped my dizziness at all! Through the visit, I'd made several trips to the bathroom and prayed that Jesus would somehow get us safely home, because Pat couldn't see at night and was now far too weak and in too much pain to drive, and I was still feeling bad.

"When the time came for Pat to anoint her brother with the tears from the Holy Icon of the Blessed Mother of God, she asked me to open the bag and help her. I was then exposed to the tears and suddenly my symptoms disappeared—praise be to God!

"My prayer had been that God would somehow bring us safely home, which He did. Pat and I even made a visit to her granddaughter's on the way home (again, her last visit) and I drove us home!

"God not only answered my prayer, but my affliction has not returned! I'm writing on February 8, 1998! Pat passed away shortly after, and so far as I know, her brother hasn't changed. Of the three of us, I received the blessing. Our Lord works in mysterious ways."

RECOVERY FROM HEART ATTACK AND DAUGHTER'S SAFE RETURN

Dolores Velasquez of Houston, Texas, wrote this note for the Monks during her visit to the Monastery on June 28, 1997:

"A few months ago I was rushed to the hospital because I had a heart attack. I lost consciousness, but yet I could see the Mother of God carrying the Infant Jesus. She helped me heal and I believe that what she did for me was a miracle. She was with me when I was in the ambulance.

"I promised her that I would visit her and give some money to help her. That is why I am here today. I also asked the Holy Virgin if she could bring my daughter back to me safely. Within a few days, my daughter came home safely, and that is a miracle to me."

SPEEDY RECOVERY FROM SURGERY

Donna Walter of Poland, Maine, wrote in a letter on September 21, 1998:

"I had surgery on August 4, 1998. I followed the instructions (given) on the anointing the morning of my surgery. My operation and discharge from the hospital was only a matter of four and one-half hours, and my recovery that week was so rapid, it was truly miraculous. I am a nurse myself and I have friends who recently had this operation (too) and are all amazed at my recovery. I was so well my family and I were able to vacation five days later on a tenting trip. A friend, who is not Orthodox, visited your Monastery earlier in the summer, and brought this (package of tears and Icon print) back to me, all prior to my knowledge of this surgery. I thank God for your Monastery and my friend for delivering the tears of the Mother of God to me. God knew I would need them."

SON HEALED

Maria Kaldis wrote on September 17, 1998, to one of the Monastics:

"I received your blessed gift of myrrh from the Weeping Icon of our Theotokos. Thank you! I gave Fr. Spyridon Kavadias the myrrh that you sent. You've asked me to write to you the miracle of my son's illness, but I find it difficult to write. It is fresh in my heart and seems to overwhelm me. I thank you for your precious gift and pray that I can come to your Monastery to venerate in front of our most holy Icon of our Theotokos."

GIFT OF A BABY

Delma Farfan wrote on September 22, 1998:

"I am now 37 years old. I have been married for ten years now. We have been happily married, thanks to God. Ever since we first got married we got along pretty good. The only thing that was lacking in our marriage was children. Years and years passed by and I just would not get pregnant.

"Ever since we got married, I was involved pretty much in the Church. Every time we got together for prayer, I prayed to the Lord that He could grant me the blessing to have a baby. But year after year went by and I would not get pregnant. Sometimes I would get very depressed because out of four sisters, I was the oldest, and the only one that did not have a baby. Everyone would ask me, 'So, when are you going to have a baby?' These remarks would only make me feel worse. Thank God, my husband would support me in every way and he would always tell me, 'Don't worry about it, we are happy and we are all right like this. If the Lord wants to give us a baby, He will.'

"Deep in my heart, I really believed this to be true, so I did not seek medical assistance to get me pregnant. I really believed that when the Lord would think that we were ready and that it was time for us to be parents, He was going to make it happen.

"One night in the Church, I was once again asking the Lord to give me a baby. One of the ladies from our Church approached me and asked me if I wanted for her to pray for me and to anoint me with the tears of the Mother of God. She had just received them from Texas, and she told me a little bit about where those blessed tears came from, and that there had already been many miracles. She anointed me and prayed to the Holy Virgin to intercede for me and heal me, so that the Lord could grant me a baby.

"That night I felt that prayer different from all the other times that I had prayed. My whole body felt moved, touched by that prayer. A warm feeling engulfed my body and I knew that something different had happened. After my friend finished praying, I had a feeling of so much peace and happiness in my heart that I had not had before.

"I told my husband about it that night when I got home, and we both thought, the Lord will do whatever He wishes. The following month I suspected I was pregnant, and two months later it was confirmed.

"There was a lot of happiness not only in us, but also a lot of people that knew my desire to have a baby. And I told all of those people of what had done the miracle. Maybe not everyone believed it, but I knew, and I believed that it was that anointing with the tears that worked the miracle. My daughter is now four years old, and she has a little three–month–old baby sister. Thanks be to God!"

COLON CANCER HEALED

Shirley Renow wrote on the 29th of July, 1998:

"I wish to tell you that last June, 1997, our dear grandson, at the age of 18, was found to have a second stage colon cancer. We began to pray to our Most Holy Lady for healing and touched him with her tear.

"Praise be to God, the doctors were able to remove it; there was no need for the temporary colostomy which they believed would be necessary. After some suffering, he healed and is yet free from cancer. His quarterly checkups have found him to be healthy.

FAITH IN GOD

James Newville wrote from Fort Pierce, Florida, on June 22, 1998:

"Several months ago, I sent in a prayer request for my wife's brother. He was working on his Ph.D., and it seemed his professor was preventing him from graduating. He was able to graduate this month.

"Also, just two months ago, he did not believe in God. Now he believes, and is preparing for baptism. His faith in God is clearly genuine. You can really see the difference. Thank you for your prayers."

ARTHRITIS CURED

On June 21, 1998, Karen Schuele wrote from Newark, Delaware:

"Thank you so much for sending me the Holy Mother's tears. I am writing to tell you about a healing that occurred when I used them on my mother, Johanna McGlensey. My mother is in her 70's and has been suffering many years from arthritis. She has had this in her knees, shoulders, and neck. She has had a great deal of pain in these areas, especially her knees. If she stood for a while, her knees would swell. Even though she experienced sharp pain in her arms and legs, she rarely complained, but we knew she suffered. She always has been prayerful and only prayed that God would not make her condition worse, since she was still capable of caring for herself. When she walked, she was always somewhat hunched over and hobbled a bit. She needed help going up and down steps and could not kneel.

"On June 2nd, 1998, I used the tears on my mother's forehead, shoulders, and knees. When she went to pray later, she would normally have said her prayers while sitting on her sofa. She found she could not concentrate for some reason, and went to her kitchen window that is situated over her sink. There she found no distractions, but had to stand the whole time. She experienced no discomfort in her knees then or later. The next day I again applied the tears. She smelled very strong wafts of roses coming and going. I was sitting close to her, but did not experience the same. That evening she prayed on her knees at her bedside. She was able to get up and down with very little problem. On June 4th , I again applied the tears and prayed. My mother's hands began shaking. She was not able to control this. It happened for about five minutes. That evening my mother discovered she was able to raise her arms without experiencing any sharp pain.

"Even though my mother still has arthritis, she walks with a straighter back, does not hobble, and she does not experience the pain she used to feel."

HEALING AFTER HEART SURGERY

Marina Markin wrote to the Monks on June 9, 1998, that she and her daughter had been to the office of a doctor and had spoken with his receptionist. She told them of her brother-in-law, a wonderful person, who had had a heart transplant. She writes:

"After (the surgery) started many different severe complications. An infection started in the 'new' heart. He was critical. He is Orthodox and Russian, too. We brought to the receptionist a cotton with the Holy Myrrh, and she gave it to the suffering critical man. He accepted it very gladly, as a Christian man. A few days ago we went to the same doctor. The receptionist told us: 'He is much better, the infection is gone, he is rapidly healing and already home.'"

RECOVERY FROM POTENTIALLY FATAL DIABETIC ATTACK

Mrs. Dorothy Muraresky wrote from Palmyra, New Jersey. Her letter is not dated, but it is written on a photocopy of a medical chart dated October 26, 1998. She writes:

"My dear friend, Elizabeth Meyer, gave me a cotton ball touched to the tears of the Holy Mother of God. By the time it arrived in New Jersey, all your literature was soaked with myrrh oil. I shared it with many. We have a severely diabetic daughter, since she was three. She is now 42 and has many complications of this disease. For some reason which none of the doctors can explain to us, Donna's blood sugar which should be in the range of 70 to 115 or so, shot up to 600. As the ambulance and the medics were rushing her to the hospital 15 minutes away, as she was being carried out, I touched her with the tear and said a quick prayer. By the time we got to the hospital her blood sugar had risen to 1546. That is totally unheard of. No books or charts have any numbers like that. She made medical history and was on the point of death—heart, lungs, kidneys, brain were all about at the point of death. Then she came to and was able to speak and comprehend. The astounded doctors said, 'She should be dead or have brain damage or kidney damage.' Donna is back to being a normal diabetic.

"The laboratory report is from the Rancocas Clinical Lab, physician, Daniel Rosenbaum, and shows blood sugar levels of 1546."

RECOVERY FROM GALL STONE

Yolanda Castaneda writes in an undated testimonial:

"I felt I was dying. I went to a doctor but she said I was fine. Still, I packed all my belongings. I gave away the things I thought my family members would enjoy. On the way from Weatherford (Texas) to San Antonio I saw a sign to the Monastery and felt drawn here to pray. When I arrived, I stayed in my car because I was wearing pants. As I sat in my car praying a gentle sweet voice told me to trust. 'All is well. Come to visit when you are well.'

"I went to San Antonio that Monday and I continued with vomiting and went to bed. I went to the hospital. I awoke on Thursday at 4 p.m. Three days had passed. I was prepared for surgery to remove a gall stone. Sixteen and a half hours later, I would not awaken.

Finally, Dr. Oliver, the surgeon, and his assistants awakened me. The stone had collapsed the gall bladder and the stones had caused internal bleeding, and the stomach wall was worn. After eight days I was released. After eight months I came to honor the voice that had blessed me. I saw the Weeping Icon and was anointed. That week I was told that my liver was healed and they could perform the second operation. This time Dr. Oliver classified me as 'one of those fast healers.'"

Yolanda also writes of a second healing she experienced.

"On Sunday, January 9th, I waited in E.R. for a bowel blockage to be removed. I had suffered pain and increasing fatigue for a week. As the pain increased while I waited, I remembered the fragrance when I was anointed here (at the Monastery). 'Come to me,' said the same sweet voice. I was helped by the E.R. doctor and went home. I came here as soon as I could. As soon as I stood in front of the Icon my fear left me. I am renewed. (My doctor in) Corpus Christi said I had been bleeding internally and had anemia. I feel fine now."

REHABILITATION FROM ADDICTION

Mrs. Laura Webber wrote from Valparaiso, Indiana, on November 9, 1998:

"Just a note to let you all know the blessings and healings our family have received. My husband James Webber and myself, Laura, visited your Monastery in

August of this year. We were anointed with the blessed tears of our beloved Lady of Vladimir. The Monks of the Monastery sent home with us more tears to anoint our family and friends. Since receiving them we have had three cases of rehabilitation from abuse of alcohol and from drug addiction. Also many of our family members have since seen their doctors and are being cured of minor ailments. We all wish to give our thanks to the people of Christ of the Hills Monastery and most of all to our beloved Mother of God."

PREMATURE BABY SURVIVES

A young single mother wrote from Falls Church, Virginia, on November 5, 1998:

"I am writing to tell you about a miracle that happened in 1997. On July 14, 1997, I delivered a premature baby that weighed 1 lb., 13 oz. He was intubated and in the isolete for almost four months. While I was still in the hospital going through pain and hopelessness, a friend of mine came to visit me and brought with her (a copy of) the Weeping Icon and the oil. She anointed my son Olisa with it when he was a day old and in the isolete. My son was discharged from the hospital on All Saints Day weighing 5 pounds.

"By the grace of God, my son is doing physically, mentally and developmentally all right. I believe the Weeping Icon oil helped my son. He now weighs 23 lb. and 5 oz."

MUCH TRAVELLED TEARS

Fr. Vasili received a letter from Fouad Farag, from Lynhurst, New Jersey. It was dated January 13, 1999:

"If you remember you sent me tears of the Mother of God. I sent them all over, especially to my family in Egypt. A miracle happened as a result. I sent one to my sister living at Heliopolis, Cairo, Egypt. To my astonishment she told me she received the letter after nine months. The letter had gone to India, Pakistan, and other countries until it reached the border of China. The letter was opened in one of these countries and it was returned back to Egypt. She received it last December, after nine months. The chief of the post office told her that they received the letter opened, and he was very amazed by the fragrant odor that was even outside the envelope. Surely everyone read the blue paper attached telling about the Weeping Icon. God knows how many people were cured at these countries. The Mother of God helped in the spreading of her good news without any intervention from us.

"My sister signed for the letter and received it but the post office insisted on taking the envelope that had so many prints from these countries before it arrived."

RELIEF FROM UNIVERSITY STRESS

Susan Morrison wrote to Father Pangratios on October 29, 1998, from Southwest Texas State University:

"Thank you so much for your graciousness in spending so much time with us on Saturday! It was a wonderful day for all of us from Southwest Texas State. We all took away something special and personal from New Sarov. One student's interest, for example, is art history, and she really loved it when you spoke about the hieratic style in art. Another has been on two other Pilgrimages, both in England, and said, 'It's a slice of medieval life in the Texas Hill Country.' I know for Liralen, who is Russian Orthodox, and for her mother it was a very moving time. One student said she had been stressed out for a year, but going to the Monastery suddenly relieved her of this oppressive weight.

"Everyone we encountered at New Sarov was totally welcoming and open to visitors, which I realize must be difficult when one is trying to focus oneself on God....I appreciate how you reminded us how life is a Pilgrimage."

NO CHEMOTHERAPY NEEDED

In an undated note written at the Monastery, Yolanda Gaita wrote:

"The first time I came, I believe I saw the Holy Mother weep one tear. When I went back to see the doctor, since I have cancer, good news came to me. I didn't have to take chemotherapy. All I needed was to take calcium for my bones. Twice I have been blessed thanks to my Most Holy Mother. It's not a cure, but she blessed me from going through a rough road, chemotherapy. I believe in God, I love Him, and I praise Him."

RELIEF FROM FEAR OF AIDS

On June 11, 1998, a woman wrote from Dripping Springs, Texas, a small town near Blanco:

"I visited your Monastery yesterday and was completely astonished with what I encountered. The whole experience was more than I expected. Let me start by saying that I've been living with AIDS for five years, and came to Blanco looking for a miracle. What I found was more than that. I can't say that I'm free of the disease, but my spirit is free once again. My experience in Blanco yesterday was one that I won't soon forget. I've only felt like that twice before in my life. I can only hope that the Lord will let me raise my children for a long while. I can't ask for more than that. I pray every day for a cure and hope He will give the doctors the knowledge to find it. I hope that God will watch over you all and keep you from harm's way. I will pray that He does. Keep on doing this wonderful thing you all are doing by sharing this miraculous gift with others. May God always be with you!"

HEALING FOR A DIABETIC

In a testimonial from Mrs. Mendoza recently given to the Monks, she writes:

"I visited the Monastery two weeks before and I took some tears of the Mother of God. I work for (a pizza parlor) and another manager went to do an inspection in my store. After the inspection I asked him how he was doing, since he is diabetic. He replied that he had no feeling in his legs, and that the doctor had told him he was going to amputate his foot to see how far his infection was. But then I told him about the tears and I asked him if he believed in the Virgin Mother of God. He said yes, so I gave him a tear. The next day he called me at work and told me that when he got home the day before he told his wife about the tears and at night he put the tears on both of his legs. (He was) rubbing and thinking he was not going to have enough next morning. He was overjoyed to feel sensation in his legs.

PEACE OF MIND AND RELIEF OF PAIN

In a letter postmarked June 6, 1998, Mary Lowery wrote from Houston, Texas:

"My brother-in-law and his sister and I came to the Monastery on Tuesday, May 2, 1998 at 4:00 p.m. I want to thank the Priest that blessed me with the holy myrrh because since I have been blessed by the myrrh I have had peace of mind, no more pain in my arm (in which I had pain for four or five months), no pain in the gums of my mouth. And most of all, I have been blessed to where I was not hooked on the pain medicine. After being on the pain medicine for one month I could not get off of it. When I wouldn't take it I would shake real bad. Since I have been off this time I have not had any more problem."

HOLE IN INFANT'S HEART HEALED

A man from the Middle East reported to one of the Monks on January 23, 1998, a miracle his granddaughter experienced. She was born with a hole in her heart. In order for her to live she would have to go through a serious and dangerous surgery. After being anointed with the holy tears she went for a checkup and the hole had healed. She is today about seven years old and as vibrant and healthy as can be.

RECOVERY FROM A STROKE

Angelita Garza wrote on March 8, 1998:

"About a month ago I came after having a stroke. The Father gave me oil to anoint myself and pray every day. One day I was just lying in my bed. All of a sudden I was overtaken by the scent of the (myrrh). I immediately started praying and anointed myself. I have recovered from my stroke rapidly. All my tests have been good. I give thanks to the Holy Virgin. I anoint myself every day."

AMPUTATION AVOIDED

On March 22, 1998, Norma Guerrero of Austin, Texas, wrote concerning her husband:

"My husband's diabetic foot ulcer got infected at Thanksgiving time of 1997. It developed into a full blown infection that seemed to require amputation of his leg. We prayed and prayed and prayed. My husband, Tony, has had seven surgeries, but his foot is still on his body. The surgeries left his foot with a hole from top to bottom and about 6 inches in circumference. Four months later it is now on the verge of totally closing—with no infection. The doctors say they have never seen a diabetic heal so completely and so fast. Tony is 53 years old."

RECOVERY FROM A DRINKING PROBLEM

On a visit to the Monastery in 1998, Miguel Dismas of Dallas, Texas, wrote:

"I came here seven years ago with my wife and daughter and son-in-law. We got in line to be blessed from the tears of the Icon. There were several people here. I was the last one in line. When I approached the Nun and she touched my head, at that very moment I felt a sensation moving very slowly from my head to my feet. It scared me a little, but I didn't think much of it. After we left here and got back on the highway, I opened a beer and started to drink it, but it tasted flat. So I opened another and another. They all tasted flat. About two hours later I forced myself to drink this so-called flat beer. Within five or ten minutes I felt so sick at my stomach I though I was going to pass out. To this day I still haven't had a beer to drink.

"I had visited my Priest several times and told him I wanted to quit drinking. That I used to get up on Sunday mornings with a hangover and go to the back yard and get on my knees and pray to the Lord to take this drunkenness away from me. I told my Priest that the Lord wouldn't answer my prayer. My Priest told me that I was just trying to get comfort from my hangover, and wasn't trying to quit.

"When I came here seven years ago that never entered my mind about quitting drinking. It just happened after I was blessed."

HELP FOR AN AUTISTIC CHILD

Suzie Twedh from Great Falls, Montana, wrote on October 12, 1998:

"Last May we visited your Monastery and the Chapel of the Weeping Mother. It was such an awesome feeling being there in the presence of the Mother of God, and of all of you. Thank you for that wonderful opportunity. Our son, Bob, was with us. He is autistic. He was going through a very trying time. Since we have been blessing him with oil from the tears, we have seen so many miracles happen for him. His speech is much clearer. His language is so much more expanded. He seems to be seeing the world around him for the first time. He examines it, smells it, feels it, tastes it, hears it. It is wonderful. He can follow directions. So many, many things are happening to him, which means that they are happening to us. We are so thankful for the healing that we are witnessing—it is nothing but a miracle. Yes, we give our thanks every day."

HEARING RESTORED

Serefina Vega of Redwood City, California, wrote on February 17, 1998:

"This letter is to update you on my hearing loss which occurred on December 29, 1997. I would also like to thank you for all of your prayers and well wishes. Today on Tuesday the 17th of February, I underwent my second audiogram and was told that my hearing had improved 64%. The good news is that if I had an audio tumor, I would not have shown any improvement, so there will be no need for an MRI. The doctor feels hopeful that I may still gain more of my hearing in time. But because it has taken so long to regain this much hearing it's unlikely that I will hear at 100% again. Even though 64% seems to be encouraging news, I continue to struggle with my inability to hear actual speech and sounds. The only thing that I do hear the sound of (is) fullness in my ear, it's like putting a sea shell to your ear. I continue to pray and keep faith and ask that you do the same."

In the same letter she appended a handwritten note on February 24, updating what she had previously written:

"Many, many thanks to you all and mostly to the Blessed Virgin Mary. The cotton blessed myrrh has healed me. I feel my hearing improving every week. I can never thank you enough."

A CHILD RECOVERS FROM ENCEPHALITIS

On October 6, 1998, Gloria Torres sent to one of the Fathers a beautiful account written by her friend, Celia Ruvalcaba, about the recovery of her child from an encephalitic coma:

"On March 16, 1995, my son Jesse was complaining of a cold. I took him to the doctor and he said that Jesse had a cold and a virus infection, so he prescribed antibiotics and sent us home. Friday, March 17, 1995, he went to school just like a regular day. He was taking his medicine. We had plans of going camping that weekend, so on Saturday morning we all got up and got ready to go. Jesse washed the motor home and cleaned and loaded up everything we were taking. On the way to San Diego Campland he was fine, did not complain of anything. He was just very excited. We got to the camping grounds around 6:00 p.m. We got set up and we ate, had a campfire and he still did not complain. Sunday morning was cloudy, cold and foggy. We all went for a walk along the shore. The water looked dirty and there were jellyfish along the seashore. We went back to the camping grounds and we had breakfast and later on the kids went swimming. Jesse was also swimming and also going in the Jacuzzi. Around 4:00 we had something to eat and Jesse did not want anything (that's when I noticed him being a little quiet and tired) so he went to sleep. We left around 6:30 p.m. And he was still in bed, quiet, and restless. We got home around 9:00 p.m. We unloaded all the stuff off the motor home. Jesse was walking very awkward. He was still quiet. I made him some chicken noodle soup but he refused. He went to the bathroom and vomited. I gave him two Tylenol and put him to bed.

"On Monday, March 20, my husband went to work around 6:00 a.m., and I woke up and woke Jesse up but he said, 'Mom, my legs hurt.' I told him, 'Well, maybe I should take you back to urgent care. Let me call my supervisor and let her know that I'm going to be late.' I went and got his clothes ready and asked him to get up, and he say, 'Mom, I can't move my legs, my neck hurts.' I told him, 'OK, I'll get you dressed.' I turned to get his socks and when I turned back he was shaking, foaming from the mouth and his eyes were open but not blinking. I yelled for my daughter (11 years old) to call 911, and I was yelling and telling God, 'I know he is yours, but don't take him. I'm not finished teaching him. You are not taking him!' He stopped shaking and I got on the phone and called the 911 operator. She told me 'Stay calm and turn him to his side.' I kept telling her to hurry up and please get somebody here. The paramedics came and tried to revive him, but he was not responding. He was breathing on his own. They took him to the hospital. My husband came from work not knowing what was going on. We followed the ambulance to the hospital. I could not believe it was happening to us, to my son. When we got to the hospital, Jesse was still like in a coma, he did not respond to anything. The doctors told us that they would have to do an MRI and that he might not make it. My daughter got down on her knees and asked God to take her instead of Jesse. We all got down on our knees and prayed in the hospital hall facing the trailer where they had Jesse. The doctors told us that they would have to transfer him to Riverside Community Hospital because (there) they had a pediatric intensive care, and here in Corona they did not have that. We followed the ambulance to the Riverside Hospital and Jesse was still like in a coma. We all went in the hospital room with Jesse. He had all these needles stuck in his arms (he hated needles). After the doctors examined him they told us that he had a viral infection and it had caused inflammation in his brain, so they were going to treat him with strong antibiotics. I called everybody that I knew and asked them to pray for Jesse. People started prayer vigils for him. I called my workplace and they all prayed for him. Monday was over and Jesse was in the same condition. His Grandma and Grandpa, his Dad and myself were in the room with him just praying and hoping he would respond and open his eyes and talk to us, but there was no change in his condition.

"The doctors told us that he had encephalitis, an inflammation of the brain. We would just have to wait and hope that all the medication would bring down the inflammation and he would respond. All this time he was breathing on his own. In the afternoon I had to leave the hospital and come to Corona to take my two daughters (eleven and three years old) to urgent care because they were both sick. They had high fevers, and of course I got all worried and afraid that they might have the same thing Jesse had. I took them to the doctor's. I mentioned to him that my son was in the hospital and he had a viral infection. He treated my girls right away and he did the meningitis test and told me they did not have that. They just had the flu. That was a relief. Meanwhile at the hospital my friend Gloria went to pray for Jesse. My husband told her that I was not there. Her response was, 'I did not come to see Celia. I came to see the little boy.'

"Jesse's grandparents were there along with my husband. They all held hands and made a circle around Jesse. Gloria prayed and blessed him with the precious tears (of the Weeping Icon of the Mother of

God). It was powerful, and everybody was crying. Gloria left, and two hours later Jesse woke up. His cousin went in to see him and he opened his eyes and said, 'Hi.' My husband jumped so high, and his cousin was speechless and his grandparents were just thanking God for the miracle. After 27 hours of being like in a coma. Jesse shook my husband's hand and told him what are we doing here. I called to find out how Jesse was doing. My husband told me, 'Hurry, come down here, Jesse is awake and talking!' I was so happy and thankful to God for this miracle. After this day Jesse was feeling better every day that went by. The doctors moved him to a regular hospital room, and my husband stayed with him day and night. I stayed every other night. My husband and I could not thank God enough for His miracle. After a week they transferred Jesse back to Corona Community Hospital, where he stayed one more week. The doctors were amazed to see him back to normal. He stayed in the hospital a total of 11 days. After his release I took him to get a neurological exam and he was back to normal. Everything was back to normal. We thanked God every day for giving Jesse back to us. I always bless him with the precious tears, and I tell him that he is a miracle, and that he has a special purpose in his life.

"It took us a while to get back to normal but we made it through with God's help. Jesse is 6'1" tall, weighs 155 lb. He is in the 11th grade, he drives, is 16 years old, soon to be 17. He plays baseball, has a girlfriend, works part time, and is his dad's mechanic helper. 'Jesse is a miracle.'"

MIRACLES OF THE MOTHER OF GOD AND OF SAINT JOHN OF SHANGHAI AND SAN FRANCISCO

Michael Dimozantos wrote to Mother Seraphima on December 16, 1998 from Nanimo, British Columbia, in Canada:

"As I mentioned in my telephone conversation on December 14, 1998, God in His great love and mercy, graced us (my family) with a number of miracles which I shall describe in the following pages. God is a truly loving God to bestow such gifts on us who are such ungrateful and undeserving sinners. Glory be to Him for evermore!

"The latest miracle was granted to us through St. John of Shanghai and San Francisco, the Wonderworker, as follows:

"Previous to the miracle, and for many months before, my wife Maria, who converted to Orthodoxy from the Catholic faith back in 1993, suffered greatly from a diseased uterus. The specialist who performed a laprascopy at the local hospital (in Nanimo) discovered that her uterus became enlarged seven times its normal size and had become spongy. He ordered an immediate hysterectomy. The operation was set for the 13th of October, 1997. In the meantime my wife suffered terrible pains. She would administer herself huge doses of Tylenol-3 with codeine, and that worried me. Even then her pains were unbearable. Besides her pain, my wife and I were very concerned over our financial future. Such an operation would require the closure of my wife's pre-school for approximately two months. As I am retired and with no other source of income apart from my pension, the loss of her income over two months was unthinkable. Besides, we were concerned that the parents would pull their children from our school and place them with another school, for it would be too much to ask or expect them to wait for two months. Then I remembered the numerous miracles of St. John (Maximovitch), some of which were granted to personal friends (of mine). I then booked a flight to San Francisco on a Pilgrimage to St. John's Relics. O what a spiritual happiness and joy I felt to be so close to a Saint! Truly God is wondrous in His ways. While I was there I was blessed with a personal introduction with Archbishop Antony. I was so astonished and gladdened beyond comprehension when he asked me, and he wrote on a piece of paper the names of each member of my family promising that he would pray for us. God is truly abundantly generous with His gifts.

"When I returned home I was greeted with great news. My wife told me that on the second day after I left home, her pains ceased completely. She could bend down to pick up things again that she couldn't before. What is wonderful is that I prayed to St. John for her healing on the second day because the first day of my trip I spent it traveling and getting settled down at some friends' house. It is interesting that while I prayed at his Relics to heal her, I also remembered and prayed for St. John to heal her of her severe cramps and pains she suffered during her monthly periods which were profuse. I remember praying to St. John to heal her uterus and restore it to that of a 22 year old's (that is the age of my wife when I first met her! She is now 40! How the years go by!) There too I was granted my wish, for as she told me on her own accord, she can hardly feel her periods any more. It is now five months and she is still pain free. Glory be to God!

"The other three miracles happened through the tears of the Theotokos from the myrrh–bearing Icon of your Monastery. Briefly, they are the following:

"1) One night my wife, Maria, felt acute pains in the back of her mouth and she had great difficulty swallowing. When I looked in her mouth I saw in the back of her mouth above the tongue a large number of fire red pimples with white dots. The next day she visited the doctor who told her that it was a virus (streptonitis) and it will take about a week or two to pass. He could do nothing because it was a virus. He warned her however that it will get a lot worse before it got better. He informed her that the pimples will grow into cankers (pussy wounds) and she will have problems even drinking. He told her though to drink water with a straw to avoid dehydration. Of course, we were very alarmed, but felt totally helpless. That same night while she was sleeping (I am a late sleeper) a thought passed through my mind to administer to her a drop of the tears of the Theotokos. I went to our Iconostasion where I keep such holy tears and squeezed a drop of the tears into a tablespoon. I added a bit of Holy Water and administered it to my wife who did not know what she swallowed, as she was half asleep. Well, the next day in the morning her mouth was completely clear of all cankers and pimples. Glory be to God!

"2) Again one night my little six–year–old son (who was 5 then) had started coughing unceasingly, and had problems breathing. For many minutes that felt like years, he continued to cough non-stop. I thought of rushing him to the hospital, but he started turning blue. Then I remembered the tears of the Theotokos, and the miracle with my wife, so I ran and prepared the same mixture of tears of the Theotokos with Holy Water in a tablespoon. My son was coughing so much that I could not administer it. I then told him to try to stop for one second. This he just managed, giving me enough time to pour it in his mouth. No sooner did it enter his mouth than all the coughing ceased completely, sharp as a razor. He slept soundly the whole night, not coughing even once. The next day, I being of such a weak faith, I took him to the family doctor to be examined. The doctor examined him and asked me what medicine I administered to him, since his lungs and everything else were just fine. He looked perplexed, having heard from me of unceasing coughs and difficulty of breathing when my son exhibited nothing wrong. I then felt strange because I did not know what to tell him. How could I tell him of the tears of the Theotokos and of the miracle. I decided to tell him the truth. He did not laugh as I expected him to do, but told me that he also believes in the Theotokos, being Catholic.

"3) A couple who are members of our Church in Victoria, of the St. Sophia Parish, and very good friends of ours, had suffered a severe financial reversal. His wife, perhaps due to the constant unrelenting stress had developed heart problems. She was tested at the hospital and was told that she had most probably three months of life left in her. They told her (that) her heart was weakened greatly and her veins were severely clogged. Of course this news was crushing. One weekend she called us and asked us if she could spend it with us by herself as a break from the stresses in her house. We were happy to have her. We cried when we heard that she had written letters to her sons who were 14 and 16 then, to be opened after her death. On her second and last night at our house I gathered enough courage to ask her if she would accept to drink the mixture of a drop of the tears of the Theotokos and Holy Water. To our delight she accepted. Great was the miracle that happened. When she went back to her home, the Vancouver hospital called her and told her that someone had canceled so if she wished she could come in for a battery of tests within a day instead of her original appointment date which was in another three months hence. She accepted and hurried to that hospital. When she returned we asked her how it went and crying she told us that the doctor (specialist) was very rude and treated her very badly. She told us that he insulted her by telling her that she lied about her condition, for her heart and veins were perfect. He apparently became very annoyed because she wasted his time which could have been used by a more deserving case. Little did he suspect that a miracle had taken place. Glory be to God!"

TRAGEDY AVERTED

A spiritual son of one of the Monastery's Hieromonks wrote on July 15, 1997:

"Thank you again for your holy prayers! My nephew that I called you about yesterday came by today with my sister and her children! He was out on bond. Also, the man that was in intensive care yesterday, who sounded as though he would not live, recovered and was home drinking beer again on his front porch the same day! Glory to God! I had asked you to pray that this man would not die at my nephew's hand, and this prayer has been answered two-fold. Firstly, the man miraculously recovered and was home again the same day. Secondly, as it turned out, my nephew was not the one who beat the man nearly to death as it were with an ax handle. It was some other people who did not live in the trailer park, and the man recovered miraculously. My nephew is still accused and must stand trial, but is 100% better–off than yesterday. Many of my relatives who are Protestants are speechless. Thank you again, Father, for your prayers, and the Mother of God for her prayers to God, her Son!"

HEALINGS WITHOUT MEDICINE

On April 20, 1998, Marina and Juan Cortez, of Canyon Lake, Texas, left the following message with the Monks:

Marina: "Thank you for the miracle of healing my knees without medicine and just (by)asking her (to heal) the hurt of the knee."

Juan: "Thank you for healing my lump that I had without medicine, and just asking her for the lump I had (to be healed.)"

RELIEF FROM TENDONITIS

Mary Marcotullio wrote from North Haledon, New Jersey, on October 2, 1997:

"I'm writing to inform you that I've been praying to the Mother of God in her Holy Icon that I would get comfort and relief of tendonitis in my wrist and thumb which were very painful, and if it didn't get better, it would (require) surgery. Through the Blessed Mother of God it doesn't bother me hardly. I'm to see the doctor on October 9. I had to keep the hand in a cast. Now I took it off because it feels much better. Thank the Blessed Mother! I put the myrrh (from the) Weeping Icon on it for healing."

RELIEF FROM MULTIPLE SCLEROSIS AND THE GIFT OF A CHILD

Mother Seraphima wrote this account of a conversation with Pilgrims in the Monastery store:

A married couple with a six–year–old little boy came into the store after going to see the Icon. The whole family and their love for each other was very moving. They have been married for about sixteen years, ten of which they were childless. They came here two years ago. The mother of the boy was at that time in a wheelchair because of multiple sclerosis. At that time the whole family was with them. Now she, the mother, is walking and still has M.S. Her sister, seeing how much they wanted a baby and could not conceive, after giving birth gave the boy to her to raise as her own. What a great blessing and what love they had for each other. They came back to give thanks to God for the relief of the multiple sclerosis and for the gift of this child. His mother named him Joseph.

RELIEF FROM A LINGERING COUGH

An anonymous note left with a Monk at the Monastery relates the following:

"The wife of a friend in New Zealand had a cough, which lingered on for some time. I sent a cotton ball with myrrh from the Monastery at Blanco, with a brochure, and told him how to anoint, and to offer prayers. At last report, there was considerable improvement in the lady's cough."

RECOVERY FROM A TERRIBLE ACCIDENT

Mary Layton wrote:

"On October 5, 1997, my son's face was split in half vertically from his upper jaw to his frontal bone. The doctor told me "he had multiple trauma to the head" and they didn't know whether he would make it or not. I went in to see him. Then I remembered I had a tear of the Mother of God in my purse. When I could not find it I went back to the car; it had fallen in the parking lot. I made the Sign of the Cross with the invocation.

"My son stayed two weeks in ICU and two weeks on other floors recuperating. All of the bones in the middle of his face were broken. He now has five plates in his face. I kept using the tears while he was in the hospital. And he has been to New Sarov a few times for blessings.

"He is now going to graduate from high school and has a full time job. Some of the doctors can't believe his brain wasn't damaged. Everyone is calling it a miracle. That's what it is!"

BABY'S CYST DISAPPEARS

S. A. E. wrote on May 17, 1999, concerning her baby son:

"My two year old son, Ryan, developed a cyst on his tiny head. It continued to grow bigger and bigger so I took him to the pediatrician in San Marcos, Texas. The doctor informed me that the only way to remove the cyst was surgically. My anxiety grew because we did not have medical insurance and our finances were in ruin.

"My family received some of the myrrh soaked cotton from the Monks of Christ of the Hills Monastery while we were visiting. One of the Monks suggested that I anoint my child on the cyst in the Sign of the Cross while saying, 'In the name of the Father, and the Son, and the Holy Spirit.'

"Each evening after our evening prayers and before sleeping, I would follow these instructions and anoint him with the cotton from the Myrrh–Weeping Icon. Each evening I noticed the cyst shrinking. When the day for the scheduled surgery arrived, to my continued amazement, the cyst had disappeared. We went to the doctor to make sure the cyst had indeed vanished. The doctor happily confirmed our miracle. He did say the cyst could return. This took place over one year ago and to this day, thanks to the intercessions of the Most Holy Mother of God and the merciful tears she gives us through the Myrrh–Weeping Icon, my son is still well."

LOST VOICE RESTORED

In May, 1999, the Monks received the following letter from Elizabeth Salcedo of San Antonio:

"On July 15, 1998, my vocal cord (arythenoid) cartilage was broken during anesthesia (tube insertion) and I lost my voice. Three weeks later, a procedure was done to relocate or fix the broken cartilage and I was given a five to ten percent chance of getting my voice back. Five days later I still did not get my voice back. On the morning of the sixth day after the operation, I wiped my throat with myrrh oil from the Weeping Icon of Our Lady of Vladimir at New Sarov Monastery and said my prayers. In the evening I got my voice back and from then on I could talk like nothing has happened to my voice box. A month later, we came back here (to) New Sarov to give thanks to our Merciful Lady."

SIGHT GIVEN TO BABY BORN BLIND

On May 10, 1999, Anne Roundtree, a member of parishioner in the Prophet Elias Orthodox Mission, wrote from Placerville, California:

"Christ is Risen! I am writing to tell of a healing of the Mother of God. Here in Placerville, California, we have a favorite coffee shop which some of our parishioners frequent on Saturdays. At this restaurant there is a waitress, named Angela, who is our favorite. One evening she took some of us aside before we left our table and asked us to pray for her four–month–old nephew, Baby Richard, who was born blind. We assured her that we would.

"During the following week I received the tears of the Mother of God from Christ of the Hills Monastery. I took an envelope with the tears and prayers, leaving them at the restaurant with Angela's name on the envelope, and a short note.

"Two days later, some of our young people visited the restaurant. Angela was very happy. She said she and her sister (the baby Richard's mother) had prayed the prayers and anointed the baby's eyes with the tears in the Sign of the Cross. The baby suddenly began to smile, which he seldom had done before, and began tracking with his eyes, as they moved their fingers back and forth in front of him. His mother began to weep. Our Parish was greatly moved by this story.

"Thank you, and glory to God!"

GLORY TO GOD FOR ALL THINGS!

Bishop Constantine

His gentleness and meekness inspired all around him. With his mind constantly fixed on the heavenly realm, he taught by example the Beatitudes of Christ.